demonstrates how and why those sources may very well give us the most fruitful way of reading the earliest of the Synoptics. An invaluable addition to our understanding of the New Testament."

—Robert Royal, Ph.D., President, Faith & Reason Institute

"This lively translation will make you feel like you're encountering Jesus for the first time as St. Peter himself preaches the Good News, and the thoughtful and accessible commentary will help you reach new insights into the Gospel."

—Ryan T. Anderson, author of *When Harry Became Sally:*
Responding to the Transgender Moment and *Truth*
Overruled: The Future of Marriage and Religious Freedom

"Michael Pakaluk manages to combine a fresh and lively Bible translation and commentary with spiritual inspiration and persuasive apologetics. It's fashionable to treat the Gospel accounts as something like historical fiction. Pakaluk, in contrast, shows that in the Gospel of Mark, we encounter the testimony of an eyewitness of Jesus' ministry, death, and resurrection. You should read this book for the health of both your mind and your soul."

—Jay W. Richards, *New York Times* bestselling author of
The Human Advantage

"There is a quiet urgency to this volume that radiates from sentence to sentence. *The Memoirs of St. Peter* is an intimate walk with Jesus—as Scripture is meant to be—for a real encounter with Christ. Michael Pakaluk's re-presentation of the Gospel of Mark is a gift. It lays out reality as it must be lived. I pray you read it with joyful receptivity to our Lord."

—Kathryn Jean Lopez, Senior Fellow, National Review
Institute, and Editor at Large, *National Review*

"With elegant simplicity, literal precision, and the conceptual graces of an Aristotelian philosopher, Michael Pakaluk brings the Lord Jesus Christ into sharp focus through the eyes of the Church's first universal pastor, St. Peter. Highly recommended."
—C. C. Pecknold, Associate Professor of Theology, The Catholic University of America

"Reading *The Memoirs of St. Peter* deepened my appreciation and enriched my understanding of the Gospel of Mark. It is a perfect companion that brings the verses of the Gospel to life. It is thoroughly researched, well written, and easy to read. I highly recommend it to all who want to experience the life, message, and mission of our Lord Jesus as recorded from the eyewitness account of St. Peter."
—Obianuju Ekeocha, international human rights activist and author of *Target Africa: Ideological Neocolonialism in the Twenty-first Century*

THE MEMOIRS OF ST. PETER

The Memoirs *of* St. Peter

A New Translation of the Gospel According to Mark

Michael Pakaluk

REGNERY GATEWAY

Regnery Gateway™ is a trademark of Salem Communications Holding Corporation; Regnery® is a registered trademark of Salem Communications Holding Corporation

Scripture quotations from The Authorized (King James) Version. Rights in the Authorized Version in the United Kingdom are vested in the Crown. Reproduced by permission of the Crown's patentee, Cambridge University Press

Scripture quotations from Revised Standard Version of the Bible—Second Catholic Edition (Ignatius Edition): Copyright © 2006 National Council of the Churches of Christ in the United States of America. Used by permission. All rights reserved worldwide.

Scripture quotations from the ESV® Bible (The Holy Bible, English Standard Version®): Copyright © 2001 by Crossway, a publishing ministry of Good News Publishers. Used by permission. All rights reserved.

Cataloging-in-Publication data on file with the Library of Congress

ISBN 978-1-62157-834-5
e-book ISBN 978-1-62157-835-2

Published in the United States by
Regnery Gateway, an imprint of
Regnery Publishing
A Division of Salem Media Group
300 New Jersey Ave NW
Washington, DC 20001
www.RegneryGateway.com

Manufactured in the United States of America

10 9 8 7 6 5 4 3 2

Books are available in quantity for promotional or premium use. For information on discounts and terms, please visit our website: www.Regnery.com.

To Mark Dominic

Contents

T he *immediacy* of the Gospels, their closeness in time and place to the events they narrate, can be a shocking discovery. A colleague of mine, as a student at the Sorbonne, came to know the remarkable philosopher and theologian Claude Tresmontant, who would argue that the Greek of the Gospels makes full sense only if construed as a translation of an original Hebrew version. (Hebrew, not Aramaic—Tresmontant also argued that Jewish believers of the time continued to speak and write in Hebrew.) It wasn't the theory of a Hebrew original that struck my colleague so much as an assumption behind it

"What do you mean?" he exclaimed. "Are you saying that these writings were so close in time to Jesus that they were written by contemporaries, in the same language he spoke? Could our evidence of Jesus really be so direct and close?"

Another colleague made this discovery as an undergraduate. He was reading *The New Testament Documents: Are They Reliable?* by F. F. Bruce, who points out that there are tens of thousands of manuscripts of the New Testament, some dating to the early second century. The combined witness of these manuscripts, Bruce argues, examined carefully through the science of textual criticism, gives strong assurance that 99 percent of the text we now have coincides with the texts that would have been used by the very first Christians. The textual tradition is so strong that it can make the intervening centuries seem to vanish.

Others are struck by the "texture" of the narrative itself. To understand what I mean by that, consider an example from my own field of ancient philosophy. When scholars translate Aristotle's *Nicomachean Ethics* for the legions of undergraduates who study it, they work from a Greek text that is based not on thousands of manuscripts but basically on two. They date from the tenth and twelfth centuries, more than 1,300 years after Aristotle composed the work. But for a scholar reading the text in Greek, that distance in time does not raise any doubt that he is encountering Aristotle's thought directly. Why? Because the thought expressed in these medieval manuscripts is so ingenious and insightful that it is clear that the text is revealing—with immediacy—the power of a great philosophical mind. Writing is, after all, just a code for speaking. A scholar reading that text can easily imagine that he is hearing Aristotle himself formulate his thoughts.

The "texture" of the Gospels is that of an eyewitness narrative, which of itself makes a claim of immediacy. C. S. Lewis makes this point very well:

> I have been reading poems, romances, vision-literature, legends, myths all my life. I know what they are like. I know that not one of them is like [the Gospel of John]. Of this text there are only two possible views. Either this is reportage—though it may no doubt contain errors—pretty close to the facts; nearly as close as [Samuel Johnson's friend and biographer] Boswell. Or else, some unknown writer in the second century, without known predecessors or successors, suddenly anticipated the whole technique of modern, novelistic,

realistic narrative. If it is untrue, it must be narrative of that kind. The reader who doesn't see this has simply not learned to read.[1]

To strengthen the argument, one might add that the historical novel, the first example of "novelistic, realistic narrative," arose only when there was a highly educated reading public ready to appreciate that sort of writing. The *Waverley* novels of Sir Walter Scott, perhaps the first in that genre, had to be lengthy to construct a fictitious past while drawing on a knowledge of history already possessed by his readers. Imagine Scott arriving on the American frontier in the 1820s and writing *Waverley* for the enjoyment of the indigenous peoples there, who had no knowledge of or interest in Scottish history and no taste for reading literature at all, and you have a good analogy for the supposition that Lewis rightly scorns.

Among the Gospels, this "texture" of immediacy is probably most evident in Mark. Scholars have long taken this for granted. "The details point clearly to the impression produced upon an eye-witness, and are not such as would suggest themselves to the imagination of a chronicler," wrote the great New Testament scholar Brooke Foss Westcott in the nineteenth century. "At one time we find a minute touch which places the whole scene before us: at another time an accessory circumstance such as often fixes itself on the mind, without appearing at first sight to possess any special interest.... In substance and style and treatment the Gospel of Mark is essentially a transcript from life."[2]

But the presumed author of this Gospel, Mark, was not a follower of Jesus and therefore not an eyewitness to the events he describes.

---

1 C. S. Lewis, "Modern Theology and Biblical Criticism," in Lyle W. Dorsett, ed., *The Essential C. S. Lewis* (New York: Scribner, 1988) p. 351.
2 Brooke Foss Westcott, *Introduction to the Study of the Gospels* (London: Macmillan, 1881), pp. 366–7, 371.

So what could be the source of this ostensible eyewitness account? We need a hypothesis.

The unanimous early tradition of the Church was that Mark's Gospel captured the narrative of the apostle Peter. According to St. Jerome, "Mark, the disciple and interpreter of Peter, wrote a short Gospel at the request of the brethren at Rome, embodying what he had heard Peter tell. When Peter had heard this, he approved it and published it to the churches to be read by his authority."[3] Jerome wrote those words in A.D. 392, but the tradition went back to apostolic times. Bishop Papias of Hierapolis, who died around the year 120, used to quote an unnamed "elder" in the Church who told him that "Mark, having become the interpreter of Peter, wrote down accurately, though not in order, whatsoever he remembered of the things said or done by Christ."[4]

Suppose Papias heard the "elder" say this in A.D. 100, and the elder was about seventy years old. This elder would have been a mature man of around forty years when Peter was martyred in Rome in A.D. 67. Papias was a disciple of John the evangelist, and he was a friend of Polycarp. Papias' testimony, then, reaches right back to the apostles.

There are many other testimonies. Irenaeus writes in about the year 180 that "Mark, the disciple and interpreter of Peter, handed down to us in writing what had been preached by Peter [in Rome]."[5] Clement of Alexandria, writing at roughly the same time, states, "As Peter had preached the Word publicly at Rome, and declared the Gospel by the Spirit, many who were present requested that Mark, who had followed him for a long time and remembered his sayings, should write them out."[6] Origen says the same thing a generation later, as does Tertullian:

---

3 Jerome, *De viris illustribus*, 8.
4 Eusebius, *Ecclesiastical History*, III.39.15.
5 Irenaeus, *Adv. Haer.*, III.1; cf. III.5.
6 *Eccl. Hist.*, VI. 14.

"the Gospel that Mark wrote may be affirmed to be Peter's, whose interpreter Mark was."[7]

In the fourth century, appealing specifically to a tradition distinct from Papias and Clement, Eusebius writes,

> so greatly did the splendor of piety illumine the minds of Peter's hearers that they were not satisfied with hearing once only, and were not content with the unwritten teaching of the divine Gospel, but with all sorts of entreaties they besought Mark, a follower of Peter, and the one whose Gospel is extant, that he would leave them a written monument of the doctrine which had been orally communicated to them.[8]

The term "interpreter" used in these passages meant what we might call an editor, or perhaps a "ghost writer," as when a famous person publishes his life story "as told to" someone who has skill in writing. Jerome, writing around A.D. 407, explains the practice:

> However much the Apostle Paul possessed knowledge of the holy Scriptures, and had a gift of speaking and abilities in various languages... he still was incapable of expressing himself, in eloquent Greek words, in such a way as to match the majesty of the divine meanings of things. Therefore, he employed the services of Titus as his interpreter, just as St. Peter employed the services of Mark, whose Gospel was composed by Peter narrating and Mark transcribing.[9]

---

7 *Adv. Marc.*, IV.5. It does not matter if these later witnesses are relying on the same tradition reported by Papias. That they wished to reaffirm that tradition and found nothing to contradict it would itself constitute separate evidence.
8 *Eccl. Hist.*, II.15.1–2.
9 Letter 120, "To Hebdia," Question 11.

For Jerome, Mark's Gospel is in effect the "Gospel according to Peter, as told to Mark"—which would explain, of course, how a Gospel composed by someone who was not even a follower of Christ could be accepted on all sides as apostolic and part of the canon of Sacred Scripture.

In fact, the title of this book, *The Memoirs of Peter*, is first used by Justin Martyr in A.D. 150. That he uses the phrase in passing—as though what he was saying were obvious and known by all—makes his reference all the more impressive. "It is said," Justin writes, "that he [Jesus] changed the name of one of the apostles to Peter. In fact, it is written in the memoirs of him [Peter] that this happened, as well as that he changed the names of other two brothers, the sons of Zebedee, to Boanerges, which means 'Sons of Thunder.'"[10] The "memoirs" here must mean the Gospel of Mark, because it is only in the Gospel of Mark, not in any of the other three Gospels, that this detail about the sons of Zebedee is reported, and because there is no evidence whatsoever for anything else that could be called by that name.

Scholars point to difficulties with this tradition, as they find difficulties with the traditions of any ancient text. For example, Irenaeus in the passage quoted above also writes that Mark composed his Gospel after "the departure," perhaps meaning the death, of Peter and Paul. Other witnesses, however, say that Peter was familiar with and approved of Mark's writing, while Clement says that Peter knew of the Gospel but neither approved of it nor rejected it. Which alternative is the true one? Perhaps this particular difficulty, like many difficulties, can be resolved by splitting the difference. Peter might have approved a draft but not a final version, or he might

---

10 *Dialogue with Trypho*, Chapter 106. In the phrase "in the memoirs of him" (*en tois apomnēmoneumasin autou*), "of him" (*autou*) is a subjective, not an objective, genitive, and refers to Peter, not Christ, as is clear from the parallelism "in the memoirs of his apostles" (*en tois apomnēmoneumasin tōn apostolōn*) in Chapter 100 of the same work.

have approved of Mark's writing something down in general but did not see a particular version to approve, or perhaps he approved a part of our current text but not all of it. For our purposes, it does not matter much, as we should expect a certain unruliness in any non-contrived, organic tradition.

One might say that the combined weight of these diverse witnesses makes Peter's role in Mark's Gospel as certain as most of what we know about the ancient world. This general conclusion would stand regardless of how one resolves certain difficulties. And yet we need not say this much. If it were merely *plausible* that Peter played such a role, then we would be justified in examining the Gospel of Mark on that hypothesis. If looking at Mark's Gospel in that way bore fruit, then to that extent the hypothesis would be justified.

Yet when we adopt that hypothesis, we find the tradition supported by two pieces of internal evidence: first, Mark's Gospel alone relays things which Peter would have known first-hand, and second, Mark's Gospel depicts Peter in a distinctive way.

Recall that Peter was not only one of the twelve apostles but also, with James and John, a member of a preeminent inner group. Sometimes Jesus took only these three with him, not all of the apostles. Matthew was an apostle but not a member of this inner group. Luke was neither an apostle nor a member of this inner group. In cases in which all three Synoptic writers—Matthew, Mark, and Luke—recount an event at which only the preeminent group was present, we can ask, Does Mark's account, over the others, show signs of its being an eyewitness account? We find that it does. For example:

- When Jesus takes only the smaller group with him to raise a small girl from the dead (Mk. 5:37–43; Mt. 9:23–25; Lk. 8:51–56), only Mark records the Aramaic words (*talitha coum*) with which Jesus brings the child back to life

- In the Transfiguration (Mk. 9:2–13; Mt. 17:1–13; Lk. 9:28–36), only Mark gives the word pronounced in Aramaic, with which Peter addresses Jesus (*Rabbi*), only Mark comments on the silliness of Peter's statement ("he had no idea what to say in response"), and only Mark gives details about the appearance of Jesus and the sudden disappearance of Moses and Elijah, details that have the character of recollections

- In the agony in the garden of Gethsemane, when Jesus, taking Peter, James, and John with him, draws apart from the other disciples to pray, only Mark gives the Aramaic word (*Abba*) with which Jesus addresses his Father, only Mark gives the Aramaic name (*Simōn*) with which Jesus addresses Peter, and only Mark comments on the thoughtlessness of the three ("they had no idea what to say to him in response")

So here the internal evidence supports Peter as the narrator and source. If Peter, telling a gathering in Rome about events back in Palestine, wished to convey what it was like to be there, we would expect him to repeat some the actual words spoken, and it rings true that Mark, in his "interpretation," would preserve them. The self-depreciating details about Peter's own shortcomings also ring true.

The accounts of Peter's denial of Jesus (Mk. 14:54, 66–72; Mt. 26:58, 69–75; Lk. 22:54–62) likewise support his role as the source of Mark's Gospel. None of the other disciples was present, and we find in Mark's account distinctive details, not found in the others, which seem intended to evoke what it was like to be there.

What about Mark's depiction of Peter? In some ways, Mark gives greater attention to Peter, but in some ways less, as one would expect if Peter were his source. Peter appears most frequently in the Gospel of Mark, who mentions him about every 450 words. Matthew and Luke mention Peter only every 720 words. Mark mentions Peter in interesting contexts in which the other evangelists do not. For example, only Mark notes that it was Peter who, strikingly, noticed the withered fig tree that Jesus had cursed the day before (11:21). Mark takes special care to report that the angel at Christ's tomb gave a message to "the disciples *and Peter*" (16:7)—a detail which would have been especially important to Peter, as this would be the Lord's first communication to him since he had denied Jesus three times.

On the other hand, it seems to be Mark's practice not to refer to Peter when doing so might draw attention away from Jesus. For example, when the woman with the issue of blood is healed and Jesus asks, "Who touched me?" Luke records that Peter chided the Lord, saying "Master, a crowd is surrounding you and pressing upon you!" Mark, by contrast, keeps the attention on Jesus. Before reporting Jesus' question, he reports that Jesus could perceive power going out of him (5:30), as if to explain in advance why he asked, and the chiding is attributed to the disciples collectively. Again, Luke writes that Jesus sent Peter and John ahead to prepare the Last Supper (22:8), but Mark records merely that Jesus sent "two disciples" (14:13), as though Peter wished to avoid ascribing to himself a special role on the occasion.

In general, Peter's appearances in Mark's Gospel are not commendatory or distracting. Mark omits the detail that Peter walked on the water with Jesus (Mt. 14:29–31) and the story of Peter's paying the temple tax for Jesus and himself with a coin taken from a fish's mouth (Mt. 17:24–27). But Mark alone in some crucial passages depicts Peter as thoughtless or foolish.

Already in the fourth century, Eusebius noted these same traits about the Gospel of Mark, offering a similar explanation:

What Mark reports is said to be a memoir of Peter's teaching. But consider someone who refused to record what seemed to him to spread his good fame. Suppose instead that he handed down in writing slanders against himself to unforgetting ages, and accusations of sins, which no one in after years would ever have known of, unless they had heard it from his own voice. By putting an advertisement on himself in this way, such a person would justly be considered to have been void of all egoism and false speaking. He will have given plain and clear proof of his truth-loving disposition.[11]

Mark's Gospel seems to exercise a certain authority over the other Gospels, directing them toward a uniform treatment of Jesus. This authority is easily explicable if we take Peter to be the source of Mark's Gospel and if the evangelists recognized his pastoral authority over how the life and teaching of Jesus should be presented.

The Gospels of Matthew, Mark, and Luke are called "synoptic," a word that means "taking a similar view of things." For the most part, they narrate the same events in the life of Jesus, in roughly the same order, and with similar words and phrases. The Gospel of John, in contrast, often strikes off on its own, relating different episodes, conversations, and sessions of teaching. The so-called "Synoptic Problem," which scholars love to examine, is the question of the source of the commonalities among these three Gospels and the causes of their differences. The most widely accepted solution to this "problem" is probably the Two Source theory, which holds that Mark's Gospel is responsible for what is in common among the synoptics and that the

---

11 Eusebius, *The Proof of the Gospel*, III.5.

different use by the three evangelists of an unknown collection of the sayings of Jesus explains the differences.

I am concerned here not with the Synoptic Problem, which takes for granted the congruence of Matthew, Mark, and Luke, but with a prior question: Why should there be this congruence in the first place? The evangelists were not locked up with nothing to base their account on except texts in a library. Jesus apparently healed thousands of people. He taught repeatedly, on many occasions, to many different groups. He presumably had thousands of memorable conversations. He was hardly ever at rest in the three years of his public ministry. Let us say, conservatively, that there were ten thousand episodes attested by eyewitnesses or their immediate associates that could have been included in a Gospel. Why do the evangelists pick out the same handful of healings and recount these? Why mainly the same parables? Why the same miracles?

Here is a plausible explanation. Suppose that Mark's Gospel reflects Peter's own pastoral concern. Suppose it was written at the time when the apostles and disciples were about to depart for different parts of the known world. Peter, then, would have faced this question: How should the Church present the life of Christ in a uniform way to those who had not followed him, emphasizing all the essential points but also keeping preachers "on message"" so as to limit confusion and distortion by those hostile to the faith? The Gospel of Mark would represent Peter's original judgment on this question. If, then, the Church throughout the centuries has meditated mainly on the same hundred episodes from the life of Jesus and not tens of thousands, it would be because we are all in a sense children of Peter, the first universal pastor. On this hypothesis, Peter's judgment in the matter did prevail. We basically know Jesus as Peter judged that we should know him.

I have been emphasizing two ideas about the Gospel of Mark, which are connected: the vividness of its narrative and its Petrine source.

These ideas guide my translation and commentary—especially the former. The main purpose of both the translation and commentary is to bring out as much as possible for a reader who does not have Greek this vibrancy and sense of reality. Peter wanted to convey what it was like to be there: we honor his intention by reading the Gospel in that spirit. Moreover, when pertinent in the commentary, I use the hypothesis of a Petrine origin to help explain the structure, order, or shape of the text.

By trying to make the translation as much like an evocative, spoken narrative as possible, I have found it relatively easy to resolve the two difficulties which confront any translator of Mark. The first has to do with sentence connectives. In Greek, sentences in a continuous narrative must be joined, each with the one before, through a "connecting particle," such as "hence," "now," "therefore," "but," and so on. Writers of ancient Greek typically vary these connectives for subtlety and argument. But Mark is famous for largely limiting himself to one such connective—the simplest one at that—"and" (*kai*). The majority of his sentences begin with "and." Translators usually deal with the problem by just leaving that word out. But Mark's usage makes more sense if we think of how we speak when we tell a story: "So I left my driveway. And I turned around the block. And I saw a man with a pig. And I thought that was strange. So I stopped to ask him about it. And he said...." And so on.

The second difficulty is that Mark varies his verb tenses in apparently unpredictable ways. Sometimes he uses the present tense, sometimes the imperfect, sometimes the "aorist." Most translations solve the problem by throwing everything into the past tense. And yet this removes the vividness that Mark's frequent use of the historic present conveys. But when one approaches the text as originally a spoken narrative, one can generally retain Mark's tense changes. For example: "So I left my driveway. And I turn the corner. And what do I see? I see a man with a pig. And I thought, that was strange. So I stopped and I asked him...." Someone speaking from memory in this way will change tenses to keep the hearer's attention, but mainly because, as he is speaking "from memory," he finds it easy to revert to the viewpoint of "what it was like to be there."

As for the commentary, again, in the service of freshness and realism, I am interested in Mark's Gospel as the narrative of an eyewitness, so I am almost solely interested in what is called the "literal" sense of Scripture. Christian exegetes have traditionally recognized four main senses of Scripture: the *literal*, that is, what actually happened; the *moral*, the practical lesson to be drawn; the *allegorical*, the parallel and higher reality that is putatively represented; and the *anagogical*, what is conveyed about the final consummation of creation in glory. If we are construing Mark's Gospel as Peter's account of what it was like to live with Christ for three years, the literal sense assumes primacy.

I am aware of three methods for drawing out the literal sense. In the first, the reader uses his imagination to picture as fully and acutely as possible what is recounted, just as a child listening to a story does. St. Ignatius of Loyola recommends this method in his *Spiritual Exercises*. The second method appeals more to the heart. The reader takes on the role of someone in an episode of the Gospel and fosters the thoughts and emotions of that person. St. Josemaría Escrivá is a great proponent of this method, as for example in his devotional book on the Holy Rosary.

But here I follow a third method, which mainly engages the intellect. In this method, the reader is invited to puzzle over Scripture, to find it intellectually interesting, by considering the question, "What must have things been like for the events recounted here to have taken place?" It is a search for reasons, presuppositions, attendant circumstances, and implications. It is a matter of mulling things over and taking them seriously as though true.

When we pursue the literal sense in any of these ways, we discover it is not narrow or restrictive. When people used to ask Flannery O'Connor what was the meaning or message of one of her stories, she would say that its meaning is what it says. Its meaning is not some philosophical proposition other than what it says. Similarly, reality speaks for itself. It says what it means. It makes an impression precisely as what is real. It does not become more real by being resolved into some kind of lesson of good behavior, psychological hygiene, or doctrinal didacticism.

The venerable project of "harmonizing" the Gospels plays some role in this third method, but it must be approached with moderation. What is harmonization? The accounts of an event in two or more Gospels are frequently untidy or even apparently contradictory. Investigators see something similar whenever there are multiple testimonies, each one truthful, about the same event. In such cases, investigators will attempt to "reconstruct" what happened by postulating a single reality that explains how these apparently conflicting testimonies arose. Likewise, scholars throughout the centuries have attempted to "harmonize" varying Gospel accounts by finding a single account that explains them. St. Augustine's *On the Agreement of the Gospel Writers* is one of the earliest but also one of the most systematic and comprehensive of such attempts.

Mark's Gospel—Peter's narrative—was obviously meant to be heard and to have an effect on its own. So that is the first way we should take it. In general, a thing should be studied in its own right before studying it in comparison with something else. And yet, comparisons with the other Gospels will occasionally bring out something important in Mark. Then too, if we want to take Mark's account seriously as an eyewitness account, we must sometimes consider the objections that arise from apparent contradictions between Mark's Gospel and other Gospels.

It can be no surprise that this book was written out of devotion, even if it is not a devotional book in the usual sense. So let me conclude this introduction with some words of St. Josemaría Escrivá that express for me the importance of the Gospel. This great saint once said to a friend, "When I made you a present of that Life of Jesus, I wrote in it this inscription: 'May you seek Christ. May you find Christ. May you love Christ.' These are three very distinct steps. Have you at least tried to live the first one?"[12] I have written this book for those who seek Christ. With St. Josemaría, I can wish and hope, "May your behavior and your conversation be such that everyone who sees or hears you can say

This man reads the life of Jesus Christ."[13]

Hyattsville, Maryland

June 29, 2018

Feast of St. Peter and St. Paul

The format of the commentary

There are sixteen chapters of Mark's Gospel and therefore sixteen chapters of this commentary. In each chapter, I will first place my translation of the entire corresponding chapter of Mark's Gospel so that it may be read without interruption. Then, for purposes of the commentary, I will break that same translation into chunks, indicated by verse numbers, matching episodes written by Mark (presumably in imitation of Peter's narration). Following each such chunk, I will comment on particular words and phrases, using verse numbers and boldface to indicate what I am commenting upon. It will be necessary

---

12 Josemaría Escrivá, *The Way*, no. 382.
13 Ibid., no. 2.

to look up the entire verse, as only a word or phrase is highlighted, but in this way the reader will be able easily to consider the text at different levels of analysis without the text's being reprinted.

CHAPTER 1

1 This is how it began, the good news of Jesus, Anointed One of God, Son of God.

2 Exactly as is written in Isaiah the prophet (Behold, I am sending my messenger before you, who will prepare your way.... ³"A voice of one crying in the desert, 'Make ready the way of the Lord, make straight his paths!'"), ⁴there arose someone baptizing in the desert, proclaiming a baptism of repentance for the forgiveness of sins—John.

5 And so the whole district of Judea, and residents of Jerusalem from every walk of life, came out to him. And they were baptized by him in the Jordan river as they confessed their sins.

6 Well, as for John, he was clothed in camel hair, with a leather belt around his waist. And for food he ate locusts and wild honey. ⁷And he cried out, "Right behind me comes someone greater than I! I am not worthy to stoop down and loosen the tie on his sandals. ⁸I baptize you with water, but he himself will baptize you in the Holy Spirit."

9 So it was in this setting that Jesus came from Nazareth in Galilee and was baptized in the Jordan by John. ¹⁰And immediately, as he was emerging from the water, he saw heaven opened up and the Spirit

coming down upon him as a dove. ¹¹And there was a voice from heaven: "You are my son, my beloved one. I delight in you."

12 So right away, the Spirit carries him out into the desert. ¹³And he was in the desert for forty days, where he was put to the test by Satan. He faced dangerous animals. And the angels ministered to him.

14 Well, after John was handed over, Jesus went to Galilee, proclaiming the good news of God, ¹⁵and saying that "It is the crucial moment: the Kingdom of God is near. Repent and believe in the good news."

16 And as he was walking along the Sea of Galilee, he saw Simon, and Andrew, the brother of Simon, in the sea casting. (They were fishermen, after all.) ¹⁷So Jesus said to them: "Come, follow me, and I will turn you into fishers of men." ¹⁸And so they, dropping their nets, followed him.

19 So continuing on his way a little bit more, he saw James, the son of Zebedee, and John, his brother. They were mending their nets in a boat. ²⁰So he called them right then and there. And so they left their father Zebedee in the boat with the hired hands, and, taking a place behind him, they walked away.

21 So they make their way into Capernaum. And right away he began teaching in the synagogue there, on the Sabbath. ²²Well, they were overwhelmed by his teaching, because he taught them as someone who had authority, and not as the scribes.

23 And right then there was a man in their synagogue with an unclean spirit. He cried out ²⁴saying, "What business do you have with us, Jesus of Nazareth? Have you come to destroy us? I know who you are, the Holy One of God." ²⁵So Jesus admonished him saying, "Be silent and come out of him." ²⁶Well, the unclean spirit convulsed him and, producing a tremendous sound, came out of him. ²⁷And the people there were all so deeply affected that they began to say to

one another, "What is this? A new teaching. With authority. He tells even unclean spirits what to do, and they obey him." ²⁸And so this report about him traveled straightway throughout the entire region of Galilee.

29 Well, after they left the synagogue, they went directly to Simon and Andrew's home, with James and John. ³⁰Simon's mother-in-law was lying down with a fever. So the first thing, they speak with him about her. ³¹And so, going to her, he raised her up by taking her hand. Well, the fever left her. So she began taking care of them.

32 In the evening, when the sun set, they brought to him everyone who had something wrong, and everyone afflicted by devils. ³³In fact, the entire town gathered at their door. ³⁴So he healed the many townspeople who were sick—suffering from diseases of every description. He cast out many devils. He did not permit the devils to say anything, because they knew him.

35 Well, the following morning, so early that it was still dark, he got up, left the house, and went out to a desolate spot. He remained there to pray. ³⁶So Simon and the others in Jesus' group went searching for him. ³⁷And they found him. So they say to him, "They all want to know where you are." ³⁸So he says to them, "Let's go somewhere else, to the neighboring villages, so that I can preach there as well. That is why I left."

39 So he went throughout the whole of Galilee, preaching in the synagogues there, and expelling devils. ⁴⁰So a leper comes up to him, and, beseeching him and falling to his knees, he says to him, "If you so will, you can make me clean." ⁴¹Well, Jesus was keenly affected, and, reaching out his hand, touched him. So he says to him, "I do so will. Be clean." ⁴²Well, his leprosy was gone immediately. He became clean. ⁴³And so Jesus was stern with him and sent him right off on his way. ⁴⁴And he says to him, "See that you say nothing about this to anyone. But go immediately, present yourself to a priest, and bring

with you, for the fact that you are now clean, the offering which Moses set down as public evidence." [45]But as soon as he left, he began to proclaim it loudly, spreading his story far and wide. Well, that is why it was no longer feasible for Jesus to enter villages openly. Instead, he stayed outside, in desolate places. And people everywhere came to him.

Commentary

1–8

1 This is how it began.

Literally, "The beginning" (Greek: *archē*). Yes, there are deliberate echoes here of Genesis, "In the beginning." John likewise opens, "In the beginning [Greek: *en archē*] was the Word."

But Mark is telling Peter's story of what it was like to live with Jesus for three years. So the "beginning" that concerns Mark is the public life of Christ, and the "good news" he is recounting is displayed in the public life and death and resurrection of Christ as witnessed by Peter.

good news

This renders the Greek word *eu-anggelion*. The root of the word is the same as in the word "angel," a messenger. The prefix indicates something good. It is a good message. A message is a communication conveyed from someone to someone by someone. Walker Percy, in *Message in a Bottle*, distinguishes a "message" from "knowledge." A man stranded on a desert island, he says, is looking for a message, not knowledge. An encyclopedia washing ashore won't help him much. But any scrap with news about how he can be rescued—this he yearns to acquire. Likewise, in this book you will find news, as received and conveyed by Peter, not systematic knowledge.

of Jesus

The message which Peter wishes to convey is not news involving a fact or thing but the person Jesus, just as the preaching of Jesus was mainly about himself.

The Church Fathers[1] used to argue that Jesus "is either God or a bad man—there is no alternative" (*aut Deus aut homo malus*). Jesus taught that he is the way of salvation for everyone—or rather, that he *is* that salvation. But he would need to be God to be that. If he were not that but claimed to be, he would be self-deceived or a deceiver.

What we cannot assert is that Jesus was a "great moral teacher." No great moral teacher makes himself the message. Right from the start Peter makes it clear that this way of interpreting Jesus is closed off to us.

Anointed One of God,

That is, he is the "Christ" (Greek *Christos*, Hebrew *Messiah*). The Anointed One is someone who is shown to have been selected by God, by an anointing, to occupy in a preeminent way the roles of Priest, Prophet, and King—as those were the roles in the Jewish tradition that specifically required anointing.

Son of God

The manuscripts are almost equally divided as to whether Mark originally included this phrase or not. Given this division, we must turn to considerations of a higher level to settle the matter. There are many considerations in favor of including it, but perhaps the most important are the following. First, there are numerous signs that Mark wants to appeal both to Jews and to Gentiles; the title "Anointed One"

---

1 The Fathers are the holy bishops and theologians from the first five centuries of the Church, and later, whose teachings are regarded as particularly authoritative because of their closeness in time to Christ and because they were given the role in divine providence of shaping definitively the teaching of the Church.

answers to the traditions of the former, and "Son of God" corresponds to those of the latter. Second, the Gospel just about ends with the confession of a Gentile—the centurion assigned with guarding the cross—that Jesus was truly the "son of God" (15:39). It makes sense that Mark would begin his narrative with that confession as a kind of confirmation of the title and office ascribed to Jesus.

2 written in Isaiah

Only the line which begins "A voice of one crying in the desert" is from Isaiah. The line before that—"Behold, I am sending my messenger"—is taken from the prophet Malachi (3:1). So has Mark made a mistake? Or was the phrase "written in Isaiah" added by a later editor who did not know what he was doing? Because of the perceived difficulty here, the phrase is changed in various later manuscript traditions from "written in Isaiah" to "written in the prophets."

And yet there is no real problem. It turns out that the line from Isaiah is an exact quotation of the Septuagint.[2] The line from Malachi is a paraphrase. So we can take Mark to be principally concerned with the verse from Isaiah, which he quotes exactly, and introducing the quotation with the line from Malachi as a kind of gloss. There are no quotation marks in ancient Greek, but in English the difference can easily be indicated by putting only the verse from Isaiah in quotation marks, as I have done.

So the apparent difficulty in **verses 1–2** can be dealt with easily enough. But what can be said about their meaning? Peter seems to have been struck by the fulfillment in his own day of the Scriptural prophecy that someone would arise in the desert and cry out there to herald the Messiah—for lo and behold, John the Baptist had done exactly that. Peter believed that the coincidence between Isaiah and

---

2 The Greek version of the Old Testament, commonly quoted by New Testament writers. It gets its name from a tradition that seventy scholars, working independently, all produced the same translation.

John was too remarkable to be an accident: it was the fulfillment of the prophecy.

2–3 "I am sending…"

If "I" is God and the "messenger" is John, who in this paraphrase of Malachi is this "you" whose way is prepared? The verse from Isaiah supplies the answer

It is the way *of the Lord.* It tells us, then, that the "you" whose way is being prepared and who ostensibly is distinct from God is also God, as he is the Lord. These verses, then, implicitly introduce the doctrine of the Trinity: the Father, who is Lord, sends the Son, who is Lord—at least two persons, then, in one God.

The Trinitarian implications of the passage are not clear without the verse from Malachi. It seems, therefore, that an inspired Mark joined the two verses from the prophets to imply the divinity of Christ, and we find the seeds of the doctrine of the Trinity right at the beginning of the Gospel of Mark.

4 someone baptizing in the desert, proclaiming

Consider the parallelism here:

someone baptizing in the desert

proclaiming a baptism of repentance for the forgiveness of sins

Mark asserts a parallelism between action and word: John *does* something, and at the same time he *preaches* about what he is doing, because he proclaims that his baptism, if accompanied by repentance, effects the forgiveness of sins. In describing John in this way, Mark (or Peter) is suggesting that John prefigures what is known as "the sacramental system"—God's free use of material signs to effect his purposes and confer graces, through his ministers, in a reliable and repeatable way. These signs *accomplish what they signify.* In a sacrament, an action signifies something, and the words clarify and effect what is done in the action.

The verb "baptize" is a transliteration of a Greek verb, *baptizo*, which means the action of immersing in a liquid, generally water. Usually, the thing immersed is drawn out again. The phrase **baptizing in the desert** is therefore paradoxical. A desert by definition lacks water for dipping.

Imagine someone encountering water in the desert and being immersed in it. He comes out again, refreshed by the water and coated with it under the sun. This is a vivid sign of what the baptism of John signified. The desert represents distance from God and loss of true life through sin. The water represents life—life with God again, and regeneration. The immersion in the water, when accompanied by conversion, effects that change because it is **for the forgiveness of sins**. That is, by God's special institution, it effects that forgiveness.

John's preaching confirms this by word. What John says gives the interpretation of the material sign. It is not that the material actions of immersion and emergence are *like* a parallel spiritual reality of repentance and forgiveness. There are not two things going on; there is one thing. John's action and preaching are a unity. Mark's use of the Hebrew poetic device of repetition emphasizes this. John's **baptizing in the desert** and his **proclaiming a baptism of repentance for the forgiveness of sins**, then, are the same thing viewed differently.

5 they were baptized . . . as they confessed their sins.

The Greek term rendered "confessed" (*exomologoumenoi*) means to acknowledge and additionally to express that acknowledgement in a binding way, somewhat as one binds oneself through a legal document. To confess sins in this sense is to bind oneself to accept the punishment due to them and to bind oneself to refrain from those sins in the future.

We cannot tell from Mark's bare description whether these people expressed their sins openly to one another, to John, or simply to

God in prayer. Given that we are told that John immersed them, perhaps the most likely alternative is that they confessed their sins to John prior to immersion.

Mark's use of the plural "sins" suggests not an acknowledgment of general sinfulness but some kind of reckoning and accounting.

6 around his waist

The phrase in Greek means, precisely, slung low just over the hips. Peter is conveying how John looked to him when he went out into the desert, presumably to confess his own sins.

7 "Right behind me comes someone greater than I!"

Let us not fail to notice that John uses the present tense, which would indicate that this one who is to come is coming soon or is alive already.

It is difficult for a modern reader to appreciate how paradoxical this teaching would have seemed to John's listeners. Someone who came after would be literally a follower. But followers were at best the equal of those they followed, never greater. That is why John had to emphasize

"I am not worthy to stoop down and loosen the tie on his sandals."

To the Fathers, such imagery implied the divinity of Christ: "He says this to extol the excellence of the power of Christ, and the greatness of His divinity; as if he said, Not even in the station of his servant am I worthy to be reckoned. For it is a great thing to contemplate, as it were stooping down, those things which belong to the body of Christ, and to see from below the image of things above, and to untie each of those mysteries, about the Incarnation of Christ, which cannot be unraveled."[3]

---

3 Chrysostom, quoted in Saint Thomas Aquinas, *Catena Aurea: Gospel of Mark,* trans. William Whiston (Grand Rapids, MI: Christian Classics Ethereal Library), p. 9.

8 "he himself will baptize you in the Holy Spirit"

Literally, "he himself will baptize you *in holy spirit*." "Spirit" (Greek *pneuma*) was regarded as akin to air, one of the four elements along with earth, water, and fire. The initial contrast is between John's immersing sinners in visible, material stuff (water) and Christ's immersing them in a finer, immaterial stuff (spirit)—not just any spirit, but "holy" spirit.

John emphasizes that *he himself* will baptize you: that is, his successor himself will be the agent of the immersion which he effects. He will not be simply a "messenger."

Accordingly, the Fathers take John's contrast to imply that the one who followed him would be God himself. "How does water differ from the Holy Spirit, who was borne over the face of the waters? Water is the ministry of man; but the Spirit is ministered by God," writes St. Jerome.[4]

9–11

9 it was in this setting

Literally, "in those days." The translation is free but also accurate. In Mark's day, ordinary people did not use a calendar. They dated events in relation to who happened to be in authority at the time or some cyclical event, such as the Olympiads. Mark is saying, in effect, "You want to know when Jesus burst upon the scene? That dates back to the time when there was that widespread religious reawakening of people going out to the desert to see John."

Jesus came from Nazareth in Galilee

John baptized sometimes at Bethany "beyond the Jordan" and sometimes at Aenon near Salim. According to John's Gospel, Jesus was baptized at the Aenon location, about a forty-mile walk from

---

4 Jerome, ibid., p. 10.

Nazareth. At either location, a pilgrimage to see the Baptist would require about a week, a substantial endeavor.

Jesus **was baptized in the Jordan by John.** It notably does not say that he was baptized "confessing his sins."

10 immediately, as he was emerging

Here "immediately" emphasizes that in Jesus' baptism, God, through the ministry of John, conferred on him a kind of public office. John did not simply prepare the way and precede "the one who was to come." He was instrumental in effecting the start of Jesus' public ministry.

heaven opened up

Literally, "heaven divided." Physical heaven was regarded as a hemispherical vault over the earth, holding back the waters above. The splitting of that vault would have been regarded as a sign of the opening of a direct and intimate path between the dealings of man on earth and the realm of God in immaterial heaven. This sign from the beginning of Mark's Gospel is comparable to the splitting of the temple curtain at the end of the Gospel, when Christ dies on the Cross (Mk. 15:38–40).

11 there was a voice

In Greek, "voice" (*phōne*) is a species of sound, so everyone present—John the Baptist, anyone in the crowd, and of course Jesus himself—must have heard it. We should therefore suppose that the vision of heaven opening and the dove descending were likewise seen by everyone. And yet Mark writes as though the vision was seen only by Jesus. Why?

Consider two possible descriptions of what happened: (1) there was a general public miracle of the splitting open of heaven, the descent of a dove, and a voice from above, which everyone in that place experienced, including Jesus, or (2) there was a miraculous vision *directed at* Jesus, and there were miraculous words addressed *to him*, an expression of the intimate relationship between Father and Son, and those persons who were around Jesus were invited to share with him in that vision.

Mark's language suggests the second. That is, this miracle was not for the benefit of the crowd but was a natural expression of the love of the Father for the Son, which others were privileged to witness.

We observed that Mark is silent as to Jesus' confession of sin. In place of such a confession, we find rather a "confession" coming from God in heaven: **"You are my son, my beloved one. I delight in you."** (The Greek is literally "You are the beloved one of mine, the beloved son of mine," and carries the sense of "only begotten son.") Instead of a man saying, "I have displeased you, God, for I have sinned," we hear God saying, "You please me, you have not sinned."

12 So right away, the Spirit carries him out into the desert.

Here, "right away" establishes a connection between Jesus' baptism and his testing in the desert. The same Spirit who descended as a dove brings him into the desert. "Conversion brings trouble," St. Augustine wrote, and if the baptism of Christ is an image of the baptism of any Christian, then we should expect that baptism to be connected, at some time or other, with spiritual dryness, temptations of the devil, and trials.

The phrase "carries him into the desert" is literally "expelled him into the desert." The verb *ekballō* typically means a violent action going against natural or habitual inclination. The Fathers take the word to emphasize that Jesus faced temptations only out of obedience, not by recklessly seeking them out.

13 forty days

These forty days correspond to the Israelites' forty years of wandering in the desert under Moses and Joshua. Jesus therefore represents the Jewish people. In the desert, he would face similar trials: temptations to idolatry (like the golden calf); temptations to grumble from hunger; and temptations to doubt God's power to rescue (see Mt. 4:1–11).

He faced dangerous animals.

Literally, "he was among wild animals." The implication is that these were threatening animals. Note that at least half the time in the desert, he would have been in complete darkness, alone.

the angels ministered

Jesus could have fortified his human nature by an act of his divine will, but since he chose to leave it weak he needed the angels to protect him. Just as Mark's mention of Satan signifies that the temptations were both real and from without, so this mention of the holy angels signifies that Jesus' weakness was real and within him.

14–15

Mark here wishes to identify two spiritual eras, first that of John and then that of Jesus. "When the Law ceases, the Gospel arises in its steps," observes the Venerable Bede.

14 Jesus went to Galilee

Unlike John, Jesus did not go to an unusual place to teach but started from his home town and places familiar from his childhood.

the good news of God

He preaches the good news of Jesus Christ, which is the good news of God, and so once again we are invited to infer that Jesus is God.

If someone were to say, "Well, what Mark means is that the good news is *from God*, although it is *about* Jesus"—this would be just as extraordinary, since John did not preach about himself but about someone who was to come. But then what about this "One who is to come"—what does he preach about? Did he preach *not* about God, but about himself? No, we must mean that he preached about God in preaching about himself.

15 "It is the crucial moment"

Literally, "the moment has reached fulfillment," but in Greek, the "moment" (*kairos*) was something which passed. It was necessary to act then and just then. There is an urgency in this preaching as great as the good which is at stake.

"Repent and believe in the good news."

We have here a progressive idea: repent in order to believe (accept trustfully) the good news. One would think it would be easy and straightforward to accept good news. But implicit in this phrase is the idea that good news may not appear good. Good news tests us: we need to change, to convert, in order to accept it. We need to convert because the good news contains something hidden. The Kingdom of God is present, indeed, but it is also concealed: it is "near."

16–20

The successive callings of the first apostles, apparently on the same day, are presented as miraculous. People wonder whether these men knew Jesus before. Perhaps they had already discussed with him the possibility of following permanently as disciples, so that these "callings" were only a matter of Jesus' telling them, in effect, "It's time." Even if that were true, there was still something miraculous about these callings.

16 he saw Simon

Simon is mentioned first in all lists of the apostles in the New Testament. Here, Mark takes pains to name Peter first. As if to emphasize the point, Andrew does not stand on his own but is simply "the brother of Peter." In such usages, we find evidence of the "primacy of Peter" among the disciples of Jesus.

in the sea casting

Sometimes this is translated "casting their nets into the sea." But "in the sea" seems to indicate where they were, not where their nets were going. Thus there is parallelism in the two callings: "they were in the sea, casting their nets" (v. 16) and "they were in a boat, mending their nets" (v. 19). They were not standing on the shore, but casting in thigh-deep water. Apparently, they simply dropped their nets in the water, a dramatic statement.

(They were fishermen, after all.)

Since Mark has just said they were in the sea casting, he hardly needs to explain that they were fishing. So this remark has two functions. First, it emphasizes that they fished by *occupation*. Thus, when they left their nets, they forsook their livelihood. Second, it is a reminder to the early Christian community, in a Gospel written twenty or more years after the event, of the humble origins of their spiritual leaders.

17 "fishers of men"

Once we understand that **"they were fishermen"** emphasizes the occupation or role these men filled, we must understand "I will turn you into fishers of men" as Jesus' saying that he will confer a new occupation, and a new role, upon them. These men are not simply chance followers: they are to occupy an office.

The point is reinforced by Our Lord's language "I will turn you into" is literally "I will make it so that you become." Their becoming Fishers of Men will be the result of some kind of effective action on Our Lord's part.

The word "fisherman" in Greek is taken from the word for "sea." Literally it means "seaman"—someone proficient with life in and around the water. It would have been impossible for anyone to have heard this phrase without imagining men adrift (and drowning?) in the sea. A fisherman takes fish out of where they belong and into where they do not belong. A fisher of men, in contrast, goes out into inhospitable places (the sea) to find men where they do not belong and brings them home.

19 They were mending their nets

Simon and Andrew were called in the middle of their work, which they left. James and John, in contrast, were called while taking a break from their work, making good use of that "down time." But their calling had its own dramatic gesture, insofar as they had to jump into the water from the boat, and they left their father behind.

20 taking a place behind him

The language indicates a simple fact we may be inclined to overlook: that the word "follower of Christ" meant not simply someone who followed the teachings of the Master but also, originally, someone who walked behind the Master as he traveled from town to town.

The word order in the Greek is "walked away, taking a place behind him." Often word order in Greek is important for meaning. Here, Mark emphasizes that they did not decide "to abandon their father" (nor did Simon and Andrew decide to abandon their work) but decided "to walk behind Christ"—and as a consequence, their father (and their work) was left behind.

21–28

Here Mark gives an account of an incident at the very beginning of Jesus' public ministry, and at the same time explains how it was the source of common, invidious rumors about Jesus. People were "overwhelmed" and "deeply affected" by what they saw. They couldn't help talking about it. But the report that came out in fragments—"new teaching," "a special authority," "superior to the scribes," "commanding evil spirits," "does what he wants on the Sabbath"—would pave the way for false charges later made against Jesus.

21 they make their way

Not "Jesus makes his way, with his disciples," but now simply "they." Because of their calling, these disciples now form a single association (*koinōnia*) with him.

21 right away he began teaching

Jesus wanted to teach in the synagogue without delay. They happened to arrive in Capernaum on the Sabbath, and that is how Jesus ended up teaching (and healing) on the Sabbath.

22 overwhelmed by his teaching

The Greek connotes an emotional impact: Jesus spoke directly to the deepest longings of the human heart.

as someone who had authority

Understand this remark not simply as Mark's explanation of why the people there felt as they did, but as how those people would have expressed how they felt.

Religion involves a search for truth. Since the truth of religion is beyond us, it requires a search for the right authority. Finding what one takes to be a genuine authority is therefore an important part of this search. Today, for example, someone might say he is a Christian because he finds that the New Testament speaks to him authoritatively. Mark and the other Gospel writers report that many people responded to Jesus in this way and for this reason.

23 there was a man in their synagogue

By noting that the man was there when Jesus and his disciples entered the synagogue, Mark indicates that this healing took place on the Sabbath, too. He emphasizes that, for Jesus, teaching and healing were integrated.

"With an unclean spirit" is literally "in an unclean spirit." That's idiomatic Greek, but it is also theologically more accurate than the English. Angels, whether good or bad, have no bodies and are not "in" things. But because a spirit has power over things within the person, such as the power to cause his muscles to convulse, it is said popularly that a spirit is in him.

23 "Have you come to destroy us?"

The devil in that man bears witness against his will. Only God has the power to annihilate, just as only God has the power to create. Implicit in this statement, then, is an affirmation that Jesus is God.

Yet the devil supposes something false about God. A rational creature by its nature lives forever. God would need to will it into nothingness to destroy it. But sound theology holds that this he cannot do, because he is good. He can punish an evil spirit forever, as that would be to confer upon the spirit the good of justice, but he cannot annihilate it.

24 "I know who you are"

Note the switch to the first person singular, from "us" to "I," suggesting that a single spirit possesses this man, not a "legion" of them, as in chapter 5 below. When this single devil earlier referred to "us," he was referring to other devils in general, not other devils possessing the man.

25 Jesus admonished him

That is, he did not agree with him; he did not support him; he was not in league with that spirit in any way. Mark wishes to make that very clear.

"Be silent"

Devils speak lies constantly. When faced with them, the first wish of any holy person, and therefore of course Jesus, is "Silence!"

26 convulsed him

Literally, "tore him to pieces." Out of spite, the devil attacks the man as much as possible on the way out. This detail emphasizes that though the devil does what Jesus commands, it is not in any way "in league" with Jesus. The devil is clearly forced to comply.

producing a tremendous sound

Literally, "sounding with a great sound." This may or may not be a voice. The devil could have used the lungs and vocal chords of the poor possessed man to produce a loud cry. But the sound could have been some "unearthly" or "supernatural" inhuman utterance, such as is sometimes reported in exorcisms.

27 "With authority. He tells even unclean spirits what to do...."

In this crucial passage, Mark indicates how rumors (the deliberately clipped phrases) arose naturally from the astonishing event.

28 this report about him traveled straightway

The force of "straightway" is that this report established itself before Jesus preached elsewhere in that region and therefore colored some persons' reception of him, while also making Jesus an object of intense curiosity.

The way in which these rumors arose and hampered his ministry explains why Jesus, when he cured the sick, would charge them to refrain from telling others about the healing.

29 they went directly

The Greek *euthus* reminds us that what takes place next is still on the Sabbath. Again, Simon is mentioned first, although it is equally Andrew's home. Again, it is noteworthy that they go to a home: the mission of Jesus is based in the homes of his followers and friends. The house in ancient Capernaum (within the so-called *Insula Sacra*) that tradition identifies as Peter's is quite suitable for gatherings, measuring a spacious thirty feet by thirty feet.

30 The first thing

Jesus had not healed anyone of physical disease in the synagogue. He cast out a devil. But faith has its own powerful logic. The disciples evidently drew the conclusion that Jesus was therefore capable of healing Peter's mother-in-law.

Note the discretion conveyed by Mark's expression "they spoke with him about her." Most likely, they made their request indirectly: "She says she is sorry she cannot greet you. She is ill with a fever."

31 going to her, he raised her up

A marvelously refined detail. Mark could have written that after his disciples spoke of the mother-in-law, Jesus raised her by the hand. Instead he takes pains to indicate that Jesus approaches her. He deals with her as a person. After he has approached her, he heals her.

He does not heal her with words. Here is another detail, like the one we noted above, which has the ring of an eyewitness account: he took her hand and raised her to her feet. We should try to imagine this. He would not have roughly pulled her to her feet. She would have had to be cooperating. This means she had to be looking him in the eyes, seeing his intention, and indicating her willingness to go along. This would imply real faith on her part that he was doing something reasonable.

We may conjecture that Peter includes this detail because later, after the resurrection, it became clear that Jesus intended this gentle act to be a sign for those present of the resurrection of the dead. Mark's language seems designed to suggest this intention: "He raised her up," which is a slightly odd expression as it stands.

Consider how compelling that sign is: Jesus approaches someone who is "sleeping" and in a personal encounter with that soul invites her to be raised back to life.

she began taking care of them

It is a reasonable inference that she was in charge of the household. The concerns of women of the day are, therefore, introduced into Mark's Gospel at its very start. Only men gather at a Jewish synagogue. But the moment Jesus leaves the synagogue and arrives at a home, he is dealing with the woman in charge there and taking her concerns to be his own.

32–34

32 when the sun set

The townspeople wanted to go to that house, but they waited until the moment the sun set, presumably from observance of the Sabbath.

How did they know to bring the sick to Jesus? Either they used the same "logic of faith" as the disciples, or word had gotten out that Jesus had healed Peter's mother-in-law.

34 he healed the many townspeople

The suggestion here is that Jesus healed them all. So "the many" is preferable to "many," as some translations have it. We know that that is the suggestion from the phrase attached:

suffering from diseases of every description

The phrase in Greek connotes striking variety—everything from goiter to leprosy. Mark's phrase implies that the healing power was evidently miraculous, even divine, because of the range of illnesses it could heal.

because they knew him

Apparently the devils did not know his power earlier, at the synagogue. The question posed then—"What do you have to do with us?"—seemed provocative and a test; it expressed dread. But then that devil's expulsion *showed* what Jesus had to do with them. They then "knew" he was a superior spiritual power and therefore, by implication, God.

35–45

These passages go together. The first reveals that Jesus would have preferred to go to the people himself and travel rather quickly from village to village, preaching the good news. The second explains why Jesus ended up taking a different approach, staying out in the countryside, crowds going out there to hear him.

35 The following morning

He preached in the synagogue of Capernaum for a day, and now it was time to go to the next town. Jesus is never depicted as delaying or taking time off.

so early that it was still dark

The daytime represents both creation and the time of work. The Son rising before the sun rises represents God's providence and wisdom, a preliminary to any action of God in the world. At the same time, his example teaches us that we should not attempt to work without first praying.

he got up, left the house, and went out to a desolate spot

As becomes clear below, Jesus did not just go out of the house for a bit. He was leaving it to move on.

36 Simon and the others in Jesus' group went searching for him

The sense of the sentence is that Simon led the others in search of Jesus.

37 "They all want to know where you are."

This statement is beautiful because it is so human. It is another of those details that point to an eyewitness account. This is exactly what we would say—not "we wanted to know where you were," but shifting the responsibility, "Everyone wants to know."

38 "Let's go somewhere else"

Another beautiful detail, so frank and direct. The disciples would have been startled by the abruptness of Jesus' statement. They had just arrived in town. Simon's mother-in-law was looking forward to showing more hospitality. The people he healed wanted to return and spend more time with him. They had questions about his synagogue preaching. But Jesus says, "Let's go somewhere else."

"neighboring villages"

Literally, the villages contiguous to this one. The phrase implies an open series: we start here, we go to the villages around this one, then we go to the villages around those, and so on.

"That is why I left."

It is now apparent that this means, "That is why I took my leave of the house and have started on the way." Literally, the language is, "That is why I came forth." In this literal sense, the word might be taken to refer to the Incarnation—"that is why I came forth from the Father into the world." In any case, it implies a *missio*, a being sent into a context to accomplish a task.

39 preaching in the synagogues there, and expelling devils

Mark does not mention healing the sick. Presumably, the sick who needed healing would not be in the synagogues: they would stay at home. But men troubled by devils would go to the synagogues, just as we see troubled persons in churches today. These are dealing with supernatural battles and are drawn to the holy places.

From this detail, it is clear that Jesus followed a plan in his ministry. He did not act at random to spread the good news. His plan was to go to a town, preach in the synagogue, expel devils there (if he found any), move on to the neighboring town, and so on. This plan is eventually frustrated, so Jesus needs to adopt a "second-best" alternative.

40 a leper comes up to him

Proclaiming the Kingdom, not healing the sick, was Jesus' purpose, as he told his disciples. In journeying from town to town, however, he would inevitably encounter lepers, banished from towns and living in desolate places. A leper along the way sees Jesus passing by and approaches him.

beseeching him and falling to his knees

Presumably this leper has heard the reports about healings in Capernaum. His actions already indicate his great faith. One is constantly astounded by the refinement of these simple people. He does not shout or implore. He does not play the victim. As far as we know, he does not even directly ask for anything. He utters a conditional sentence, "If you wish, you can heal me."

41 Jesus was keenly affected

The Greek participle rendered "keenly affected" is *orgistheis*, which means literally "becoming angry." That Jesus would be angry at the poor leper is absurd. Not surprisingly, most ancient manuscripts softened the statement by changing the word to *splangnistheis*, which means "feeling compassion in his guts." ("By the bowels of Christ" used to be an expression in English meaning "by the mercy of Christ.")

Yet *orgistheis*, when properly understood, can stand. In the ancient world, it was thought that there were two centers of emotional reaction in man. One such center, desire (*epithumia*), found things pleasant or unpleasant and therefore simply sought or avoided them. The other center, anger (*orgē, thumos*), came into play whenever there was a struggle to prevail against challenges.

Mark chooses a word that means that Jesus' reaction to the leper came from the latter emotional center. We should presume that Jesus did indeed feel pity, but it was an indignant pity. That is, he is "angry" not *at the leper* but *about his sickness and suffering*. We know exactly what Mark means by this. The term also brilliantly implies that Jesus is highly motivated to do something.

St. Thomas Aquinas defines mercy as "a heartfelt identification with the suffering of another which moves us to do something to relieve his suffering." This seems precisely what Mark wants to indicate.

reaching out his hand, touched him

This is another beautiful detail. The leper, out of self-disgust and regard for the feelings of others, would not have dared to touch Jesus. He kneels down at Jesus' feet, apparently within arm's reach. Now think of the boldness of someone who reaches out and touches such a leper. Note too how Jesus touches him even before he declares that he will heal him. Such a gesture proves that he would have touched him, even if he did not heal him. He touched him, then, simply because he was a fellow man who was afflicted. But he also touched him as a visible sign of healing power.

The dialogue in faith between the leper and Christ is impressive: "If you so will," spoken with tears, in faith, and "I do so will," spoken in solidarity and with indignant pity.

43 Jesus was stern with him

The Greek means literally "he snorted in through his nostrils"! It might mean being aroused like a restless horse—surely reporting the impression of any eyewitness! In the context, it implies that Jesus visibly expressed his seriousness about what he next did and said.

Presumably the very human emotional arousal in Christ, which came from looking with indignation at his suffering, affected, as emotions do, his statements and actions that followed.

We are meant to infer from the account that Jesus did not merely "say," out of some contrived sense of humility, that the man should say nothing about the healing. He really meant it; this was an utterly sincere and a serious business for him.

44 "See that you say nothing about this to anyone...."

These words are given at length and with great care. They are precise and represent an accurate understanding of the requirements of the law of Moses for recovery from leprosy, the intentions underlying that law, and how the man should satisfy those requirements,

even though his healing was miraculous. They show Jesus to be a
master of that law and a lawful Jew.

45 that is why...

Christ tried to avoid this result. And so here Mark's account is
complete. He has explained how Jesus initially wanted to proceed
and why he was compelled to change his approach.

Jesus has already been presented as such a remarkable and compelling figure that here we wonder what is next. Will Mark relay his
teaching in synagogues or what he says when crowds come to him
in desolate places? What other healings will he accomplish? What
does he say about himself and his mission? How will the religious
authorities in Jerusalem respond to him?

CHAPTER 2

1 When some days had passed, he went into Capernaum again. Word got out—he's in his house! 2So many men gathered there that it became impossible to move. There were not even any open spaces around the door.

So he was speaking his message to them. 3And here they come bringing a paralyzed man, carried by four men! 4When they couldn't bring him through, because of the crowd, they pulled away the roof above the spot where he was. And after they've dug up the tiles, they lower the pallet down—where this paralyzed man was lying. 5So Jesus sees their faith and says to the paralyzed man, "Child, your sins are forgiven."

6 There were some scribes sitting there. And they are thinking to themselves, 7"How can he talk like that? He is blaspheming. Who has the power to forgive sins except God alone?"

8 So Jesus—who knows immediately in his spirit that this is how they are thinking among themselves—says to them, "Why are you thinking those things? 9Which is easier, to say to the paralyzed man, 'Your sins are forgiven,' or to say, 'Get up, take your pallet, and walk'? 10 ... But so that you may know that the Son of Man has authority on

earth to forgive sins…"—now he speaks to the paralytic— [11]"I say to you, get up, take your pallet, and return home!" [12]The man got up. Without delay, he grabbed the pallet and left—right in front of everyone. The effect was that everyone was overcome with amazement. And they gave glory to God, saying, "We have never seen anything like this."

13 So again he went out along the sea. And the entire crowd went out to him. So he taught them.

14 He was traveling along and saw Levi, the son of Alphaeus, sitting at his desk in the customs house. And he says to him, "Follow me!"—So he got up and followed him.

15 So he is reclining at table in his house.—Now, many tax collectors and many public sinners used to recline at table with Jesus and his disciples. They were many in number, and they were among his followers.— [16]So some scribes who belonged to the party of the Pharisees, when they see that he is eating with public sinners and tax collectors, had a word with his disciples about it: "Why does he eat with tax collectors and public sinners?" [17]So Jesus overhears this and says to them, "It's not the strong who need a physician but the infirm. I have not come to call righteous men, but sinners."

18 The disciples of John, and the Pharisees also, were men who would keep fasts. So they come to Jesus and they raise this with him: "Why is it that the disciples of John, and the disciples of the Pharisees, keep fasts, but your disciples on the contrary never fast?" [19]Jesus said to them, "Can the friends of the bridegroom fast, when the bridegroom is with them? No. So long as the bridegroom is with them, they cannot fast. [20]Yet the days will come when the bridegroom is snatched away from them. Then they will fast—on that day."

21 "No one sews a patch of unshrunk cloth on an old garment. If he does, the patch tears away from it, the new from the old, and a worse tear results. [22]And no one puts new wine into old wineskins. If

he does, the wine will burst the skins, and the wine gets destroyed along with the wineskins. No, he puts new wine into fresh wineskins."

23 One time he was traveling on the Sabbath through a field of grain. So his disciples started plucking off heads of grain as they made their way through. ²⁴So the Pharisees said to him: "Look! Why are they, on the Sabbath, doing a thing which is not allowed on the Sabbath?" ²⁵So he says to them, "Did you never read what David did, from necessity, when he and the men in his group were hungry? ²⁶How he entered into the house of God, in the presence of Abiathar, high priest, and he ate the loaves for the offering, which only priests are allowed to eat? He gave them also to the men who were with him." ²⁷He told them, "The Sabbath was made for man, not man for the Sabbath. ²⁸It follows that the Son of Man is Lord of the Sabbath as well."

Commentary

1–3

Mark is recording Peter's telling of the life of Jesus. Since there would have been thousands of stories to relate about the public ministry of Jesus, Peter is faced with the pastoral question: Which stories should he select to present Jesus to others quickly and with the least possibility of misunderstandings? To begin, he picks a story which not only is dramatic but also shows how Jesus revealed more about himself to those around him over time. Here, specifically, Jesus reveals that he has "authority on earth" to forgive sins.

1 Word got out—he's in his house!

Mark loves to use the historic present, and each time he does so it has a special purpose and effect. Here his writing seems to echo what people actually said.

2 So many men gathered there...

A detail that reads like an eyewitness report. Mark is conveying what it was like to be there. "It became impossible to move" is what someone would say who experienced the inconvenience.

his message

"Message" here is *logos*: "He was speaking the *logos* to them" is what the text literally says.

Logos is notorious for having many different meanings. It can mean "word," "story," "reasoning," and "message"—among other things. Here, it serves as a placeholder. Peter does not want to burden his story by giving the content of what Jesus was saying. He simply wants to set the scene by explaining that Jesus was focused on speaking to the people gathered there (see 1:14–15).

3 here they come bringing a paralyzed man, carried by four men!

The language suggests there were more than five in the group: the paralyzed man, four men carrying him, and others, perhaps female relatives. Two men can carry a pallet, so why does Mark mention that in this case it was four? So that readers will not be surprised by what he relates next. His audience, familiar with these tile roofs, know that two men alone cannot go up with a man on a pallet and lower him down.

4–12

4 When they couldn't bring him through...

Mark puts this description of their intent at the start, to convey their audacity. "The way is blocked? Oh well, there's nothing for it— let's remove the roof!"

5 Jesus sees their faith and says...

Faith obviously includes works, if Jesus, in seeing their works, is said by Mark to see their faith. The audacity, ingenuity, exertion, and even willingness to face embarrassment that these men display are the visible measure of their faith. And everyone sees it, not simply Jesus.

says to the paralyzed man

He is paralyzed. He cannot climb ladders or dig up tiles. If he was like other sick people, he would not wish to inconvenience his friends. He would not have been the one to propose coming down through the roof. So when Jesus sees "their faith," he sees the faith of the friends. And yet this man's sins are forgiven in view of their faith. Here we see clearly the communal, not individualistic, character of Christianity. The sins of one man are forgiven in view of the faith of his friends. We can easily understand, then, how for early Christians the newborn babe—essentially a "paralytic"!—might be baptized in view of the faith of the parents, who carry him and lower him into the baptismal font.

"your sins are forgiven"

Forgiving the man's sins is the best thing Jesus can do for him. We are meant to suppose that it corresponds to what the paralyzed man most wants, and it dramatically illustrates the message Jesus has been teaching—repent of your sins and believe that the Kingdom of God has arrived. The forgiveness of this man's sins is the response to repentance, and Christ's exercise of his "authority on earth to forgive sins" reveals the presence, then and there, of the Kingdom of God.

6 There were some scribes...

Scribes were educated men, experts in written texts of the Jewish religion and law. They combined aspects of what in our society are distinct types: bureaucrats, intellectuals, lawyers, journalists, consultants.

they are thinking to themselves

Literally, "carrying on a dialogue in their hearts." Thinking was understood as the same as spoken dialogue, but carried on silently, in the heart.

7 "Who has the power to forgive sins except God alone?"

The Pharisees think that the answer to this question is no one, and certainly no man. Jesus' use of the phrase "Son of Man" in response, then, is aimed directly at this implicit answer.

To blaspheme is to attribute to God what does not belong to him or to deny what does belong to him. The scribes are not saying that Jesus is blaspheming because he makes himself equivalent to God, but rather that he blasphemes because, thinking he has the power to forgive sins although he is not God (they suppose), he is denying that God exclusively has that power.

Their position is generous, in a sense. They do not deny that the paralyzed man's sins might have been forgiven by God through Jesus' agency—as sins were forgiven by God through John's baptism. What riles the scribes is Jesus' speaking as though the forgiveness is coming from him.

The main question here is not whether the man's sins are forgiven, but whether Jesus forgives them on his own authority.

8 who knows immediately in his spirit ...

Peter, narrating the story, says that Jesus "knew" what they were thinking; it was not a conjecture. He knew "in his spirit," not as an inference from sensed signs.

The description is meant to help us imagine how the scene appeared to those who were there. Jesus says to the paralyzed man, "Your sins are forgiven," and then, unexpectedly, he turns and addresses some of the others present. Imagine how startling it would be if your friend were standing in the middle of a crowded room speaking to one person and then suddenly turned around, looked at someone else across the room, and said, "You are wrong in what you are thinking!"

9 "Which is easier ...?"

By using the verb "to say," Jesus invites us to draw a distinction. If "to say" means the mere articulation of words, then neither statement is more difficult than the other. All the words are easy to pronounce. But if "to say" means to command by speaking, again neither seems easier or more difficult than the other, because both require the same power. To forgive sins requires the same power as to create, as shown in an instantaneous healing.

A scribe who reasoned in this way would realize that Jesus was chiding him for not having inferred already that if Jesus, by direct command and therefore on his own authority, could heal, then he could also forgive sins on his own authority. The common people in the room had sensed this intuitively; the scribes ought to have been able to reason to that conclusion.

The question in play here is actually whether Jesus is God incarnate. Those who say that Jesus slowly came to the realization that he was God, or that the doctrine of God incarnate developed over centuries in the early Church, are not paying careful attention to the text here.

Jesus' question invites the scribes to reason carefully about the healings they have already seen and supplies the reasoning by which they should evaluate what comes next.

10 "But so that you may know"

Jesus' question has a third sense too: "Which is easier to say?" can also mean "Which is less important?" Then the answer is to heal the man. Jesus did not come into the world to heal but to forgive sins. In forgiving the man's sins, then, he had done the less easy thing, and in healing him he will do the "easier" thing.

Jesus therefore sets down here a general principle for the interpretation of his miraculous works: those that are bodily are for the sake of the spiritual. He is not a wonder worker who does amazing things solely to impress. The miracles are also signs, which reveal and teach.

Jesus thus endorses the search for the "spiritual" senses of Scripture—the moral, allegorical, and anagogical. The man's infirmity stands for something; that he gets up and walks points to something; that Jesus tells him to go home stands for something and teaches. The miracles do take place on the physical level, yet they are "easier" than the spiritual realities they point to.

"the Son of Man has authority on earth to forgive sins..."

The authority to forgive sins is divine. He is not invoking this power. He *has* this power. The person who speaks is therefore both human and divine. By referring to himself as "Son of Man," he indicates that this authority is his own, not something extrinsic.

"Upon earth" emphasizes that this power is incarnate. The "earth" is fleshly; it is the place where animals dwell. A new power is at work in this domain, possessed by a living being here: the divine power to forgive sins.

12 Without delay, he grabbed the pallet and left—right in front of everyone.

Jesus asks a question about giving a command; he gives the command; and what he commands happens immediately. This is as clear a display of power originating directly from him as could be sought. That is why Jesus allowed this to happen as it did, and why Peter narrates it as he does.

Suppose I were to say in front of a crowd and I said, "Which shows the most power, to tell a shrub or to tell a tree to be uprooted and fly into the sea?" Then I turn to the shrub and say, "Be uprooted and fly into the sea!" And the shrub is uprooted and flies into the sea. My having contemplated giving the command, my giving it at my pleasure, and the accomplishment of what I command—no one else having been consulted or impetrated—show that I myself have that power.

Although Jesus commanded the man to go home, Mark does not write, "without delay, he grabbed his pallet and went home"—because the people there did not see that he went home. They saw only that he left. Mark is relaying what it was like to be there.

But why did Jesus tell him to return home? Presumably because, if he stayed there, his presence would have been a disruption. As in other cases of healing, Jesus is practical in foreseeing their consequences and making due provision.

everyone was overcome with amazement...

If "everyone" was amazed, were the scribes amazed as well, and did they too give glory to God? Presumably so. Perhaps some of them returned to Jerusalem, where their continued "amazement" led authorities there to turn against Jesus.

When Mark writes "gave glory to God," does he mean "gave glory to God in heaven" or "gave glory to Jesus as God"? It seems too much to say that the crowd regarded Jesus as God, even though this is the only logical conclusion. The mystery of the Incarnation is so surprising that even practicing Christians must "realize" it repeatedly through meditating on Christmas and saying the Creed. It is an act of faith always to affirm it, even if it is "only logical." Indeed, that is why Arianism, which denied the divinity of Christ, could become an influential heresy in the early Church.

Mark's fundamental point is that the witnesses to this healing were good Jews. They did not ascribe the forgiveness of sins to anyone but God. They would not derogate from God by attributing this power to any being except God.

People intuitively sense that where God is, their happiness is. Take this together with Jesus' having clearly displayed that he could heal everyone and remove every evil and infirmity if he so willed, and it was natural that his appearance was seen as a harbinger of some kind of radical translation of the whole world into a perfect state. It would not be necessary for the Jewish people of his time to turn to Messianic scriptures and tradition to suppose these things. Jesus' preaching about a new "kingdom of God," looked at superficially, would only tend to confirm this expectation.

One must meditate on these things to appreciate how shocking and astonishing it later was that he was captured, tortured, and put to death. If he then rises again and tells others to take up their cross too, he is conveying the disturbing message that this sought-after happiness from being with God is attained only through a comparable suffering. The Passion, although perhaps equally "logical" and inevitable, is as surprising a mystery as the Incarnation.

We saw earlier that Peter faced the problem of selecting what was important and putting it in order when telling about the life of Christ. When we reflect on this healing, we easily see why Peter might have placed it near the beginning of his account. It affirms the Incarnation, demonstrates the forgiveness of sins, and foreshadows the Resurrection.

14–17

14 He was traveling along and saw Levi...

This is the story of the calling of the man whom Mark and Luke call Levi, also known as Matthew. "He saw" must mean not simply that Jesus "saw," but also that he "looked at" him, and they made eye contact. Jesus did not say "Follow me" to get Matthew's attention; he said it when he already had his attention.

sitting at his desk

Mark mentions "sitting" here in conjunction with "he got up" in the next line. Is Mark's concern that a sitting man stood up? No, it is that a man in the midst of work answered the call by getting up and leaving his work. Matthew's response is just like that of Peter and Andrew dropping their nets and leaving them behind. The desk work of the tax collector and the manual labor of the fishermen are dealt with in the same way.

in the customs house

Taxes supported an occupying power, and tax collectors generally enriched themselves by charging extra and pocketing the difference. And given the location of the custom house by the sea, Matthew would have been collecting taxes on catches of fish. So his interests as a tax collector were at odds with the human interests of Peter and Andrew. Peter wishes to emphasize that they nevertheless became united as followers of Jesus.

He got up and followed him

The calling is as extraordinary as that of the fishermen. For all we know, there was a long line of taxpayers waiting to see him, and money and records on his desk. But he quits his job.

The calling of a tax collector raises the question how the group that Jesus formed differed from zealous religious groups of his time: (1) they did not separate themselves from public sinners, (2) they did not fast or engage in other visible forms of mortification, and (3) they did not take care to observe the Sabbath according to the strict customs of the Pharisees. Mark deals with these matters by recounting episodes not presented as occurring successively in time (recall the remarks of Pappias).

The rejection of Jesus by the Jewish religious authorities is a theme that runs throughout this Gospel. We can understand why it would be important for Peter. After all, he himself is now a religious authority in the Church founded by Christ. But people who are in authority feel a kinship for others who are in authority also. They look to them, and especially their predecessors, to understand better their own authority.

15 So he is reclining at table in his house.

Again, the vivid historic present: Peter recounts the incident as he remembers it. Mark is not concerned with the temporal placement of this episode, which may or may not have occurred soon after the calling of Levi.

reclining at table

In the ancient world, people did not sit in chairs around a table but reclined on couches, which connoted a closer bond than our conventions of eating at table. It is as if Mark wrote, "he used to be at ease and enjoy his time with tax collectors and sinners."

16 when they see that he is eating with public sinners

The Pharisees did not eat with sinners, to set an example of uprightness, as they thought. Pharisees were widely admired for their zeal.

There are many good reasons not to associate openly with public sinners, even those who are trying to change their ways: to avoid giving the appearance of approval, especially to children, who cannot easily draw distinctions; to take care not to become corrupted oneself; to protect the reputation of an institution that one represents. But when these or other special reasons are absent, and there is a good purpose for association, then nothing can be said against it.

Among the Pharisees, those who are also scribes seem to be more inclined to find fault. Their legal training apparently made them cold and harsh.

"Why does he eat with tax collectors and public sinners?"

The question is not sincere. They want to correct Jesus but decline to speak with him directly. Peter wants to teach something by contrast. If we believe that someone needs to be corrected, we ought to examine ourselves before God as to whether we show the same fault and then, approaching the person directly and privately, state the correction with charity, calmly and objectively. When we fail to do this, both we and the person we correct become confused as to what we are doing. Indeed, we seem to ask a question, but it is not really a question.

17 So Jesus overhears this

Did the scribes intend to criticize him through stating the criticism to his disciples loudly, or did he catch them attempting to undermine him quietly?

"It's not the strong who need a physician"

Jesus likens himself to a physician—a physician whose method of healing is spending time with people. This is remarkable. He has accomplished many healings instantaneously and miraculously. These healings, as we have seen, also stand for spiritual healings. Now he is apparently saying that his ordinary means for spiritual healing is befriending people, conversing with them, and teaching them.

If, as the Fathers would say, the sacramental system is the continuation of the Incarnation in time, then what holds of Christ's presence applies to sacraments also.

"I have not come to call righteous men"

Theologians have disputed about whether God would have become incarnate if man had not sinned. But only revelation can give us insight into the reason for the Incarnation, St. Thomas observes, and whenever Scripture addresses the Incarnation, it is presented as a response to sin, as in this verse.

"Sinners" is the same word rendered above as "public sinners," but as the context has changed, the meaning has changed. Here it clearly does not mean only public sinners but all men, who are sinners. Jesus is also speaking ironically. If anyone supposes that he is righteous (perhaps some of those scribes?), then he has no need of Jesus' company. But actually, no one is righteous, and everyone needs his company.

The phrase "I have not come to call" in this context therefore has the sense "to invite to dine with me." The Greek word for "church," *ekklesia*, means "the association of those who are called." Peter as pastor of the Church recognizes that Jesus' remark mirrors several parables (presented in other Gospels). Invitations go out only to sinners. Since all men are sinners, they go out to all men. But the invitation is ignored or despised if the person who receives it regards himself as righteous.

Note that when Jesus says, "I have come to call sinful men," the underlying presumption, once again, is that he is God. If men are sinners specifically in relation to God, against whom they sin, who but God has the authority to call men precisely as sinners? The divinity of Christ is implicit in almost every sentence of the Gospel of Mark.

18–20

Now Mark addresses the criticism that Jesus and his disciples do not fast.

18 they raise this with him

This seems to be a sincere question, rather than a criticism disguised as a question, because it is addressed to Jesus directly. We know from other Gospels that people slandered Jesus as a glutton and drunkard because he and his disciples did not fast (Mt. 11:19, Lk. 7:34). Having discovered the true basis for those exaggerations, these men ask Jesus his reasons.

"your disciples on the contrary never fast"

Peter wishes to confirm the extraordinary fact that although they are highly devoted, they engage in no austere religious practices.

19 "Can the friends of the bridegroom fast...?"

Literally, "sons of the bridegroom." The term "son," like "child," is a term of affection. Yet unlike "friend," it also expresses subordination. They are not his "chums."

We have seen Jesus compare reclining with him at table to the feast of the Kingdom of God. Here he continues with the comparison, now likening the feast to a wedding celebration, also in line with many parables.

"So long as the bridegroom is with them"

There are two main motives for fasting: sorrow for sin and the desire to become closer to God by rejecting created goods. These motives are absent only if someone is in the presence of God. If those who are with Jesus have no reason to fast, then they are in the presence of God, and he is God.

20 "Yet the days will come…"

Jesus refers first in the plural to "days" but then switches to the singular, "day." Why?

The "days" the bridegroom is taken away from them must mean primarily the three days when he is betrayed, put on trial, tortured, crucified. Secondarily, they mean all the days after his Ascension ("Where I am going, you cannot follow," Jn. 13:36).

The Church from earliest times observed a fast on Fridays and sometimes also another day of the week (typically Wednesdays).

We therefore take Jesus' statement to mean that the practice of fasting will begin among Christians after the days of his passion. Christians will not be unrelenting in their austerity, but they will fast on certain occasions, especially "on that day," Friday, which represents their separation from him.

21–22

Jesus came to preach what he called the "good news." News is something previously unknown. It is essential to the message of Jesus that he is preaching something new. There arises, then, the question of the relationship of this new thing to traditions that appear to have divine approval, such as the zealous practices of the widely-admired Pharisees.

"No one"

Given what is at stake, namely, divine traditions stretching back to Moses, this appeal to what "no one" would do is intended to bring in the providence of God. Jesus is, in effect, asking his listeners to consider what they themselves would do, out of prudence, if they were in God's position. At the same time, he is presenting this divine prudence as his own.

"the patch tears away from it"

If one puts a patch of new cloth on an old garment, then when the garment is washed, the patch shrinks, and it tears the old garment even more. Obviously, if one's purpose is to save the old garment, one should use a patch of old cloth instead, or at least one that has already been shrunk. Jesus, however, suggests that the *patch* needs to be saved, and the old garment thrown out!

The comparison is designed to make us think our way past an initial absurdity and reach an intelligent conclusion that takes into account his double meanings and irony: it will do no good to receive his new teaching as a patch. It is not a fix for something pre-existing. And if you did misguidedly receive it in that way, from an attachment to the old thing, you cannot keep the old thing. His teaching will destroy the old thing, even though you want to accept it solely as a patch.

Jesus, then, would not be a "reformer." He would not be "one among many reforming rabbis who appeared at that time." A patch is less than the thing patched. Likewise, a reformer is less than the tradition that he reforms. Jesus emphatically rejects that description of himself and his teaching.

23–28

23 plucking off heads of grain as they made their way through

This is familiar to farmers: walking through a field and, while talking, unreflectively pulling off the head of ripened wheat, rolling it in your hands, blowing away the chaff, and eating the sweet grains from the palm of your hand. They "make their way" in the sense that there is no pre-existing path. They "started" to do this—that is, their acts were spontaneous.

24 "Look!"

The behavior of the disciples is not something that the Pharisees criticized later, when someone told them about it. The Pharisees were there and saw it for themselves. Presumably following Jesus from one town to another, they passed through the fields with him and his disciples. It makes the most sense to imagine that they were alongside Jesus, and that, looking back, they pointed out to him what the disciples were doing in the distance. Perhaps they had already gotten through the field with him and were pausing with him for a rest.

"Why are they, on the Sabbath..."

Their legalistic accusation is similar to a criminal charge: "The law says that you are not allowed to do *x* on the Sabbath. But they are doing *x*, and it is the Sabbath. So they are breaking the law."

"not allowed"

This is meant in the sense, "we human beings are not given authority to do this." The charge is that something is being done that is against the law, *on the precise grounds that no authority for doing it has been conferred.* That is why Jesus replies to them by saying, in effect, that authority need not be conferred on him.

25 "Did you never read what David did"

Jesus argues with the Pharisees as a rabbi among rabbis. He cites a text, makes an analogy, proposes an argument, and does so with subtle twists designed to baffle and impress his interlocutors. Compare how Jesus speaks here with how he addresses simple workers in his sermons. He adapts his manner of speaking to the persons he is addressing.

"from necessity"

It is not that Jesus' disciples are eating grains of wheat out of necessity comparable to that which David and his men faced. The point is that even things set aside as holy must give way when the human good requires it.

26 "in the presence of Abiathar, high priest"

The Greek here would ordinarily mean "at the time of Abiathar, high priest." However, Ahimelech was high priest at that time (1 Samuel 21:1–7). So did someone—Jesus, Mark, or Peter—make a mistake about who was high priest?

That is unlikely. Jesus is referring to a well-known episode in the history of the Israelites, which these Jews would probably have committed to memory from an early age. Everyone would have known it, and any uncertainty could have been resolved by consulting the Scriptures.

A good way of resolving the problem was suggested by the Venerable Bede in the seventh century. Ahimelech and Abiathar were both high priests; Abiathar succeeded Ahimelech, his father, and became much more renowned. Both were present in the episode referred to, but Jesus mentions only the son because of his greater distinction: "There is no discrepancy, for both were there, when David came to ask for bread, and received it.... [T]he son became of much greater excellence than the father, and therefore was worthy to be mentioned as the High Priest, even during his father's life-time."[1]

---

1 Bede, quoted in Saint Thomas Aquinas, *Catena Aurea: Gospel of Mark*, trans. William Whiston (Grand Rapids, MI: Christian Classics Ethereal Library), p. 39.

That is to say, the phrase "Abiathar, high priest," as used by Jesus identifies not the reign of Abiathar as high priest but the office which Abiathar was famous for holding. It's like saying "when President Lincoln was a young man in Springfield, Illinois." We do not mean that Lincoln was president then; we are using the office to identify the man before he held the office.

But even if this explanation is correct and there is no error in the text, why would Jesus refer only to Abiathar and not Ahimelech as well? Perhaps Abiathar, for some reason not known to us, had great authority with the Pharisees. Or perhaps by ignoring Ahimelech and relying on the authority of the priest who would succeed him, Jesus intends to suggest, very subtly, that in this matter of the observance of the Sabbath his own authority supersedes, and will be seen to supersede, that of the Pharisees.

27 "The Sabbath was made for man, not man for the Sabbath."

The Sabbath represents the "day" on which God rested from his work of creation. God commands that man rest also, so that he can be more like God, who is his good, because man is made in the image of God. What Our Lord says here presupposes a principle that St. Thomas Aquinas expressed admirably: Anything God commands he commands because it is for our good. God wills something because it is our good; it is not our good because God wills it.

28 "It follows that"

This is the argument: The Son of Man has authority over all of creation and over what counts as the human good; the Sabbath is a creature and for the sake of man; therefore, the Son of Man has authority over the Sabbath.

Here, as in the healing of the paralytic, the phrase "Son of Man" indicates that Jesus' authority over the Sabbath is his directly. It is not conferred and does not come down from above by invocation or petition. By implication, the Church he founds will exercise in his name and on his authority a derivative authority over the Sabbath also. This is how the early Church abolished the celebration of the Jewish Sabbath and replaced it with the Lord's Day.

In giving this argument about his authority, Jesus settles the original concern of the Pharisees over whether what the disciples were doing was "allowed": Jesus is allowing it to happen; therefore, it is allowed.

CHAPTER 3

1 He entered the synagogue again. A man with a withered hand was there. ²They were watching him intently, to see if he would heal the man on the Sabbath, so that they could accuse him. ³So Jesus tells the man with the withered hand, "Stand up in the middle." ⁴He says to them, "Is it allowable, on the Sabbath, to do good or to do evil? To save a life or to put to death?" They were silent. ⁵He looks around at them with anger, pained that their hearts are like stone, and he says to the man, "Stretch out your hand." The man stretched it out. His hand was restored to normal. ⁶The Pharisees walk out, and immediately started to scheme against him, with the Herodians, to find some way to destroy him.

7 Jesus left that district with his disciples for the sea. A huge crowd from Galilee followed—people from Judea too, ⁸and Jerusalem, and Idumea—and from across the Jordan—and from Tyre and Sidon as well—it was a vast throng, who had heard stories of what different things he had done. ⁹He told his disciples to keep a boat handy for him, because of the crowd, to keep them from crushing him. ¹⁰(Keep in mind that he would heal lots of people. As a result, anyone with any kind of affliction would press forward, towards him, to touch

him. [11]Also, spirits would lunge at him the moment they saw him —crying out at the same time, "You are the Son of God!" [12]He had to order them strictly and firmly not to make him known.)

13 So he goes up a mountain, and he summons the men he himself had decided upon. They left and came to him. [14]He created Twelve (whom he also named "apostles"), who would be with him; and he would send them out to preach; [15]and they would have authority to expel evil spirits. [16]He appointed the Twelve men: Peter (the name he gave to Simon), [17]and James the son of Zebedee, and John the brother of James (he gave them the names Boanerges, that is, Sons of Thunder), [18]and Andrew, Philip, Bartholomew, Matthew, Thomas, James the son of Alphaeus, Thaddeus, Simon from Cana, [19]and Judas Iscariot (the man who actually betrayed him).

20 He goes to his house. Such a crowd again gathers there, that they could not even eat a loaf of bread.

21 Some of his supporters, when they heard the reports, set out to seize him. They were saying, "He's not himself any longer." [22]Some scribes, too, who had come down from Jerusalem, were saying, "He is possessed by Beezebul," and "It is only by the ruler of the evil spirits that he expels evil spirits."

23 Jesus asked these men to come to him and spoke to them using comparisons: "How does Satan have the power to expel Satan?" [24]And, "Suppose a kingdom should be divided against itself, it cannot remain standing—no, that kingdom cannot! [25]Or suppose a household should be divided against itself, it will not be able to remain standing—no, that household will not! [26]Or suppose Satan should rise up against himself and be divided against himself: then he is not able to stand. He is finished!" [27]"Isn't it rather the case that no one has the power to enter the house of a strong man, and plunder his possessions unless he first ties up the strong man? And only then he will plunder his household."

28 "Amen, I tell you that everything will be remitted for the sons of men—their sins, and their blasphemies, whatever blasphemies they utter. ²⁹But anyone who blasphemes against the Holy Spirit attains no remittance in eternity, but is responsible for eternal sin." ³⁰—This because they were saying, "He has an unclean spirit."

31 So his mother and his brothers arrive. They are standing outside, and they sent word to him, asking him to come to them. ³²The crowd was sitting in a circle around him. They say to him, "See, your mother and your brothers are outside! They are looking for you!" ³³He says in answer to them, "Who is my mother?...Who are my brothers?" ³⁴So he turns around and looks at those who were seated around him in a circle, and he says, "Here you see my mother and my brothers. ³⁵Is someone doing the will of God? Then he is my brother, sister, and mother."

Commentary

We have said in effect that material in the Gospel of Mark can be ascribed to Peter if (1) it conveys a vivid sense of "what it was like" to be there, (2) only Peter or Peter and a small number of others would have known about it, (3) it is important to Peter in his role as general pastor of the Church, (4) it substantiates the authority of the Apostles—especially Peter, the first among them—in contrast to that of the religious authorities of the day, or (5) it corresponds to what we know of his character. Also included would be anything that is connected by common principles of association and storytelling to Petrine material. We can call these criteria, respectively, Peter's (1) witness, (2) intimacy with Jesus, (3) teaching role, (4) authority, and (5) character.

There are three scenes in this chapter—in the synagogue, on the mountain, in Jesus' house. We can attribute the first two to Peter on the basis of authority and the third on the basis of his teaching role.

1–6

1 withered hand

A hand atrophied from lack of movement, either from birth or because of disease or injury. Luke adds the detail that it was the right hand, which would have prevented the man from working.

2 They were watching him

We expect this "they" to be the Pharisees, but the Pharisees are not mentioned until the end, when they storm out after the healing. But the suggestion is that everyone was infected with the Pharisees' suspicion, turning this scene into a showdown between Jesus and the Pharisees' leadership.

so that they could accuse him

What Jesus does becomes a matter of public evidence. Only the Pharisees witnessed the disciples plucking grain in the fields. Christ cast out a demon in the synagogue on the Sabbath, but since speaking and commanding are allowed on the Sabbath, the evidence was inconclusive. Healing Simon's mother-in-law was not a public act. The Pharisees are looking for a flagrant act as proof of Jesus' violating the law. It is even possible that they arranged for the man with the withered hand to be present as a trap.

3 "Stand up in the middle."

Jesus meets their demand for something flagrant head on. He might have declined the confrontation, healing the man secretly. But like a father whose authority has been challenged by a child, he must claim his proper authority immediately.

4 "Is it allowable..."

That is, "Have *you* been allowed...?" And in Jewish law, they *were* allowed, since rescuing someone on the Sabbath was permitted. That admission serves as a premise for Jesus' conclusion: If *you* are permitted to do good on the Sabbath, then the Lord of the Sabbath will naturally not hesitate to do so.

They were silent.

The ancient world identified thinking and speaking. The Pharisees, then, would not grant Jesus' premise. Had they done so, he might have reasoned with them gently. But they refused to give him even this minimal opening, provoking Jesus' anger and pain in the next verse.

5 He looks around at them with anger, pained that their hearts are like stone

Jesus presumably confided his interior feelings on this occasion to Peter. If so, it shows that he shared his human feelings with his followers—spontaneously, as friends do, but also deliberately, to bring home to them his full humanity.

He looks around

The verb suggests that he looked in a circle around the room, perhaps dramatically, by pivoting around and not simply turning his head.

pained that

Literally "pained along with." The verb suggests sympathy. If Jesus could see directly into hearts and did not simply infer that their hearts were hardened, he would also "feel" the infirmity with pain. Jesus' feelings were complex: anger at the Pharisees, sadness over their hardened hearts.

like stone

Literally, the "petrification" of their hearts. If the verse represents Jesus' own report to Peter of what he felt, then perhaps Jesus himself chose this precise word to express his experience. The word is a medical term referring originally to how bones mend after a break.

Could he have selected this word from his experience with the man's withered hand? Suppose the hand were atrophied from a broken wrist that fused: Jesus would have seen the "petrification." That image would have provided, then, an apt word for the hearts.

he says to the man

Mark does not write "he told him" but "he told the man," using the term that emphasizes his human nature, *anthrōpos*, for the second time in this episode (see verse 3). This man, this *anthrōpos*, stands for you and for me.

"Stretch out your hand"

This could mean "stretch out your hand" or simply "hold out your hand." Either alternative leads to an interesting consequence.

If we understand it in the former sense, then the verse suggests that the man's hand was healed in the very act of attempting to stretch it out. Trying, in response to Our Lord's command, to do what was impossible for him proved to be the faith "needed" for Our Lord to heal him.

If, however, the command simply means "hold out your hand," then we should understand that he kept his unsightly hand hidden, and Jesus asked him to hold it out so there could be no doubt of the healing.

restored to normal

We are meant to envision the change from ugly and twisted to fresh and new.

6 The Pharisees walk out

After the man was healed, the Pharisees could sense that they had lost the support of the astonished crowd. The Pharisees gave up trying to turn the people against Jesus and began conspiring in secret.

Nothing is known about the Herodians apart from what is mentioned here and in a few other passages (Mk. 3:6, 12:13; Mt. 22:16; see also Mk. 8:15, Lk. 13:31–32, Acts 4:27). In each case, they are represented as aligned with the Pharisees. Mark seems to trace the alliance of the Pharisees and Herodians against Jesus to this healing.

7–12

Mark recounts a scene in which crowds came from a much wider area than ever before. The circumstances that led to his teaching from a boat are presented as extraordinary: *he was so much in danger of being crushed that he told us to keep a boat handy.* Elsewhere Jesus is represented as teaching from a boat. This scene tells how the practice arose.

This is the fourth time that Mark depicts Jesus teaching without relaying what he was teaching. Mark is clearly more interested in Jesus' deeds and relationships—a detail not consistent with the interpretation of Jesus as merely a "great moral teacher."

7 Jesus left . . . for the sea.

Jesus regards the sea as a highly suitable backdrop for what he wants to teach, perhaps because he is "fishing for men."

8 and Jerusalem, and Idumea . . .

The list is given in a hurried, disorganized way, as if a narrator were searching his memory. The implication is that Jesus was drawing crowds from every area from which people might reasonably attempt to see him.

7–8 A huge crowd . . . it was a vast throng

The Greek has the same two words but in different order, *polu plēthos . . . plēthos polu,* as a narrator might repeat a description for emphasis—"an enormous crowd . . . the crowd, enormous."

10–11 would press forward . . . would lunge at him

A vivid and subtle difference in how persons would behave near Jesus, as if relayed by an eyewitness. Presumably the sick would surge towards him, whereas the demon-possessed would lunge violently.

12 not to make him known

Why? Presumably because he wishes to make himself known. Also, his revelation consists not merely in the words but also in how he reveals it. He does not want the devils to "control" how he reveals himself or to serve as intermediaries of his revelation.

13–19

13 So he goes up a mountain

This is the first time that Jesus goes up a mountain. He has been by a river, in the desert, along the sea, and in towns. Mountains in Jewish thought stood for authority (kingdoms, in Old Testament imagery), the origin of law (Mount Sinai), and the presence of God (Mount Horeb).

These simple words introduce all these meanings: what follows is an act of fundamental law, conferring authority, originating from Jesus, who is God.

he summons

That is, he calls them to himself—a calling that is fundamentally a calling *to be with Jesus*. A call from Jesus is subtle. It is stronger than being invited but weaker than being commanded. It is solemn but leaves room for freedom.

the men

"The men," to be sure, not "those," because the Greek pronoun is masculine. One could not infer from this one word that only males are called, and yet Mark did not have to include this clause and this word at all—but he did.

he himself had decided

The language emphasizes that this was a deliberate act originating from Jesus and only him. He is issuing fundamental law, not interpreting or applying prior law.

They left and came to him

To respond to a calling to be with Jesus, it is necessary to leave: "Peter began to say to him, 'Behold, we have left everything and followed you'" (10:28).

14 He created the Twelve . . .

There are seven important points about this carefully crafted sentence.

created

The Greek verb (*poieō*) means to make. The same word occurs in verse 16, where it is rendered "appointed," to distinguish between the erecting and the subsequent filling of an office.

Twelve

The word for "twelve" is used twice in this passage, here and in verse 16. The first time there is no definite article ("he created Twelve"), whereas the second time there is a masculine plural definite article ("he appointed the Twelve men"). The meaning of "Twelve" without the article is explained in the phrase that follows: they are to be with Jesus, to preach with authority, and to cast out devils. That is their "office."

whom he also named "apostles"

Apostles means "authoritatively sent men." Here, the noun is plural and without a definite article, suggesting that although the original holders of this office numbered twelve, one would not necessarily have to have been among the original Twelve to be authoritatively sent. That is, the number of authoritatively sent men could expand. Paul would insist that he was equally an apostle (Eph. 1:1, Col 1:1), and Barnabas would be called an apostle (Acts 14:4, 14). In the letters of Clement (late first century) and of Ignatius of Antioch (early second century), we are told that Jesus instructed his apostles to appoint successors before their death. These are the "bishops," who continue the role of the original apostles.

who would be with him

The first job of the apostle is to be with Jesus, which seems different from simply following him, presumably because his other tasks—preaching and casting out devils—depend on his being with Jesus.

he would send them out to preach

In chapter 1, Jesus said that the reason he entered the world was to preach. The apostles are sent because the Son is sent into the world. If the Son is sent to preach, the apostles too are sent to preach. But their preaching is not a finite errand. Henceforth, the purpose of their life is to be sent and to preach.

to preach

Not "to preach about Scripture," since the New Testament had not been written yet. The spoken word passed down, "tradition," was the equal of any account that they would put in writing.

15 authority to expel evil spirits

Was this authority understood then as including the authority to forgive sins, since doing so also frees men from the devil?

16 He appointed the Twelve men

Literally, "He made men to be the Twelve." In this verse, Jesus makes particular men holders of the offices he had created.

Peter

Peter is mentioned first, implying priority. By mentioning the conferral of the name Peter, or "Rock," in connection with the appointment of men to the Twelve offices, Mark suggests that the role of Peter, too, is an office. In the case of the Twelve, the offices are established first and then men are appointed to them. In the case of Peter, however, the man is first chosen and given preeminence, and then the name is conferred on him. The name "Peter" indicates that the office itself is identified with Simon Peter. If it can be passed down, it must be as the office of *this* man, Peter.

Simon was given the Aramaic name *Cephas*, which means "Rock." But as Greek was the universal language at the time, Mark uses the Greek *Petros*, from *petra*, "rock" (think of our word "petrified").

Petros, which is masculine, means "pebble," while *petra*, which is feminine, means a large rock that could serve as a foundation. Some have objected that because Jesus did not call Simon *petra*, Peter was not foundational. This objection is misguided. First, Jesus gave Peter the name *Cephas* in Aramaic, which *does* mean a large rock that could serve as a foundation. Second, when Mark and others searched for a Greek word that conveyed the same meaning, they naturally chose a masculine noun with the appropriate root, since it was a man's name. And finally, why would Jesus solemnly change anyone's name to "Pebble"?

17 Sons of Thunder

This seems a nickname, with no juridical significance: Why isn't Peter, then, also a mere nickname? For two reasons:

Listing the apostles, Mark uses the conferred name Peter and mentions incidentally that this is the man originally referred to in his narrative as Simon. That is, the conferred name has supplanted the original name. His name as an apostle is Peter, not Simon. Nicknames don't have that kind of priority.

We do not know with certainty why Jesus called James and John "Sons of Thunder" or why only these two apostles had a special name. So we do not know that it was only a nickname. Yet certainly it has no juridical import, because the names of these apostles remained James and John, not Sons of Thunder, whereas the name of the first apostle became Peter.

19 Judas Iscariot

Judas is mentioned last in the list for a reason, just as Peter is listed first.

20–23

20 Such a crowd again gathers there, that they could not even eat a loaf of bread.

Another detail that conveys, concisely but effectively, what it was like to be there, caught in that crowd. Incidentally, it implies that the meeting was two to four hours long, as it ran over into a meal time.

21 when they heard the reports

What reports? Possibly that Jesus had gone up to a mountain and publicly summoned some of his followers to himself, in effect establishing a government and presuming to confer power on these followers. The violent and critical reaction of some described in verses 13–19 seems to reflect how significant that juridical act was held to be.

A "report" typically contains gossip or distortion. Perhaps they were saying, "He's made himself into a king," "These fisherman are now full of themselves," "A tax collector is an official in his kingdom also," and so on.

Mark seems to distinguish between those who traveled with Jesus and those who supported him without following him. It is this latter group that responds in the next verses.

"He's not himself"

Literally, "he is outside himself." The phrase connotes a departure, not for the good. These people had some image of what they thought Jesus was or ought to be, and he no longer conformed to that image. Confident in the superiority of their own judgment, they would even compel Jesus and the apostles to follow their own ideas.

23 Jesus asked these men to come to him

Tellingly, these Pharisees on a fact-finding mission did not ask Jesus directly; he had to approach them. It seems their purpose was to find evidence that confirmed their settled view. Yet Jesus tries to reason with them on their own terms, using "comparisons" or "parables." A parable means something "thrown alongside" something to illuminate it. Our word "comparison" is a close match. "Analogy" is a good term also. He picks comparisons that ought to be compelling for them.

Mark now presents three distinct arguments Jesus gave to these Pharisees. In presenting them so early in his narrative, Mark is appealing to Jewish readers who may have heard distorted "reports" about Jesus.

"power to expel Satan?"

To expel is to act upon something with force. Since anything someone does to himself he does of his own accord, no one has the power to force or to expel himself. Neither has Satan the power to expel himself.

24–26

The Greek is unusual here. One easily supposes that Mark is trying to capture or convey how Jesus' statements, as Peter relayed them, sounded—for example, the emphatic repetition of "that kingdom" and "that household" at the end of the sentences. There is a question-and-answer element in the conversation as well, as if Jesus were first asking the Pharisees to contemplate a case and then drawing the conclusion he thinks they will affirm with him.

Jesus argues astutely here. He first offers an "induction": a kingdom divided against itself does not stand; a household divided against itself does not stand; therefore, every system of authority divided against itself does not stand. Then he offers an argument from cases involving a reduction ad absurdum. Either (case 1) Satan has authorized me or (case 2) Satan has not authorized me. If he has authorized me (case 1), and I expel devils, then Satan is divided against Satan, and his kingdom will not stand, which is absurd. But if he hasn't authorized me (case 2) and I expel devils, then it's as though I've tied up a strong man to despoil his house.

28–30

Here we find not an argument but a warning, and it seems to be addressed to more than the Pharisees. "Amen, I tell you" seems to be aimed at his disciples. And the phrase "for the sons of men" widens the scope to include all men and what they do.

The key question for the interpretation of the passage is this: When Jesus says, "attains no remittance in eternity, but is responsible for eternal sin," does he mean (1) attains no remittance of that sin (blasphemy against the Holy Spirit) but is eternally guilty of that sin, or (2) attains no remittance of any sin but is eternally guilty of all his sins.

It is common to take the first answer as correct and to think that Jesus is identifying a kind of sin that, unlike other sin, is unforgiveable. But if Jesus had wanted to say that a person who blasphemes against the Holy Spirit attains no remittance of that sin, he could have said precisely that. He seems in this context to be concerned with how the Pharisees, who said, "He has an unclean spirit," had cut themselves off from him and therefore from forgiveness in general. It was in their power, moreover, to repent of this sin and become his followers, in which case they would be forgiven, and the whole bounty of grace would open for them.

St. Augustine comments, "Impenitence itself is the blasphemy against the Holy Ghost which hath no remission... not because there is a blasphemy, which cannot be remitted, since even this might be remitted through a right repentance."[1]

31–35

Jesus' juridical acts of establishing the offices of apostles and appointing to those offices men who left everything to be with him are the focus of this chapter. Mark then considers some consequences of those acts. First, some supporters thought Jesus had lost

---

1 Augustine, quoted in Saint Thomas Aquinas, *Catena Aurea: Gospel of Mark*, trans. William Whiston (Grand Rapids, MI: Christian Classics Ethereal Library), p. 52.

his way and tried to correct him. Second, the Pharisees saw that he was establishing a distinct authority in matters of religion and attributed his acts to the devil. Third, Jesus teaches that the bond between men in this Kingdom of God that he is establishing are closer than the bond of blood within a natural human family.

His reference to "brother, sister, and mother" amounts to another retort to the Pharisees. When they accused him of casting out devils by the Prince of devils, he replied that a household divided against itself will not stand. Pointing to his "brother, sister, and mother," he shows what his "household" is truly like, a unity under the will of God.

Several details indicate an eyewitness account: Jesus' mother and brothers standing outside the crowded room, unable to get in but sending word through a chain of messengers; the shouts from some in the crowd who wanted to be of help; the people seated in a circle around Jesus, who looks around them in a circle before giving his reply.

31 his mother and his brothers arrive

In the Aramaic and Greek of the time, the word for "brother" could be used, and often was used, to mean any close relative (see Gen. 13:8). Bede writes, "The brothers of the Lord must not be thought to be the sons of the ever-virgin Mary... nor the sons of Joseph by a former marriage, as some think, but rather they must be understood to be His relations."[2] From the earliest days it was the considered obvious among Christians that Joseph would not have approached Mary, typified by the Ark of the Covenant and the Mother of a new creation. That was not his role.

they sent word to him, asking him to come to them

Presumably they had something important to ask him, and they may have waited a long time before making the request. As we have seen, these meetings might last more than two hours.

---

2 Bede, ibid., 53.

32 The crowd was sitting in a circle around him.

This detail conveys that he was very much "with" them and "among" them. He would need, vividly, to exit from the circle to see his mother and kinsmen.

Is the image of a circle is meant to suggest a new mother? After all, he does call his followers his mother. He is enfolded within this circle: perhaps it represents a kind of womb. There can be no mother without a womb, no mother without an embrace.

"See, your mother and your brothers are outside! They are looking for you!"

The crowd expects him to go out to his mother and brothers. They assume at least the ordinary priority and close affection that a mother and relatives would have at the time.

33 He says in answer to them, "Who is my mother? . . . Who are my brothers?"

He says, literally, "Who is my mother, *or* who are my brothers?", not "Who is my mother, *and* who are my brothers?" Why? Perhaps because the latter would suggest that *some followers are both mother and brothers*, whereas the former suggests that *some followers are, as it were, mothers and some are, as it were, brothers*. That is, his relationship to his followers does not wipe out relationships within the family but preserves them in a fuller form.

34 "Here you see my mother and my brothers."

Given the way he posed the question, he must have answered it in looking around in the circle, making it clear while doing so that some were "mother" and some were "brother," perhaps looking at a woman as he said the first and at a man as he said the second.

35 "Is someone doing the will of God? Then he is my brother, sister, and mother."

Four points:

The followers in the room were presumably doing both the "general" will of God, keeping the commandments, but also the "particular" will of God, since they went to Jesus to hear his preaching.

Why does he now add "sister"? Perhaps because female relatives were waiting outside also, or perhaps in deference to the younger women in the household.

Yet while he adds "sister" to "brother," he does not add "father" to "mother." Why? Perhaps because it would imply an absurd subordination, or perhaps because the relationship that someone has to Christ by adoption, through Christ's taking on flesh, is a matter of an earthly relationship transformed, yet Christ had no human father. Later there will indeed be "Fathers" in the church, but presumably these are not fathers "to" Jesus but men who are "other Christs." Or one might say that by not mentioning "fathers" here, Jesus indicates that there will be a special class of "fathers" within the Church. His silence now points to the ministerial priesthood, which will come later. A man is that kind of "father" not because he does the will of God but because of a special ordination.

Mark does not say that Jesus failed to go out to see his mother and relatives. For all we know, he did, after first affirming that his family included those followers sitting at his feet.

CHAPTER 4

1 He began to teach again beside the sea. Such a large crowd gathered around him that he had to get into a boat and take his seat there in the sea. The entire crowd was on the land right up to the sea.

2 He used to teach them many things by drawing comparisons. When he taught, he would say the following to them: 3"Listen carefully. Look: The sower went out to sow. 4In his sowing, it happened that some seed fell beside the path. Birds came and ate it up. 5Other seed fell on rocky ground, where it did not have much soil. It sprouted quickly from not having deep soil. 6After the sun rose, it got scorched. Because it lacked roots, it dried up. 7Other seed fell among thorns. The thorns grew up. They choked it off. It yielded no fruit. 8Other seed fell on the good soil. It did yield fruit as it grew and increased in size. One yielded thirty, another sixty, and another a hundred." 9He would add, "If anyone has ears to hear, let him hear!"

10 When they could be alone with him, the men in his company, with the Twelve, would ask him about his comparisons. 11He used to say to them, "To you, the mystery of the Kingdom of God has been given as a gift. But to those who are on the outside, everything comes

through comparisons, ¹²so that 'when they see, they might see—and not see—and when they hear, they might hear—and not hear—lest they turn back and be forgiven.'"

13 So he says to them, "So you do not grasp this comparison—and how will you grasp every comparison? ¹⁴The sower sows the word. ¹⁵Some men are beside the path where the word is sown. For these men, when they hear, immediately Satan comes and takes the word that was sown in them. ¹⁶Other men, in the same way, are those sown on rocky ground. For these men, when they hear the word, immediately they receive it with joy. ¹⁷They do not have roots within them. Rather, they grow only for a season. After that, when there is affliction, or harassment because of the word, they take offense and abandon it. ¹⁸Other men are sown in thorns. For these men, although they do hear the word, ¹⁹the cares of this present world and the deceit of wealth and covetousness for everything else insinuate themselves and choke off the word. It yields no fruit. ²⁰Finally, there are those men who have been sown in good soil and who hear the word and receive from it fully and yield fruit—one yielding thirty, another sixty, and another a hundred."

21 He also used to say to them, "Is a lamp brought in only to be placed under a basket? Or perhaps positioned under a bed? Isn't it placed—on a lampstand? ²²Well, a thing is not kept hidden, except for it to be seen openly. Nor is anything concealed, except for it to come out into the open. ²³If anyone has ears to hear, let him hear."

24 He also used to say to them, "Take care how you listen. By the measure with which you measure, it will be measured out to you. It will be applied to you. ²⁵Well, to the man who has, more will be given, and to the man who has not, even what he does have will be taken away."

26 He used to say: "The Kingdom of God is like this. It's as though a man should broadcast seed over the soil. ²⁷He goes to

sleep and rises up, night after night, and day after day. The seed germinates and sprouts. How it does so, he does not know. ²⁸The soil spontaneously yields its fruit: first the blade, next the head, then the ripe kernel in the head. ²⁹But the moment the fruit hangs ripe, he sends in the sickle because the harvest is at hand."

30 He used to say: "How should we find a likeness to the Kingdom of God? How might we draw a comparison? ³¹It is like a grain of mustard. When sown on the soil—there it is!—smaller than all of the seeds on the surface of the soil. ³²Yet also, when it is sown, it rises up and becomes something greater than all the garden plants. It puts forth large branches, so that birds of the air can make nests under its shade."

33 Using many comparisons like these, we would tell his message to them, adapted to what they were able to hear. ³⁴He would not express anything to them except in a comparison. But when he was alone, with his disciples, he would explain everything.

35 That day, as night was approaching, he tells them, "Let's go across to the other side." ³⁶After they dismissed the crowd, they took him along with them—he was in his boat, and other boats were with him. ³⁷A violent squall rose up, with high winds. The waves were spilling into his boat, so that the boat was just about filled to the top. ³⁸As for Jesus, he was at the stern, on a pillow, sleeping. So they wake him up and say to him, "Teacher, does it make no difference to you that we are going to die?!" ³⁹Getting up, he rebuked the wind, and he spoke to the sea, "Be silent! Quiet down!" And the wind abated. The sea became completely still. ⁴⁰He said to them, "Why are you so cowardly? Don't you have faith yet?" ⁴¹They were overcome with fear. They kept saying to one another, "So who is he then, that even the wind and the sea listen to him?"

Commentary

So far Mark has been mainly interested in telling us about Jesus' nature and authority as Messiah and Son of God. Now, depicting a particular day by the sea, Mark turns to Jesus' teaching. The astounding miracle in the evening seems, naturally enough, to have dominated Peter's memory of the day, and Mark seems to report not so much the particulars of what Jesus said on that occasion as much as the sort of thing he typically said when teaching. That is, Mark uses the occasion of that miracle to convey some of Jesus' introductory teachings.

We know they are introductory for three reasons. First, they are mainly about the growth of the Kingdom of God from small beginnings. Second, they are brief. It takes a scant five minutes to read the teachings in this chapter aloud, though presumably they are drawn from hours-long sessions. The burden of conveying the teachings of Christ is on the apostles, Mark seems to presume, for Jesus explained his teaching plainly only to them. Third, these teachings seem precisely designed for those who are approaching Jesus for the first time.

1

1 he had to get into a boat

A boat was kept ready and now had to be used. We can detect a certain surprise in the narration, as if to say, "Can you imagine?"

on the land right up to the sea

A simple but most interesting detail. Three comments:

Of course the crowd was on the shore! But Mark is conveying the impression the scene made on someone in a boat looking at the vast crowd. Later we will learn that there were several boats besides the one that Jesus was in. Presumably, Peter was in one of them.

This is an "elemental" scene, meaning that Jesus is depicted here in the midst of the basic elements of earth, water, air, and fire. Jesus is positioned among the elements, while presenting the elements of his teaching.

"On the land" is literally "upon the soil," (*epi tēs gēs*). The same or a similar phrase is repeated frequently in the parables of this chapter, as if the soil upon which the seed (the word) is broadcast is the very crowd which is "on the soil." Jesus preaching from the boat is broadcasting seed upon soil. That is, telling the parable of the sower, he is engaged in the very activity he is talking about.

2–9

In Mark's first presentation of Jesus' actual teaching, the Lord explains to us how to receive his word and then how to interpret a parable. We are invited to interpret the other parables for ourselves, following this model.

2 He used to teach them many things by drawing comparisons.

This could mean that Jesus used comparisons (parables) to teach many things but used other methods as well, or that he always used comparisons. Perhaps recognizing the ambiguity, Mark resolves it below in verse 34.

"Many" emphasizes the scope and multiplicity of the teaching. By implication, we have only a few excerpts here, while the ordinary and authoritative source for Jesus' comprehensive teachings will be the apostles.

When he taught...

The suggestion is that when Jesus taught, he would typically include this parable about how to receive his teaching.

Notice the repetition: "He used to teach *them* many things...," he would say "to *them*." These are the crowds, the ones "outside," not the apostles and disciples, to whom he would explain everything "in private."

3 "Listen carefully."

Literally, "Hear this!" which also meant *pay attention, recognize who is speaking to you and heed him.*

How would Jesus teach a parable like this? It is difficult to believe he would insist that the crowd listen carefully and then say it only once. Would he have stated it several times, elaborating sometimes, speaking at different speeds, perhaps varying the language with different repetitions?

"Look: the sower went out to sow."

No other parable of Jesus begins with the word "look." It is not that he needs to gain the crowd's attention: he already has it. Is Jesus pointing to himself? He himself is the sower who goes out into the world. He who utters the words "the sower went out to sow" is the Sower, and he is sowing—right now. *Look!*

"the sower"

Literally, "the sowing man." Jesus does not say, "A man went out to sow." The man is identified with this task of sowing. One might render the sentence, "The one with the task of sowing went out to sow."

4 "In his sowing"

That is, "in the course of his sowing." The phrase is consistent with the idea that the teller of the parable is the Sower himself. In the course of his sowing—*now*—this is what happens.

5 "where it did not have much soil"

Jesus does not say, "where there was no soil." That is, he speaks about the seed, not the place. The seed, as it were, "looks" for soil. On the rocky ground, it ends up not "having" the soil it is looking for.

"It sprouted quickly"

The problem is with the ground, not the seed, which does the best it can in what soil there is.

6 "it got scorched..."

The light and heat of the sun work on both the plant and the soil. Because the soil is not deep, the sun dries it out, and so the plant gets no more water and withers.

7 "The thorns grew up."

The choking isn't incidental but purposeful: the thorns are competitors with the seed.

8 "good soil"

Good soil is beautiful besides fruitful. It is as if Jesus is inviting us to think of a farmer scooping up a big handful of topsoil, feeling its moistness and texture, and admiring its richness.

"It did yield fruit"

Jesus describes the plant's yielding fruit as coincident with its growth. The plant wastes no time in yielding fruit; it does so the moment it can. This is its purpose.

9 "If anyone has ears to hear..."

A pithy phrase, with a strong element of rhythm and repetition in the original. It is an expression Jesus probably used frequently after parables or at the end of a segment of teaching. Like all good teachers, Jesus used memorable "slogans."

Jesus had begun the parable with "Listen!" which meant not simply hearing but also grasping, recognizing the speaker, and heeding. We now see that the command includes making oneself able to hear, as if Jesus were saying, "Apply this parable to all the other parables I tell you. Be good soil for them."

10–12

11 "has been given as a gift"

Literally "has been given," but the manner in which it is given is implicit, so one should say, "given as a gift," gratuitously.

A mystery is a rite, a truth, or a reality that we can grasp only in part, mainly through comparisons. Here, "the mystery of the Kingdom of God" seems to mean the reality of Christ's presence in the world.

For those "inside," since they have the mystery itself—the reality—the parables illuminate that mystery.

"those who are on the outside"

By contrast, the ones who are "outside" are those who do not possess the mystery by being in the presence of the reality. They must approach Christ through words and images, as if by inference. They have the riddle but not the answer.

"everything comes through comparisons"

Literally, everything happens to them in comparisons (parables). Jesus does not say this is how things "ought" to be. It is simply the way things are in the circumstances. Because these people are not with Christ, they approach him as best they can through the comparisons.

12 "'they might see—and not see'"

If the phrase "lest they turn back and be forgiven" is taken to qualify the whole sentence, then it seems as though Jesus deliberately makes things obscure to keep men from repenting. But presumably it qualifies only the last clause, "and not hear." So understood, it means that people who will not trouble themselves with repentance can choose not to "see" ("see" is included by implication) or "hear" the reality to which the parable points.

13–20

13 "how will you grasp...?"

As we have seen, this parable about receiving the teachings of Christ is fundamental. To understand *any* comparison requires being like the good soil of *this* comparison—receiving it, meditating on it, and living it, so as to grow in one's possession of the mystery of the Kingdom of God.

14 "The sower sows the word."

Jesus is the Word, so the Word sows the word. Does he sow himself, then? Yes, the purpose of the word is that those who hear it possess the Word.

The seed (the word) is also referred to as "that which is sown." So "the Sower sows that which is sown." This formula expresses a classical understanding of causation: the actor draws what is acted upon to itself, making it like the actor. Here, the Sower makes the ground into which he sows like the seed that is sown—that is, like himself.

15 "Some men are beside the path"

In these words, we see clearly the way a comparison illuminates a reality by being set beside it. Certain men respond to the word in a certain way. They are "men beside the path where the word is sown." That is to say, put this image next to these men, and then you will see what these men are like. The immaterial and spiritual reality, which is hard to grasp, is clarified by the vivid and simple image from everyday life.

Some Fathers said that men are to the side of the path because of their evil thoughts. By cultivating bad thoughts, they take themselves off the path and place themselves to the side of it.

"these men, when they hear"

Hear what? There is no object of hearing supplied. Well, they do not hear the word. These men fail to receive the word at all. They are described as hearing, and yet they do not hear.

"the word that was sown in them"

This also has the sense of "the word beginning to spring up in them." It seems especially devilish to attack incipient life as it arises.

16 "in the same way..."

Jesus says "in the same way" not because these men are similar to the first sort, but because we are meant to apply and interpret the parable in a similar way, so as to illuminate these men too.

"immediately they receive it with joy"

These men, unlike the first sort, do hear the *word*. But what happens next comes quickly—"immediately."

17 "They do not have roots within them."

So far in this parable, men have been identified with soil that receives the seed. But now there seems to be no distinction between them and the plant—he says *they* lack roots. It is as if the soil is for the plant; it is meant to become the plant. It is a sobering comparison, implying that Jesus looks at men as soil meant to become the plant, which in turn is meant to yield fruit.

"when there is affliction..."

The sun is hot and therefore noxious to a plant. No plant could survive being out in the sun all day. The same sun that produces rapid growth in a healthy plant kills a plant without deep roots. For a follower of Christ, trials, harassment and persecution are the analogue of the heat and light of the sun.

"they take offense and abandon it"

Literally "they are scandalized." Lacking roots, they cannot view the sunlight as anything other than an assault. They conclude the world is not hospitable to plants, and abandon that life—and yet it is not as though there were any other life for them.

19 "deceit of wealth..."

Alternatively, "the fraud that is wealth." Wealth appears to have a great value, but ultimately it does not. It is not an end, and to pursue it as such is to be defrauded.

20 "who have been sown in good soil"

With the earlier groups, there was a certain distinction between the seed and the ground in which the seed was sown. Whether rocky or covered with thorns, the ground was at odds with the purpose of the seed and therefore of the sower. But the term Mark uses for these men connotes a successful and unified completion of sowing. This last group is described from the point of view of the sower, as those who are in no way at odds with the purpose of sowing.

who hear the word ... and yield fruit

Jesus says that it is *these men*, not the seed or the soil, who bear fruit. The seed bears fruit in them, indeed, but they are one with him, and so are honored for bearing fruit. In these men, apparently, the Sower has indeed sown himself.

From fruit comes seed, and seed is for sowing. Thus, in the conclusion of this explanation is also a plan for the Church's growth by the assimilation of his listeners into him: hear the word; be deeply receptive to the word; bear fruit; cooperate with the Sower in sowing anew.

21–23

Here are three brief parables. The latter two fit with the Sower because they too involve sowing seed "upon the soil." The first, the parable of the lampstand, is a little different. In Matthew 5:13–15, Jesus applies the comparison to his disciples: "let *your* light shine before men...." Here, however, the parable seems to refer to Jesus himself. How so? Because verse 22 seems to give the interpretation of verse 21. But verse 22 speaks not about the light but about what the light is brought in to illuminate. After all, it makes little sense to say of a lamp that it is hidden to be seen. Rather, what the lamp illuminates, hidden previously, is made manifest in the light of the lamp. Jesus, then, would be the lamp that is brought in to illuminate what is hidden. What would be hidden? Presumably men's hearts. And though the Sower was concerned with whether men showed themselves to be fruitful, this parable adds that what a man is like in his heart is revealed by whether he is fruitful.

24–25

We said that Mark presents Jesus as teaching fundamentals in this sermon by the sea. Here, he seems to set down three basic principles of Christian life: prudence; reciprocity; and growth. Prudence: one cannot avoid living by some rule or other, so one must take care that the rule one follows is a good one. Reciprocity: one's relationship to his fellow man and one's relationship to God are of a piece. How we treat our fellow man determines how God will treat us. Growth (and decline): "to the man who has, more will be given, and to the man who has not, even what he does have will be taken away." In the spiritual life, there is no such thing as standing still—only growth or decay.

24 "It will be applied to you."

Notice throughout these verses the use of an impersonal "it will be applied," "it will be given," "it will be taken away." Presumably, these principles do not depend on a discretionary choice of God but rather on the nature of God and of human beings. Jesus, we might say, is articulating something he has responsibility for but not discretion over.

26–29

This parable, like any parable, illuminates the reality to which it is applied in some aspects but not others. The comparison is never comprehensive. Jesus apparently wishes to emphasize here that the Kingdom of God operates according to its own internal principles, without divine intervention. The man acts only at the beginning and at the end: he casts seed and sends in harvesters. Between the beginning and the end, he is attentive—he acts "the moment the fruit hangs ripe"—but he allows things to take place of their own accord, without his intervening.

26 "seed"

The seed is the source of the internal principle of growth and development. The plant is contained within the seed. The seed is not meant to remain a seed. John Henry Newman emphasized these ideas in his work on development of doctrine, arguing that if early Christianity continued, night after night and day after day, to look like a seedling, then it would not be the plant that Jesus had intended to emerge from the seed.

27 "he does not know"

That is, the farmer's skill and oversight do not extend to intervening in the growth of the field. Likewise, God does not ordinarily intervene from without in the growth of the Church. No such intervention is needed because a natural principle of growth is at work.

28 "first the blade..."

The growth of the grain according to a set sequence shows that it is taking place according to a spontaneous and internal principle.

29 "the moment the fruit hangs ripe"

The man does not intervene before he needs to, but the moment his intervention is called for, he does.

The parable seems to be a commentary on the relationship between nature and super-nature. Both the Christian life and the growth of the Church carry on as though they were spontaneous and natural. Nonetheless, it would be a mistake to hold that things continue on that way forever. God who allows the harvest to grow spontaneously at last sends in the sickle.

30–32

30 "How should we find a likeness"

By posing the question twice in the first person plural ("we"), Jesus seems to suggest that the Kingdom of God is too great for any comparison. This sets up our surprise at his paradoxical (and humorous) answer.

31 "a grain of mustard"

A grain of mustard is about one millimeter wide. To see what this looks like, consider a zero printed in a four-point type like so: ₒ.

"there it is!"

This is humorous because Jesus invites his listeners, many of whom were experienced farmers, to "see" the tiny mustard seed atop a layer of tilled soil. Of course, they could not.

32 "birds of the air..."

The birds of the air, which are here friendly to the Kingdom of God, stand for good angels, as in the earlier parable the hostile birds suggested devils. That the tree reaches up to heaven, where the birds are, and invites the angels to dwell there, shows the familiarity of concourse between this Kingdom and heaven.

What does it mean that they make nests under its shade? Perhaps it is an allusion to the "shadow of God," an image used in the Jewish Scriptures. Psalm 91, for example:

> He who dwells in the shelter of the Most High,
> who abides in the shadow of the Almighty,
> will say to the Lord, "My refuge and my fortress;
> my God, in whom I trust."
> For he will deliver you from the snare of the fowler
> and from the deadly pestilence;
> he will cover you with his pinions,
> and under his wings you will find refuge. (ESV)

The phrase therefore implies the presence of God.

33–34

33 adapted to what they were able to hear

The suggestion is that Jesus used different parables with different audiences. As we saw, it is reasonable to understand the parables of this chapter as among the most basic.

34 he would explain everything

In this chapter, Mark reports four parables but offers an explanation of only one. For Mark's contemporaries, the obvious implication of this sentence would be that they ought to seek out one of the disciples for an authoritative explanation of the parables.

35–41

36 other boats were with him

Apparently, Our Lord's boat was being towed. The disciples were in the other boats rowing, and Our Lord was allowed to rest.

37 the boat was just about filled

Surely an eyewitness detail!

38 So they wake him up

Considering their fear, it showed tremendous deference, if not faith, to wait so long to wake Jesus. Possibly they expected him to awake at any moment, until the delay began to seem absurd.

"does it make no difference to you…?!"

The question shows they believed he would have knowledge of the storm even though he was asleep. And they seem to assume that Jesus is not going to die, for they do not appeal to him as though his own life were at risk.

39 rebuked the wind…

The chapter began in an elemental setting, and now Jesus addresses the elements. Mark says that he spoke separately to the wind and sea. Presumably the first command is what he said to the wind, and the second what he said to the sea.

The sea became completely still.

A flat sea is eerie. No one who has seen such a thing is likely to forget it. This is another detail conveying what it was like to be there, evidently from Peter's point of view.

40 "Why are you so cowardly?"

Alternatively, "Why are you afraid?" but "cowardly" seems more appropriate, since a coward gives in to fear against reason. Jesus' point is that they have more than enough reason not to be afraid.

"Don't you have faith yet?"

Jesus healed of his own power; only God can do that. He forgave sins of his own authority; only God can do that.

That Jesus charges the disciples with a lack of faith, then, reveals how he understands faith. Faith has evidence and grounds; it is based on reasons and reasoning. But it shows itself in holding fast to reason, from devotion to Jesus, even when appearances seem to contradict what reason knows. Jesus asleep during the squall, the boat filling with water and on the point of getting swamped—these experiences appear to contradict the belief that Jesus is God, with complete authority over nature.

41 "So who is he then..."

They know the answer to this question. They repeat it to marvel at the answer.

CHAPTER 5

1 So they arrived on the other side of the sea, in the district of the Gerasenes. ²As soon as he got out of the boat, a man with an unclean spirit came out of the tombs and confronted him.

3 This man made his home among the burial caves. There was no longer any possibility of anyone's tying him up, even with chains—⁴he had been repeatedly tied up with chains and shackles, and the chains were pulled apart by him, and the shackles crushed. No one had strength to overpower him. ⁵Constantly throughout the night and during the day he would be among the burial caves and hills, shouting out loud and cutting himself with rocks.

6 So when he saw Jesus from a distance, he ran to him, and kneeled down in front of him. ⁷Shouting out in a loud voice, he says, "What do you have to do with me, Jesus, Son of the Most High God?! Swear by God that you will not torment me!" ⁸(The reason is that Jesus was saying, "Come out, unclean spirit, from the man.") ⁹Jesus asked him, "What is your name?" So he says, "Legion is my name, because we are many." ¹⁰He begs and begs him not to send them out of that district.

11 There was a large herd of swine feeding there, at the base of the mountain. ¹²They begged him, "Send us to the swine—let us enter into

them." ¹³He permitted them to do this. So the unclean spirits came out and entered into the swine. The herd rushed headlong over an embankment into the sea, two thousand in number. They were drowned in the sea. ¹⁴The herdsmen who had been watching them fled and told about it in the town and in the fields.

Streams of people came out to see what had happened. ¹⁵So they come to Jesus, and they see the demon-possessed man sitting there, clothed and of sound mind—the "man who had the legion of devils"—and they were filled with fear. ¹⁶Those who saw it related to them what happened to the demon-possessed man and the swine. ¹⁷They began begging him to leave their region.

18 As he was getting into his boat the formerly possessed man begged to go along with him. ¹⁹But Jesus did not allow him. He tells him, "Go to your home, to your own people, and tell them what the Lord has done for you and how he showed you mercy." ²⁰So he left and began to proclaim in the Decapolis what Jesus did for him. Everyone was amazed.

21 Jesus crossed back to the other side in his boat, and a large crowd gathered around him. He was beside the sea. ²²So one of the leaders of the synagogue comes to him, named Jairus. When he sees Jesus, he throws himself at his feet. ²³He begs and begs him, "My little daughter is dying. Please—come—place your hands on her—then she'll be cured and live." ²⁴So Jesus departed with him.

A large crowd was following him. It was pressing against him from every side. ²⁵There was a woman who suffered from a hemorrhage for twelve years— ²⁶she had undergone many treatments from many doctors, and had spent everything she had, but she had not improved from it but only gotten worse and worse— ²⁷when she heard the reports about Jesus, she came up to him in the crowd, and touched his clothing from behind, ²⁸since she was telling herself, If only I can touch even a bit of his clothing I'll be cured. ²⁹Then immediately the flow of blood dried up. She knew in her body that she was healed of her affliction. ³⁰Right then Jesus—since he fully recognized in himself the power going out from him— turned in the midst of the crowd and said, "Who has touched my clothing?" ³¹His disciples said to him, "Look at this crowd pressing upon you from every side. And you wonder 'who has touched my clothing?'" ³²So he was turning around and looking to see the woman who had done this. ³³The woman, who was afraid and was trembling, after she realized what had happened to her, came and threw herself at his feet. She told him the whole truth. ³⁴He said to her, "Daughter, your faith has made you well. Go in peace. Be healthy and free of your affliction."

35 He was still speaking with her, when men come from the household of the leader of the synagogue, who say, "Your daughter has died. Why should you bother the teacher any longer?" ³⁶Jesus could hear what they were saying and says to the leader of the synagogue, "Do not be afraid. Only have faith." ³⁷He did not permit anyone to accompany him, except Peter, James, and John the brother of James. ³⁸So they come to the house of the leader of the synagogue. He sees the clamor, the people sobbing and wailing to an extreme. ³⁹So entering in, he says to them, "Why are you making such a fuss and weeping? The little child has not died, but she is sleeping." ⁴⁰They ridiculed him. But he sends everyone out the door and takes aside the father and mother of the little child and his companions who were with him, and he goes in where the child was. ⁴¹So he takes the hand of the little child, and he says to her, "Talitha koum"—that means, "Little child, I say to you, arise." ⁴²Right then and there, the little girl gets up and starts walking around. (She was twelve years old.) Just like that, they are out of their minds with ecstatic joy. ⁴³Then he instructed them

strenuously that no one should know of this. He told them to give her something to eat.

Commentary

In the previous chapter, Mark introduced us to Christ's *teaching* by explaining that he taught using comparisons or parables, by giving an authoritative example of the interpretation of a parable, and by actually presenting some parables, especially three involving the growth of the Kingdom of God. The parables conveyed fundamental truths about Christian life in a setting that itself was elemental. The organizing idea of the chapter was "upon the earth": Christ has come to sow the seed of the Word upon the earth, and the earth is meant to receive this seed and bring forth fruit.

This chapter, in contrast, presents three remarkable *healings*. Its organizing idea is a command placed in the middle: "Go...to your people, and tell them what the Lord has done for you and how he showed you mercy."

Mercy is heartfelt sympathy with someone's distress joined with a resolve to help him. The distress varies in each healing: a man possessed by devils (agony of soul), a woman suffering from hemorrhage for years (agony of body), a father whose daughter has died (emotional agony of grief)—all terrible cases that show the effects of sin in the broad sense, that is, the alienation of the human race from God. Jesus' mercy in these terrible cases is meant to show his even greater mercy in saving us from sin.

All three healings take place "off scene," as it were, showing how little Jesus wanted to be regarded as a wonderworker. The first takes place on the other side of the Sea of Galilee, far from the crowd. The second occurs when a woman touches the cloak of Jesus in a crowd, unseen, as she thinks. The third takes place, intimately, at the bedside of a young girl.

They all seem to be hopeless cases. The man has not one devil but many. No doctor can heal the woman, who is getting worse and worse. The little girl dies.

They also represent different ways in which Jesus' healing power can work. The devil-possessed man himself is oblivious to Jesus. In no sense is his healing in response to his faith or in proportion to his faith. The woman has faith, but her healing seems entirely a consequence of her particular initiative. Jairus is the only one who has a reciprocated relationship with the Lord.

The healings are intertwined: coming back from the cure of the demoniac, Jesus is besought by Jairus, to whose house he is going when he is approached by the woman with a hemorrhage. Thus linked, these sufferers reveal something about our solidarity with one another.

1–5

1 on the other side of the sea

It seems the reason Jesus crossed the sea was to help this man. He leaves a crowd of thousands, gets into a boat with his disciples to row some six miles across a lake—a passage that would take several hours in good conditions—and endures a ferocious squall, all to help this one, pitiful, demon-possessed man, who spends his time among tombs howling and cutting himself.

If Jesus indeed made the trip expressly to help this man, then the squall takes on new significance: it represents the wrath of the forces of evil, which possess the man, just as Jesus' inducing perfect stillness on the lake becomes a picture of what he will do for that troubled man.

4 repeatedly tied up with chains

An example, it seems, of the very different way Mark writes when he is merely recounting a *description* relayed to him by Peter, rather than an eyewitness detail. When Mark conveys "what it was like to be there," he uses vivid language and particular details that evoke an entire scene all at once. Here he gives us a run-on sentence, plain words, and the passive voice.

5 shouting out loud and cutting himself

These torments are meant to give us a picture of the spiritual reality of a man enslaved by sin. He is not in his right mind. He already dwells among the dead. Instead of praying and engaging in prudent thought, he thinks and speaks in vain. He cannot rest. His sin causes him to harm himself, and his self-wounding is a pitiful cry for help.

6–10

6 kneeled down in front of him

The characteristic gesture of worship, but as the man is possessed by demons, it is probably a mocking gesture.

7 "Swear by God…"

Literally, "I demand you make a solemn oath before God that you will not torment me!" This is a strange thing for the demon to say. Some comments:

Matthew reports Jesus' teaching in the Sermon on the Mount, "Let your yes be yes and your no, no, and anything further comes from the devil." Here we see that something further coming from the devil.

There is an extreme lack of reverence in the devil's suggestion, maliciously frivolous, that Jesus should bind himself by an oath, as when a devil suggests that a man jump off a cliff.

The phrase "that you will not torment me" contains falsehoods, since there is more than one devil present, and devils are always tormented.

8 The reason is that Jesus was saying...

This is a strange sentence too, one that makes it easy to imagine Mark's telling this bizarre story just as he heard it from Peter. Nothing in the account has been tidied or polished.

It is puzzling that the unclean spirits apparently do not come out at Christ's command. How can this be? We may suppose that Jesus "allowed" the spirits to stay in the man after his initial order so they could demonstrate their terrible power, which we would not appreciate otherwise.

9 "What is your name?"

Jesus at first spoke as if to only one devil, but now he demands that the devil reveal its name—in the ancient world, tantamount to revealing one's nature—and we learn the extent of the evil present there.

"Legion is my name, because we are many."

A legion was the largest unit in the Roman army, consisting at that time of around five thousand heavily armed men. The irrationality of one being's saying that he is multiple represents how the devil attempts to destroy a person's unity of life.

10 not to send them out of that district

Another strange detail that is hard to explain. Incidentally, it illustrates that there are motives at work in the supernatural realm that Jesus and the devils recognize but are hidden from us.

11–20

12 "Send us to the swine—let us enter into them."

Apparently a two-fold request: first, send us to the area of the swine, instead of outside the district; second, permit us to possess the swine. When Jesus expels a spirit, it seems he controls both its location and the scope of its power.

13 The herd rushed headlong

Large herds of swine tend to scatter as they move, but these swine move together; picking up speed as they run downhill, heedless of danger as they plunge over the embankment and fall into the sea. As there was an embankment, the water was deep. Apparently, they did not pile up in shallow water but were swallowed by churning water, vanishing quickly.

were drowned

It is not that water came over them: it choked and strangled them. Just as the violent, irrational movement of the herd represents the power of the devils, the violent strangling is a picture of what the devil wishes to do to us.

This episode troubles many people, so it makes sense to pause and give it special attention.

The first thing to say is that the episode is meant to be disturbing: the tombs in darkness, the blood-curdling cries of a madman with superhuman strength, the strange assumed voice that must have come from the man when "Legion" was speaking, the desperate behavior of the swine, the frightened townspeople who begged Jesus to leave. We are meant to understand that evil here is never really vanquished. At best, it is contained. Considered carefully, the episode implies that hell exists, for spirits and souls dedicated to evil must be separated from everyone else—and God—for eternity.

Second, these supernatural spirits are beyond our full understanding. Their purposes and actions ought to remain, for us, "occult"—hidden, not something to think about or meddle in.

In connection with the swine, there are special difficulties:

Can nonhuman creatures be possessed? There seems to be no reason in principle that they cannot, but one supposes that devils typically have little interest in them, since their goal is to deceive and destroy human beings made in the image of God, and animals do not give them a foothold through sin.

Why would the devils want to enter the swine? Probably from sheer frivolous malice: seeing their time of possession was coming to an end, they wanted to leave with an intensely destructive act.

Why would Jesus allow this destruction? Perhaps he wanted us to have an unforgettable demonstration of the power and destructive evil of demons. But what about the apparently devastating loss of an enormous herd of swine? Yet that is a loss we are not in a position to measure. Perhaps the swine were owned by an extremely wealthy man or by a very bad man who required correction, or by a very good man whom God knew would be purified by the suffering. We simply do not know, and not knowing, we should not assume the worst.

15 demon-possessed man

By continuing to call him this, Mark writes from the standpoint of those who were there, who did not "see" this man as definitively cured and were worried that his calm will not last.

sitting there, clothed and of sound mind

The word for "of sound mind" is almost the same as the word for the virtue of temperance (moderation). In fact, in the culture of the time, having that virtue was thought to be the same as having sanity and self-possession.

17 begging him to leave

Fear is the expectation of evil, often born of ignorance. These people had no idea Jesus was the Son of God. They saw only that he could and did engage with demons.

18 begged to go along with him

Yet the man who was possessed does recognize Jesus as his savior. He does not fear but loves Jesus, who leaves him to teach his own people the truth, not as a bystander in an eerie display of supernatural power but as a rescued man who was shown mercy.

21–24

22 One of the leaders . . . comes to him

The historic present brings us immediately into this developing action.

23 He begs and begs him

No coolly restrained request: Jairus is probably sobbing, and his heart is affected—an image of petitionary prayer.

"My little daughter is dying."

Not daughter (*thugater*), but the diminutive, "little daughter" (*thugatrion*): this child is everything to him.

"is dying"

Is dying now—there is no time to waste.

24 Jesus departed with him.

The suggestion is that Jesus left with Jairus as he might leave with anyone for any purpose, not in great haste.

24–34

These verses are entirely in the past tense; in verse 35, Mark switches again to the historic present. The change in tenses allows Mark to present this episode as an interruption in the ongoing action. The past tense, moreover, is "slower." As Mark tells the story, reflecting the dramatic way in which Peter told it, we feel the urgency of the little girl's condition and the agony of the slow and interrupted progress of Jesus to save her.

25 There was a woman who suffered . . .

A run-on sentence, unusual for Mark. Again, when he writes in this way, we can assume he is not relaying an eyewitness account but reporting a third-hand description.

29 immediately the flow of blood dried up

"Immediately" is a mark of a miracle, as immediate healing implies God's power to create. At Lourdes today, for instance, the medical examiners inquire whether a reported healing took place instantaneously, since a natural recovery rarely would.

30 the power going out from him

The woman knows *in her body* that she is healed, but Jesus recognizes that he has healed, not in his body, but *in himself.* That is, he healed her not as man but as God. Mark's language probably comes from Jesus' own report.

"Who has touched my clothing?"

Peter would include this detail the way friends remember funny incidents in their friendship. We can easily imagine Jesus laughing when he hears his disciples' reply. He knows who was healed, of course, but by asking the question he turns the healing into a personal encounter.

33 who was afraid

She is afraid because she believes she has taken something without asking. In reverence, her first reaction to knowing that he knows about her is fear.

came and threw herself at his feet

Mark uses an intensified form of the same language that he used to describe how Jairus implored Jesus. Perhaps the woman had seen Jairus make his successful appeal and now does the same. Although afraid, she was emboldened by his example.

34 "Daughter, your faith has made you well."

"Daughter." He puts the woman in the same relation to himself as the sick little girl is to to Jairus.

"your faith has made you well"

Jesus addresses the woman's fear, assuring her that her trust in him established a personal relationship with him, and so he willingly healed her.

35-43

35 He was still speaking with her

With the historic present, we return to the ongoing action, which had been interrupted.

"Your daughter has died."

They say this to Jairus while Jesus is speaking with the woman. That is, they arrive soon after Jesus stops and asks who touched him.

"Your daughter"

Jairus had called her his "little daughter," but because of their different relationship, they use the less familiar form.

"the teacher"

Not the Aramaic word (*Rabbi*), but the Greek (*didaskalos*), perhaps a detail reflecting Peter's narration, for the servants would have addressed Jairus in Greek.

36 Jesus could hear what they were saying

Jairus would have been standing there impatiently throughout Jesus' encounter with the woman.

"Do not be afraid. Only have faith."

We can imagine that Jesus whispers these words, speaking in Jairus' ear as a friend. If so, no one else would have heard, and therefore no one had reason to think that Jesus was planning a miracle.

37 He did not permit anyone to accompany him

Presumably Jesus told the crowd to return to the seaside or to go no further toward Jairus' house. Having heard that the girl was dead, they would not have expected to see anything more.

38 the leader of the synagogue

Referring to Jairus by this title rather than by his name, Mark invites us to see the miracle as a favor for the whole Jewish community.

39 "The little child has not died, but she is sleeping."

His question is meant to teach, not to rebuke. He wants his followers to view death as temporary, like sleep.

"little child"

A familiar, diminutive term, which again indicates that he regards the girl as his own dear child.

40 They ridiculed him.

They were contemptuous. It is not clear they even knew who he was. A man walks in, apparently without good information, and says something which seems foolish.

41 "Little child, I say to you, arise."

How can he speak to *her* if she is dead? Or does he address the body as the little girl, which would show the importance of the body in Christianity?

He does not summon the soul of the girl from another world or command the soul to re-enter the body. His words, rather, make the little girl in her body-soul integrity present—a sign that he is the Creator.

"Talitha koum"

The words were seared into Peter's memory. Writing is a recording of spoken sound: here we have the ancient equivalent of a sound recording of that moment.

"I say to you"

He raises her immediately, by his own power, just as we saw earlier that he directly forgave sins of his own authority.

"arise"

This is strange, as one might expect, "Come back to life." It is the same word he applies to his resurrection but also what one might say to a sleeping person: "Time to get up!"

42 the little girl gets up . . .

The girl behaved just as she would if she had awakened from a good sleep. Mark notes her age—twelve—to explain why she was able to walk around.

they are out of their minds

This detail conveys how ecstatically happy they were, not simply the mother and father, but also Peter, James, and John. The detail, then, conveys how Peter himself felt at that moment.

43 give her something to eat

This instruction impresses upon them that she really was risen and not a ghost. Also, after being ill for so long, she would be hungry, a detail they might easily overlook in their joy.

CHAPTER 6

1 He left that place. So he goes to his home town. His disciples follow him. ²When it was the Sabbath, he started to teach in the synagogue. The many people who heard him were thrown off guard and said, "Where did he get these things?" "What is this wisdom given to him?" "Did powerful works like that really get accomplished through his hands?" ³"Isn't he the town carpenter, the son of Mary and the brother of James and Joses and Judas and Simon? Aren't his sisters right here with us?" They found him offensive. ⁴Jesus kept saying to them, "A prophet is not without honor, except in his home town, among his relatives, and in his own household." ⁵He could not do any powerful work there, except for healing a few sick persons by placing his hands on them. ⁶He kept wondering at their lack of faith.

He was making a circuit through the villages, teaching. ⁷So he summons the Twelve. (This was when he started to send them out two by two.) He gave them authority over unclean spirits. ⁸He told them to pack nothing for their travels except a staff. They should not take bread or a bag or any money. ⁹But they should wear sandals, and they should not put on two tunics. ¹⁰He would say to them, "If at a certain place you enter a home, stay there until you leave that place."

¹¹Also, "In case any place does not welcome you and listen to you, then as you leave that place, shake off the dust from the soles of your feet in witness to them."

12 And so they went on their way, provoking men to repentance with their preaching. ¹³They expelled many devils. They anointed many of the sick with oil and healed them.

14 King Herod heard the reports. (Jesus' name was becoming well known. People used to say, "He is John the Baptist, risen from the dead. That's how those powers are at work in him." ¹⁵Others would say he was Elias. Others used to say, "He is a prophet, like one of the prophets of old.") ¹⁶Herod, in view of the reports, would say, "This is indeed that John whom I beheaded come back to life."

17 Here is how that happened. Herod himself sent men to arrest John and chain him up in prison on account of Herodias, the wife of Philip his brother, because Herod had married her. ¹⁸This was because John was saying to Herod, "It is not allowable for you to have your brother's wife." ¹⁹Herodias held it against him and was wanting to put him to death. She was not able to do so. ²⁰The reason is that Herod feared John, as he knew he was a righteous and holy man. He would protect him. He would be perplexed at what John had to say. He used to enjoy listening to him.

21 Herodias had her opportunity when Herod held a feast on his birthday for his lords, his military commanders, and the leading men in Galilee. ²²Herodias' own daughter came in, dancing and delighting Herod and the dinner guests, and the king said to the little girl, "Ask me for whatever you want, and I will give it to you." ²³He swore an oath to that effect: "Whatever you ask me for, I will give it to you, up to half of my kingdom!" ²⁴She went out and said to her mother, "What shall I ask for?" She said, "The head of John the Baptist." ²⁵Without delay, she rushed back to the king and presented her request: "My wish is

that you should give me, on a platter, the head of John the Baptist." ²⁶The king became very upset. But because of his oaths and the dinner guests, he was unwilling to reject her. ²⁷So right then and there, the king sent his executioner with the orders to bring back his head. The executioner departed and beheaded him in the prison. ²⁸He brought back his head on a platter and gave it to the little girl. The little girl gave it to her mother. ²⁹When his disciples learned of it, they came and took the body and buried it in a tomb.

30 So the apostles gather around Jesus. They reported to him everything they had done and had taught. ³¹He says them, "Come with me, just you by yourselves, to a secluded spot, and take a little bit of rest." He said this because there were large numbers of people constantly coming and going. They could hardly find time to eat. ³²So they went away in a boat by themselves to a secluded spot.

33 Many people saw them going and figured out the spot. They ran there together on foot from all the cities and got there ahead of them. ³⁴He saw the vast crowd as he got out of the boat. He felt compassion for them, because they were like sheep without a shepherd. He started teaching them many things.

35 When it was already very late, the disciples went up to him and were saying, "This place is desolate." "It is getting very late." ³⁶"Send them away. That way they can go to the surrounding farms and towns and buy themselves something to eat." ³⁷He replied to them, "You give them something to eat yourselves." They say to him, "We are supposed to go out and spend two hundred denarii on bread and give it to them to eat?" ³⁸He says to them, "How many loaves do you have? Go find that out." They make a determination and say, "Five. And two fish as well." ³⁹So he told them to have everyone sit down and form as it were dinner parties, side by side, on the green grass. ⁴⁰And they sat down in groups of a hundred and groups of fifty, looking like flower beds

set side to side. ⁴¹So, taking the five loaves and two fish, he looked up to heaven, blessed and broke the loaves, and gave them to his disciples to serve to them. He also divided the two fish among all the disciples. ⁴²Everyone ate and was full. ⁴³They brought back twelve baskets full of broken pieces of bread and leftovers from the fish. ⁴⁴The men among those who ate the loaves numbered five thousand.

45 Immediately after, he made his disciples get into the boat and go across to Bethsaida while he dismissed the crowd. ⁴⁶After he sent the crowd away, he went off to a mountain to pray.

47 When evening came, the boat was in the middle of the lake. He alone was on the dry land. ⁴⁸After seeing them struggle to move the boat forward, as there was an opposing wind, sometime around the fourth watch of the night he comes to them walking on the lake. His intent was to walk right past them. ⁴⁹When they saw him walking on the sea, they thought, "It is a phantom!" They cried out, ⁵⁰because all of them saw him. They were terrified. But he addressed them right away. He says to them, "Have courage! It is I. Don't be afraid." ⁵¹So he got into the boat with them, and the wind ceased. They were completely beside themselves with amazement, ⁵²since they did not learn from what happened with the loaves, as their heart was hardened.

53 When they got across to the land they went to Gennesaret and anchored the boat close to shore. ⁵⁴As they were disembarking from the boat, the people there recognized him right away and ran throughout that whole district. And so people began to bring the sick on pallets, carrying them around to wherever they heard he was. ⁵⁶Wherever he would enter—villages, cities, or farming communities—they would place the sick down in the marketplaces. The sick would beg "to touch even the hem of his garment." And anyone who touched it would be made well.

Commentary

Our working assumption is that the Gospel of Mark represents an account of the life of Jesus from the point of view of Peter, who gives that account when he is the universal pastor of a newly-founded Church. The earlier chapters present ideas especially important to Peter, such as Christ's extraordinary powers, the transition of ministries from John the Baptist to Jesus, the unsuitability of the Pharisees and scribes to be genuine religious leaders and the authority that Jesus gives Peter and the apostles by contrast, and how mercy and the forgiveness of sins are the purpose of Christ's mission. Now Peter raises the question of Christ's identity. He will answer the question definitively in chapter 8, but here Peter is assembling the basis for that answer.

This is not to suggest that Jesus' consciousness of his own identity developed gradually or that he kept it hidden. The divinity of Christ and his role as Messiah have been implicit from the start of his public mission. Yet because of what Peter thinks is the "hardness of their hearts" (including his), it takes the apostles some time to grasp what was already evident.

1–5

1 His disciples follow him.

They need not have followed him. They made a free choice each day—Judas also, whose act of betrayal after following so long is all the more shocking.

2 When it was the Sabbath

Presumably he waited until the Sabbath to avoid what might strike people as scandalous. Precisely because "a prophet is not without honor, except in his home town," he took every practical step to win them over.

thrown off guard

Literally, these persons were "driven out...of their senses." The intensity of their dismissal of Jesus shows that he is not someone to be dismissed. Perhaps some contrast with the demon-possessed man is intended. He who had been "out of his mind" returns home sane after his encounter with Jesus, but when Jesus returns to his home, his presence provokes a kind of insanity—revealing something about his fellow Nazarenes, not Jesus.

"Where did he get these things?"

Highly compressed comments in colloquial language: they perhaps represent Peter's memory of some of the questions voiced.

The questions progress from better to worse: an initial acknowledgment that he has something special ("Where did he get these things?"), then doubts about whether his teaching really is wisdom ("What is this wisdom...") and whether he really accomplished any of his miracles ("Did powerful works like that..."), and finally a pat answer that there is nothing special about him ("Isn't he the town carpenter?").

3 "the town carpenter...?"

Since they do not refer to him as "the son of the town carpenter," presumably Joseph has passed away.

"Aren't his sisters right here with us?"

This one line settles the matter that "brother" and "sister" are used in the Gospels in the extended sense of "relatives." If Jesus had come from such a large family—seven or more siblings—it would be prominent in the Gospels, and we would know more about his brothers and sisters through the tradition.

They found him offensive.

Presumably their attitude showed up in how they acted toward him. He was shunned, isolated, humiliated, ridiculed, and dismissed. It is a proto-crucifixion, foreshadowing when "his people" (the Jewish people as a whole, and the whole human race, too, as represented by the Romans) reject, humiliate, and expel him, putting him to death.

4 Jesus kept saying to them

Mark uses the name of Jesus infrequently, typically to clarify an otherwise ambiguous reference. If he names Jesus here, there is a reason. We might infer that he is invoking the name his townspeople knew him by to underline that they knew him.

"among his relatives"

Did these relatives encourage the townspeople to think as they did, or were they perhaps bullied by the people? We don't know. In any case, their rejection was most bitter.

5 could not do any powerful work

What we call "miracles" are literally "powerful works." So "He lacked the power to do works of power" is deliberately paradoxical. He continued to have divine power over creation but was unable to exercise this power because doing so in the circumstances would have been harmful.

Working a miracle for someone resistant to faith could (1) provoke a worse, unworthy reaction, (2) suggest, wrongly, that Jesus did not prioritize his relationship to the person, and (3) coerce the person, forcing a good deed on him.

except for healing a few sick persons

A lively detail with no significance for the narrative other than that is what happened and Peter recalled it. People often introduce exceptions in narratives when contradictory memories arise.

6 He kept wondering

Jesus is repeatedly wounded by their lack of faith, and on multiple occasions he expresses astonishment at it.

We wonder at what we do not see the reason for. Sin and faithlessness seem irrational—there is no *reason* for them, even if they can be explained. Even Jesus, apparently, could not account for those closest to him taking the lead in rejecting him.

6–13

6 a circuit

We glimpse again Christ's method. He liked to teach on the Sabbath in the synagogue. Perhaps he went to a new village each week, teaching there on the Sabbath, spending the following days healing the sick, visiting farming communities, going to isolated spots to pray, and instructing his disciples. After a couple of months, he could repeat the circuit to provide accountability and deeper instruction.

The Jewish Sabbath was the last day of the week. But if the pattern just suggested is correct, then Jesus' visit to a town would *de facto* turn the Sabbath into the first day of the week—foreshadowing the change to be instituted after his Resurrection.

7 summons the Twelve

The sudden intrusion of the historical present indicates that Jesus acts like someone without much time—in this case, rapidly laying down a pattern for the future growth in the Church.

The Twelve are his authoritative representatives, and they in turn are to send out their own authoritative representatives. This successive "sending" is known as the Apostolic Succession—literally, the "sequence of those sent."

This was when he started to send them

With this phrase, Mark refers to a new way of proceeding in Jesus' public ministry—one in which the apostles now go about on their own as his representatives.

Where were they sent—to the same villages, as "follow up," or to new villages, so that he could reach more? Probably the latter. Mark has said that sometimes it became impossible for Jesus to enter a village, and then large crowds would come out to meet him. When these persons—perhaps tens of thousands of them—returned to their own villages, they were willing to host the teachers Jesus sent.

two by two

He sends them out as friends, and friends find it easier to work with friends. Friends also protect and strengthen each other. The prudence of Jesus: he was physically present with his disciples; he taught them directly; they went away only for a short time; they had to give an account of themselves when they returned; and he takes care to send them out two by two.

He gave them authority

The apostles do not just "happen to have" this authority because they are close to the Lord or because they love him a lot. This authority is deliberately conferred on them. Presumably Jesus did so with some public sign accompanied by explanatory words—the rudiments of holy orders.

8 pack nothing . . . except a staff

Presumably they took staffs not for walking or protection, but because they were to represent shepherds.

They should not take bread . . .

They are to be supported, providentially, by the goodwill of those they teach and help.

9 But they should wear sandals

Sandals, yes; extra tunic, no. The spirit of poverty that the disciples are meant to assume should not, it seems, interfere with their *mobility*. They should wear sandals, contrary what we might expect, because they needed to cover a lot of ground quickly. That they should not take a second tunic signals that their comfort is unimportant (and that comfort is not the reason for use of sandals).

10 "stay there until you leave that place"

By following this sensible prescription, the apostles will avoid offending their hosts, patiently endure inconveniences, show gratitude, express Our Lord's affirmation of that household (since they are his representatives), and not fall into cliques.

11 "shake off the dust"

This declaration that the apostles will not be coming back seems harsh. At the same time, Jesus merely poses a hypothetical case of total rejection, with no opening for the Gospel at all. However unlikely such a total rejection might be, if it were to happen, would such a gesture be unduly harsh?

13 They anointed many

Like Jesus, these first missionaries are sent into the world to teach, to expel demons, and to heal. Unlike him, however, they do none of those things of their own power. For example, they do not usually heal simply by laying their hands on the sick. They also anoint, presumably saying words as they do so, signifying that the power is not theirs.

14–16

14 King Herod heard

The king is so impressed by what he heard that he posits a miracle to account for it—John the Baptist is returned from the dead! But in contrast, the people in Jesus' home town concluded that he was only the village carpenter. These stories, taken together, sharpen the question of Jesus' identity.

"He is John the Baptist ... "

The people who thought this knew nothing about Jesus' origin or his life prior to John's death. Having heard that some "Jesus," about the same age as John, was teaching something similar to John's teaching, they concluded that Jesus was John, risen from the dead with newfound miraculous powers.

Note that no one asserts that John, supposedly raised from the dead, is the Christ. They regard dying and being raised as proof of a kind of resistance to long-term harm. It is not what a Messiah "must" do.

16 Herod... would say

The superstitious Herod regards himself as authorized to decide, as king, which rumor about Jesus is true. His official endorsement of the view that "Jesus is John" makes it necessary for Peter in his narrative to say something about John's death.

17–29

17 Here is how that happened.

Mark does not tell the story chronologically, beginning with Herodias and Philip's marriage and concluding with John's imprisonment. He sees that the heart of the story is the conflict between the king and the prophet, an echo of similar conflicts in the Old Testament. Perhaps this is Peter's sense for good storytelling coming through.

Philip his brother

As Philip is still alive, Herod and Herodias are committing adultery.

18 "It is not allowable..."

John the Baptist proclaims publicly that Herod is bound by the natural law and is violating it by adultery. A proud king, Herod does not want to acknowledge that he too is under the natural law, nor does he want to overcome his lust. So he imprisons this prophet who, because he speaks with the voice of reason, speaks also for God.

19 Herodias held it against him

She not only has a guilty conscience but also is afraid John may convince Herod, in which case she will lose both her man and her privileges as royal consort. People who act wrongly do not take a principled position against those who criticize them but turn hostile, like a dog when someone threatens to take its bone.

21 Herodias had her opportunity

The language opens the possibility that she taught her daughter dancing precisely to use her in such a way.

22 delighting Herod

Mark discreetly omits that the dance was erotic and caused the king to desire the daughter as he desired the mother.

23 He swore an oath

This oath, provoked by sexual desire, has no more solidity than a man's promise to marry later a woman he wants to bed now.

"up to half of my kingdom!"

He is saying he will treat her as his partner and consort, a veiled sexual proposition that everyone understood.

24 She went out and said to her mother

The mother was not in the room. Her absence made it psychologically possible for this young girl to perform an erotic dance for this group of powerful men, giving their imaginations free rein. Even though Herodias was a schemer, the mere presence of the mother in the room would have prevented the evening from developing this way.

25 "My wish is that ... "

This formulaic statement of the girl's wish binds Herod to his oath. At the same time, the word "wish" makes it inescapably clear that the great prophet John is going to be executed on the whim of a child. The contrast between cause and effect is grotesque and sickening.

The detail that the head should be placed on a platter seems to have been added by the girl. By including it, Mark shows how thoroughly the mother has corrupted her.

28 and gave it to the little girl

Mark uses the same diminutive for Herodias' daughter as for Jairus', intimating a contrast between the humble concerns of the poor, and the depraved whims of the wealthy and powerful.

Many capital sins are at work in this story: *lust*, excited by the daughter's dance; *gluttony*, indulged at the feast; *pride*, causing Herod to suppose himself exempt from the law; *vainglory*, keeping Herod from retreating from his rash oath in the presence of his lords; *anger*, stoking Herodias' burning grudge against John; and *envy*, fueling Herodias' resentment toward women who have their men without the reproach of adultery.

30–32
30 the apostles gather around Jesus
The interposition of the story of John the Baptist has conveyed the impression of a substantial lapse of time—very good storytelling, reflective perhaps of Peter's telling the story many times.

They tell Jesus everything, presumably because they want him to examine and correct their service.
31 "take a little bit of rest"
He invites them to a "retreat." The phrase "just you by yourselves" is full of attention and love.

33–34
33 Many people saw them going and figured out the spot.
Jesus, then, had gone there before. It was likely a spot across the water, visible from where these people stood.
34 He felt compassion for them
How did Mark know how Jesus felt? Did Jesus share his feelings with Peter there in the boat, or did he tell him later?
He started teaching them many things.
The retreat, it seems, is postponed as Jesus immediately assumes the role of shepherd. In response to the love they showed in running to him, he teaches them.

35-44

35 and were saying

The disciples seem to have been reluctant to say outright what they thought, simply suggesting, "This place is desolate." As it gets late, they become bolder and perhaps even impatient, telling Jesus, "Send them away." As if teasing them for their impatience, Jesus replies, "You give them something to eat yourselves."

36 "buy themselves something to eat"

Some interpreters say that the feeding of the five thousand was not miraculous but rather shows that Jesus inspired the people to share with others, so that everyone had more than enough. But such a reading is inconsistent with the reported facts: the disciples see that the people do not have food. Having spontaneously hurried out to see Jesus, the crowd would not have planned to stay late listening to him.

37 "spend two hundred denarii on bread"

A denarius was a day's wage for a laborer. One denarius might purchase enough for sixty meals. "Two hundred denarii," which would not come close to feeding this crowd, might have idiomatically stood for a large number.

38 "Go find that out."

Jesus' testing and teasing continues, because the disciples doubtless thought that the exercise was pointless. Yet they carried it out diligently, adding that they had even come up with "two fish as well."

39-40 dinner parties...flower beds

These are fascinating lines. Mark uses two idioms that occur only here in recorded Greek literature: "dinner parties, side by side" and "looking like flower beds set side to side."

The phrase for the first is *sumposia sumposia*. A symposium is literally a drinking party, though we would say dinner party. The phrase for the second is *prasiai prasiai*. A *prasia* is a flower bed. Mark repeats each word so that the position of the words in the sentence, side by side, is like the position of the things represented by the words, side by side. It is very clever.

But notice this. Jesus *commands* the disciples to seat everyone in groups like dinner parties. But in *following* the command, the disciples seat everyone in groups of fifty or one hundred, in rectangular formations. The first sentence records the Lord's command; the second is Peter's vivid description of how it looked after the fact.

The contrast between the two expressions shows that Jesus would leave the details to the disciples' discretion as they followed his command. The apostles are given scope to set down definite realizations of what the Lord intends.

39 on the green grass

A gratuitous but vivid detail that gives an impression of what it was like to be there. Incidentally, it explains why Our Lord's command that they be seated was not unreasonable. Green grass indicates spring, the season of Passover, a fitting time for a miracle that was a reflection of the feeding by manna and a sign of the Eucharist, which Jesus would institute at the Paschal meal.

41 blessed and broke the loaves

He blesses the loaves, not the fish. He breaks the loaves, but he divides the fish. Each disciple gets a piece of bread and a piece of fish.

42 Everyone ate and was full.

Presumably the food, like the "best wine" at Cana, was excellent. By implication, too, everyone was aware that he could eat until he was full without denying others—another fact that is incompatible with the idea that people were simply sharing their hidden stock.

43 twelve baskets

If we assume a loaf is not "ready to eat" until it is broken (that is, the unit of bread for eating is really a broken loaf), then the feeding starts with twelve items for eating (ten half-loaves and two fish), and it ends with the superabundance of an entire basket corresponding to each.

44 The men ... numbered five thousand.

Assume one adult man for every five persons. The crowd would be about twenty-five thousand in number.

45–52

45 he made his disciples

Literally, he compelled them. Especially after the storm, they hardly wanted to get into a boat without him.

47 He alone was on the dry land.

Why "he alone"? If he often drew apart with only Peter, James, and John, Peter needs to clarify here that none of those three was with him.

48 the fourth watch

He was praying, but he also watched them struggle against the wind, perhaps as long as eight hours. He is testing them once again. These arduous twenty-four hours show that following the Lord is not easy. In addition to the difficulties of human nature and of circumstances, there are difficulties deliberately imposed by the Lord.

he comes to them walking on the lake

It is the middle of the night, far away from any lights. If it were near the Passover full moon, they could see some distance, but the silvery moonlight would make the vista only eerier.

His intent was to walk right past them.

Mark says not that he acted as if he was going to walk by (as on the road to Emmaus), but that planning to pass them by, he changed his intention ("I'll just keep walking past them until they cry out to me for help").

50 because all of them saw him

When the men in the boat saw the spectral figure, they asked one another whether they saw it too. When it became clear that everyone else saw it—that it was not a hallucination—they became terrified.

He says to them, "... It is I. Don't be afraid."

Mark relates in the historic present the friendly and comforting words, as Peter heard them, with which Jesus calmed his disciples.

51 beside themselves with amazement

Here is a vivid detail about the disciples' inner feelings—literally, "they were extremely, overwhelmingly beside themselves with amazement." Their fear dispelled, relieved that their hard work is over, and astonished at the miracle, they rejoice at seeing Jesus.

52 as their heart was hardened

We said that in this chapter Mark raises the question of Jesus' identity from Peter's perspective. This sentence indicates that Peter believed, in retrospect, that by this time the apostles should have affirmed that Jesus was "the Christ, the Son of the Living God." Peter offers both a basis for that affirmation and an explanation for what was hindering them.

The basis was the feeding of the five thousand. We might think that miracle was not more astounding than, say, raising the daughter of Jairus. Yet Peter is clearly assessing miracles not simply as interventions in the laws of nature but as revelations. Looking back at the feeding, he would naturally think, "We should have concluded then that he was a second Moses and therefore the Messiah."

Peter's explanation for his and the other disciples' slowness is their hardness of heart. We saw that Jesus was angry with the Pharisees for their "hardness of heart," and he later rebukes the disciples for it also. "Hardness of heart" seems to be Jesus' main concern with sinful man.

53–56

56 place the sick in the marketplaces.

The market would be the central meeting place and the most "public" place. The marketplace—not law courts, halls of power, or even the synagogue—is the main meeting place between Christ and those needing his help.

"even the hem of his garment"

Word of the healing of the woman with a hemorrhage must have traveled. The sick wanted to imitate her.

CHAPTER 7

1 So the Pharisees, and certain scribes who had come from Jerusalem, hold a meeting to confront him— ²because they had seen some of his disciples taking their meals with "defiled" hands, that is, with unwashed hands.

3 (Now the Pharisees, and all of the Jewish people, do not eat unless they first ritually wash their hands, observing the tradition of their elders. ⁴When they return from the market, too, they do not eat unless they first wash themselves. And there are many other traditions which they observe, such as rituals for washing cups, pots, and utensils.)

5 So these Pharisees and scribes pose the question to him: "Why do your disciples not keep step with the traditions of the elders? They take their meals with defiled hands." ⁶He said to them, to the contrary, "Isaiah was right to prophesy about you hypocrites, as is written: 'This people honors with me their lips, but their heart remains distant from me. ⁷In vain do they worship me, since they teach as doctrines the precepts of men.' ⁸While you put aside the commandment of God, you observe a tradition of men!"

9 He also said to them, "How true it is, that you set aside a commandment of God to safeguard your tradition. [10]Moses said: 'Honor your father and your mother,' and 'Let anyone who reviles his father or mother be put to death.' [11]But you say, 'If a man says to his father or mother, "Whatever help you might have gotten from me is Corban," (that is, 'dedicated as a gift'), [12]then he no longer needs to do anything for his father or his mother,' [13]thereby cancelling out the word of God with your tradition, which you have handed down. And you do many other things just like that."

14 Once again summoning the crowd of people, he told them, "Listen to me, all of you, and understand. [15]There is nothing that goes into man from outside man that has any power to defile him. No, rather, only things that come out of man from within can defile man. [16]If anyone has ears to hear, let him hear!"

17 When he went into his house, leaving the crowd, his disciples started to ask him about that parable. [18]He says to them, "So even you fail to understand? Do you not see that everything which goes into man from outside has no power to defile him?— [19]that it does not enter into the heart but into the gut, and it proceeds out from there, into a latrine?" (He thus made all foods clean.)

20 He said, to the contrary, "What comes out from within man, that is what defiles man. [21]For it is from within the hearts of men that evil plans proceed outward—fornications, thefts, murders, [22]acts of adultery, greedy takings, depraved acts, deceit, insolence, an evil eye, blasphemy, pride, foolishness. [23]All of these evil things proceed out of man from within, and they defile man."

24 He left that place and went up to the districts of Tyre. He entered a house, wanting no one to know. Yet it was not possible for him to remain unnoticed. [25]Rather, right away a woman who had heard about him—whose little daughter had an unclean spirit— came and fell at his feet. [26]The woman was Greek, a Syrophoenician

by birth. She asked him to cast the evil spirit out of her daughter.
²⁷He said to her, "First, let the children eat their fill. It's not right to
take the children's bread and throw it to the dogs." ²⁸She had a ready
reply. She says, to the contrary, "Lord, even the dogs under the table
eat the children's crumbs." ²⁹He told her, "Because of what you
said—go your way, the evil spirit has come out of your daughter."
³⁰She did depart to her own house and found her child lying on a
bed, the evil spirit now gone.

31 Again, after leaving the region of Tyre, he went to the Sea of
Galilee through Sidon and right through the region of the Decapolis.
³²So they bring him a man who was deaf and dumb. They beg him to
place a hand on the man. ³³So, leading the man by himself, away from
the crowd, he placed his fingers into his ears. Spitting, he touched his
tongue. ³⁴Looking up to heaven, he sighed deeply. He says to him,
"Eph-phatha." (That is, "Be opened!") ³⁵The man's ears were opened,
the binding on his tongue was loosed, and he spoke fluently. ³⁶He
instructed them that they should tell no one. But the more strenuously
he instructed them, the more openly they proclaimed it. ³⁷People were
astonished beyond measure and said, "He has done all things well. He
makes the deaf hear and the mute speak."

Commentary

From the Acts of the Apostles (chapter 10 and 11:15–16), we know
that Peter and the other apostles believed at first that the good news
was intended for the Jewish people alone. It was only after Peter saw,
among other things, the Holy Spirit poured out on Gentiles too that
he recognized that the good news was intended for the entire world.

On our working assumption that Mark's Gospel is his interpretation of the life of Christ as recounted by Peter, we interpret chapter
7 as Peter's assembling of teachings and acts of Christ that, he saw

in retrospect, revealed Jesus' intent that the Gospel go out to all peoples, although the Jewish people would enjoy a certain priority.

It makes sense that Peter would clarify this idea now, before describing how Jesus was rejected by the Jewish religious authorities, and indeed by the Jewish people as a whole, who were incited to cry out for his crucifixion. Peter felt keenly the contrast between what Jesus deserved and how he was treated. It forms the core of his first public sermon as the leading apostle (Acts 2:22–23).

That contrast is likewise an important theme in the First Letter of Peter, especially in relation to the prophecy about the cornerstone. "Come to him, to that living stone," Peter writes, "rejected by men but in God's sight chosen and precious; and like living stones be yourselves built into a spiritual house, to be a holy priesthood, to offer spiritual sacrifices acceptable to God through Jesus Christ," (1 Pt. 2:4–5).

This image of a living temple must have been particularly vivid for Peter, whom Jesus named "Rock." And in his account of the trial of Jesus, the crucial charge is that he said he would destroy the temple and rebuild it in three days.

1–5

These scribes, and some of the Pharisees too, have traveled all the way from Jerusalem to investigate Jesus. When they have the chance to speak to him, however, they neither ask him deep questions of religion nor beg him to heal, nor seek forgiveness. Instead, they waste their encounter with the Son of God on a petty accusation disingenuously cloaked as a question.

Let us grant that they saw some disciples of Jesus eating without first performing the traditional ceremonial cleansings. As a matter of courtesy, the scribes ought to have verified the facts and then discreetly informed the men's teacher, rather than humiliating them and insulting Jesus. In any case, their accusation has many flaws. It overgeneralizes—they saw *some* disciples not washing their hands, not all. It assumes a lack of piety toward the traditions of their ancestors, when haste or thoughtlessness might explain the disciples' behavior. And it blames Jesus, though the scribes did not know whether he approved or even knew about the supposed infraction. They also fail to ask Jesus' view about the principle behind the system of ceremonial washings.

Recognizing that the question is not sincere but a trap, Jesus refuses to answer. Instead, he changes the focus to their own behavior, citing Isaiah, an authority whom these men would accept.

2 with "defiled" hands

Literally, "with common hands." The Jewish people believed themselves to be set apart from other nations by their covenants with God. To become "common" was to abandon this holy status and become profane. Jesus does not reject the notion that a people can be set apart or subject to defilement. For him, the question is not *whether* a man can be defiled, but *what* defiles him.

with unwashed hands

This is presumably Mark's explanation for Christians in Rome, including former pagans, who would not know what the Pharisees and scribes were talking about. For these Pharisees and scribes, a man was rendered profane not by going to the market, for example, or touching food that has been prepared by pagans but by *ingesting* these profaned things, unless, by ceremonial washings, he set the food—and himself—apart.

4 unless they first wash themselves

Literally, "unless they are baptized [immersed] in water." Similarly, "baptizing" cups and pots and utensils.

In the background is the question: What kind of immersion makes someone holy? The Pharisees and scribes rejected the baptism of John, but here they defend the baptism of pots and pans.

5 pose the question to him

Apparently having conferred among themselves, they deliberately raise this question as a challenge to Jesus.

"keep step with the traditions of the elders"

Literally, "walk in accordance with." It is a striking phrase because these disciples, after all, are walking behind Jesus. Since the Pharisees and scribes view themselves as the caretakers of these traditions, their question contains a complaint: Why do these men follow you and not us?

6–13

6 "'This people honors with me their lips....'"

The full verse is Isaiah 29:13, which reads, "... *this people draw near* with their mouth and honor me with their lips, while their hearts are far from me, and their fear of me is a commandment of men learned by rote." Jesus does not quote the first phrase of the verse (italicized here) because the Pharisees and scribes do not, in fact, draw near to him outwardly but are public critics.

Note the ease with which Jesus takes as his own a verse that gives God's point of view.

9 "to safeguard your tradition"

Jesus refers to "the traditions of men" in verse 8 but here to "your tradition," emphasizing that a person who hands down a tradition is responsible for it, since he must freely choose to embrace that tradition and pass it down. So the tradition of ceremonial washing is "their" tradition as much as if it originated with them.

10 "Moses said"

Moses was a prophet, someone who, by speaking the word of God, is a mediator between God and man. Jesus can say "Moses said" and let that stand for "God said" precisely because Moses was such a mediator. But what Moses said was transmitted by a tradition. A tradition is like a chain: it can support something only if what it hangs from is stable and strong. In referring to Moses, then, Jesus is introducing the principle that conveyance from God to man is greater than conveyance from man to man.

"'Honor your father and your mother'"

The commandment enjoined not only obedience and respect but also support in their old age. This reciprocity of the generations is known as "piety."

The Pharisees and scribes had implicitly charged Jesus with a lack of piety toward his ancestors. Here Jesus turns the tables: do they practice piety or, disregarding the commandment, observe merely human precepts?

"'Let anyone who reviles his father....'"

Why does Jesus cite two commandments of piety when one would suffice? Perhaps because of the double hypocrisy of the Pharisees and scribes, reviling for a lack of piety him to whom they owed piety.

11 Corban

"Corban," a common word in the Old Testament, means a sacrifice to God. Apparently, these men taught that someone could pledge his possessions to the temple while retaining control over them. He might use some of these possessions occasionally to support the temple and argue that, his responsibilities of piety having been fulfilled, he was justified in refusing help to his parents. Both the man who made the pledge and the temple authorities would profit, while the parents were neglected.

13 "canceling out the word of God"

By "word of God," Jesus means the *commandments* of God—an important reminder that for God, belief and practice cannot be separated.

"many other things"

Jesus is not criticizing human decisions by which a commandment of God is reasonably specified or filled out. For example, one could imagine human laws that determined what kind of support was to be rendered to elderly parents (for example, for sustenance but not for entertainment). Such laws do not fall under Jesus' criticisms.

14–15

Truth and boldness characterize Jesus' public ministry. Immediately after pointing out the hypocrisy of the Pharisees and scribes, he raises the substantive question they should have asked but did not. Since the religious authorities are not interested in the truth, he addresses the people, undermining with his teaching the traditions upon which the Pharisees and scribes were insisting. He is likewise imploring the people to follow him, not them.

14 "Listen to me, all of you, and understand."

He calls for heeding ("listening") first, as typically we come to understand his teaching only after we begin to follow it.

15 "nothing that goes into man from outside"

Literally, "There is nothing going into *the man* from outside *the man* that has the power to defile him"—deliberately abstract language by which Jesus conveys a moral truth about human nature.

17–23

17 ask him about that parable

What Jesus said about the power to defile was so abstract that his disciples thought it was an obscure parable.

18 "fail to understand"

Christ's habit is to address the crowds in parables but to explain everything directly to his disciples, so when he does address the crowd in direct language, he is astonished that his disciples fail to grasp it.

19 "it does not enter into the heart"

Jesus illuminates his direct teaching with this parable. It is a parable because the "heart" here is not on a par with the intestines. Nothing that flows into the heart as an organ is capable of defiling a man.

He thus made all foods clean.

Literally, "he thus cleansed all foods." He did not merely pronounce them acceptable but actually made them clean. Only what pertained simply to human nature—the virtue of moderation, precepts pertaining to gluttony, and so on—would bind his followers. In this way, becoming a Christian was opened to the entire human race.

This important observation is made as if in passing—Peter's judgment in retrospect, it seems, of the significance of what Jesus said on that earlier occasion.

20 "that is what defiles man"

What is voluntary is that for which the starting point of action lies within someone, as Aristotle taught. Jesus endorses that principle here, saying, in effect, that only actions attributable to a man as their source can defile him. He thus endorses the notion of defilement and, by implication, what later became known in moral theology as "mortal sin." A mortal sin is a definite act that kills the supernatural life of the soul and separates a person from fellowship with God. No longer set apart for God and holy, he reverts to a condition as if yet unredeemed.

21 "within the hearts of men"

Jesus identifies the heart as the center and source of a man's actions. St. Jerome famously remarked that in classical philosophy, the chief part of a man is his mind, but for a Christian, it is his heart.

21–22 "fornications...depraved acts"

Jesus' list of twelve acts that defile roughly corresponds to the Ten Commandments. The first six are outward actions, given in the plural, presumably to make clear that he is speaking of definite acts rather than thoughts alone.

The first defiling action is "fornication," which in both Greek and Hebrew encompassed any kind of sexual impurity besides adultery, including masturbation, sodomy, premarital sex, use of pornography, and cohabitation. These are often thought to be victimless crimes. They are not, but it is true that in the New Testament, the evil of fornication lies less in the offense against neighbor than in the offense against the Lord. It is an abuse of the body, which is a temple of God.

Why does Jesus put fornication first? Because it is one of the first manifestations, within a man's own body, of evil cogitations within the heart. Almost everyone struggles against these sins, the shame of which clearly appears to "defile" us.

22 "depraved acts"

Or "malicious acts," that is, any act we do for the sheer evil of it. We typically steal because we want the good thing which we take, but if we were to steal just because theft is forbidden, without even wanting the thing stolen, the theft becomes "depraved" in this sense. In his *Confessions*, St. Augustine writes that in such cases, casting off what we recognize as constraints, we are chasing an illusion of omnipotence.

"deceit...foolishness"

The next six defiling sins pertain to motives. These acts, more hidden and interior, can be more serious than the first six defiling sins if they become more than occasional faults and come to express our character.

"evil eye"

It is not clear what an "evil eye" means in the context. Perhaps the term is related to Mt. 6:23, "if your eye is wicked, your whole body will be dark."

23 "… and they defile man"

There is a treatise on sin implicit in this list that Jesus gives, as well as a helpful checklist for an examination of conscience. The logic of the complete list seems to be this:

- Visible acts that offend the Lord by offending the body (fornication)
- Visible acts that offend the Lord by offending one's neighbor (theft, murder, adultery)
- Visible acts that offend against body or neighbor and are intended to offend the Lord (deliberate depravity)
- Invisible acts—especially when habitual, indicating a vice—that offend against the Lord, one's neighbor, or the body

Did Peter deliberately memorize this list? Perhaps Jesus used the same list on different occasions. Or perhaps, besides giving the list, Jesus spent time on it, explaining its structure and the meaning of the items on it, giving his disciples the opportunity to memorize it. Instruction has traditionally been closely linked to memorization.

24-30

24 districts of Tyre

Jesus was at Genesarret on the northwest shore of the Sea of Galilee, which is about six hundred feet below sea level. To get to Tyre, on the Mediterranean coast, he had to pass over a ridge of mountains.

That is why Mark describes him as "going up from there." Jesus did not just happen to end up in Tyre; it was a deliberate choice.

The ancient Phoenician city of Tyre occupied an island just off the shore. Alexander the Great had built a causeway to conquer and raze the city. At the time of Jesus, it was a prosperous Roman port and commercial center.

A carpenter's journey from Nazareth to Tyre would be comparable to a tradesman's journey from rural China to Hong Kong. Christ's journey to Tyre, then, signifies something. If this chapter of Mark's Gospel reflects Peter's retrospective understanding of Jesus' sayings and deeds as pointing to the mission to the Gentiles, then Peter would see Jesus' journey to Tyre as representing the spread of Christianity to the entire Roman Empire.

wanting no one to know

Jesus apparently had a friend in Tyre who wanted to help him stay unnoticed. He was in need of rest. Fame is a burden from which he would need occasional relief. The bustling port city offered anonymity.

By refraining from public preaching in Tyre, Jesus indicated that although the Gospel was to be preached to the Gentiles, the time had not yet come.

25 whose little daughter

Jesus is constantly dealing with people afflicted by evil spirits, yet today demonic possession, though real enough, seems rare. What explains this difference?

Here are three possibilities: (1) There are degrees of affliction by demons that fall short of possession, and these are just as common today, but we do not notice them. (2) Many who were thought to be afflicted by demons were in fact suffering from mental illness, described as "an unclean spirit"; illness in an indirect and mysterious way is often traceable to the actions of evil spirits. (3) In Christendom, the realm of evil spirits has been pushed back and weakened, whereas in missionary areas, malign activity is frequently encountered, to a degree not unlike what seems to be reported by Gospel writers.

These explanations are not mutually exclusive. Perhaps the best answer is to say that there is truth in all three.

26 The woman was Greek

Peter, realizing later that Jesus' cure of the Syrophoenician woman's daughter stands for the future opening of the Gospel to all the nations, emphasizes her ethnicity.

27 "to the dogs"

Anyone offended by Jesus' remark should consider that it is clear that the woman herself was not offended by it. Taking it in good humor, she offered a witty repartee. In any case, Jesus is speaking in a parable, proposing an image for comparison, though not necessarily in every respect. The woman evidently understands the limits of the comparison.

What is the parable? Jesus has traveled to Gentile territory to rest, not to preach and heal. It is not yet time for the Gospel to be preached to the Gentiles. (That time will come, after the Resurrection.) His task for now is to preach the Gospel to the Jewish people, who have inherited the covenants with God and the promise of the Christ. Explaining this priority with the figure of a household, he says it is unheard of that parents prepare a nice dinner which they throw to the family pets while the children are seated at the table. This is the point of the parable. The figure of the dogs does not suggest that Gentiles are subhuman.

In this parable, Jesus likens himself to food. We have often commented how, in what he says and does, he takes for granted that he is God. This presupposition is so pervasive in his life that one would not say he "asserts" that he is God. You do not "assert" that you are yourself. Jesus simply presumes that he is given to us, and in particular, that he is food for us, in anticipation of the Eucharist.

28 "Lord, even the dogs.... "

As Jesus told the parable, the dogs have to wait until the children have "had their fill"; it is a parable about priority. Now the woman adds a twist—the dogs are under the table eating the crumbs even before the children have finished. Her parable is about realization, not order.

29 "Because of what you said"

Jesus does not wish to heal Gentiles at this time, as doing so would offend the order of "Jews first, Gentiles second." He will, however, heal the daughter if that healing is understood under the description the woman provides, "incidentally befalling."

Jesus praises the woman for the way she has changed the parable, as it shows that she has prayed and thought about Jesus beforehand—an expression of her faith. The Greek word here rendered as "what you said" is *logos*, which means not simply *word* or *statement*, but also *reasoning*. "Reasoning" is an appropriate secondary meaning to see in the word here, because Jesus rewards her for her resourcefulness.

30 She did depart to her own house and found her child lying on a bed, the evil spirit now gone.

According to Bede, Jesus' healing of the woman's daughter is an image of Christian baptism: "On account then of the humble and faithful saying of her mother, the devil left the daughter; here is given a precedent for catechizing and baptizing infants, seeing that by the faith and the confession of the parents, infants are freed in baptism from the devil, though they can neither have knowledge in themselves, or do either good or evil."[1]

31–37

This chapter has been concerned with the rejection of Jesus by the religious leaders of the Jewish people and the eventual opening

---

1 Bede, quoted in Saint Thomas Aquinas, *Catena Aurea: Gospel of Mark*, trans. William Whiston (Grand Rapids, MI: Christian Classics Ethereal Library), p. 109.

up of the message of salvation to the Gentiles. For Peter, a crucial sign that the Gospel was to be preached to the Gentiles was their receiving the Holy Spirit, as shown in the gift of tongues (Acts 10:44–46). It would make sense, then, for Peter to include here this healing of the deaf and dumb man, signifying how the Gentiles later would "hear" the good news and would prophesy and speak in tongues.

31 the region of the Decapolis

The Decapolis was ten pagan cities in the region southeast of the Sea of Galilee.

Some critics have said that Mark's description of Jesus' journey betrays an absence of geographical knowledge. Sidon is twenty-five miles north of Tyre on the Mediterranean coast. No one would go *through* Sidon to get to the cities of the Decapolis. Yet Jesus liked to teach by making a circuit among villages. A circuitous route back to the Sea of Galilee, tracing a clockwise path, is entirely plausible. Indeed, one might say that it is only because Jesus took such a circuitous path, through pagan regions, that Mark thought it worth recounting. And such a long journey through pagan territory is exactly what would be of interest, in retrospect, to Peter.

32 deaf and dumb

It is unusual for Mark to describe an incident like this without providing the context of the place and the persons involved. We presume that, for Peter's narration, the important detail is that it takes place in pagan territory.

They beg him to place a hand on the man.

It is not clear why it was important to these pagans that Jesus place his hand on the man. Perhaps in that culture, there were stories of healers who did so.

This passage is striking for its groups of similarly structured sentences, a construction that may reflect one of Peter's methods for remembering the details. Consider the similar structure in this group of three sentences:

> *Leading the man . . . away from the crowd, he placed his fingers into his ears.*
> *Spitting, he touched his tongue.*
> *Looking up to heaven, he sighed deeply.*

And in this group of three sentences:

> *The man's ears were opened.*
> *The binding on his tongue was loosed.*
> *He spoke fluently.*

34 he sighed deeply

This is not for the man's benefit: he can't hear yet. Nor for the crowd's: they were too far away to hear it. Jesus' sigh is simply a spontaneous expression his mercy and pity. Again, Peter is conveying what it was like to be there.

He says to him, "Eph-phatha."

Here we have once again Peter's "sound recording" of what it was like to hear Christ speak.

Note that Jesus does not heal the man by touch alone but by a word that gives the interpretation of the touch. The seven sacraments are like this. They involve a tactile gesture, like washing or anointing, and yet the imparting of grace requires the added verbal dimension, which gives the interpretation of the action and relates to the action as form to matter.

35 he spoke fluently

Literally, "he spoke rightly." The miracle is not simply that the man was now able to speak, but also that he was immediately able to speak fluently, without any training or practice. This effect would be even more startling than a simple healing of dumbness.

36 He instructed them that they should tell no one.

As Jesus made his circuit through the Decapolis, he presumably instructed the people on multiple occasions not to repeat the story. The result of his injunction, however, was that they told the story more enthusiastically.

37 "He has done all things well."

The Gentiles have no religious traditions stretching back to Moses and Abraham by which they can evaluate whether Jesus is the Anointed One of God. All they can know is his "virtue," that is, his ability to do things well, and they judge him by that.

"the deaf hear and the mute speak"

Peter quotes the prophetic utterances of these Gentiles, who were destined to receive the Spirit. In most prophesy, the prophet does not fully understand the meaning of what he is saying. The same thing holds true here. These pagans thought they were speaking only about a particular healing of sensory muteness and deafness. But they were prophesying as to the opening of hearts and minds of the pagans to the Gospel later—as Peter well sees in retrospect.

CHAPTER 8

1 There was a time, in those days, when there was another great crowd of people, who did not have anything to eat. So he calls his disciples and tells them, ²"I am deeply concerned about this crowd. They have been with me for three days now. They do not have anything to eat. ³If I send them back to their homes fasting, they will collapse on the way. Some of them have come a long distance." ⁴His disciples said to him in reply, "Where in this remote place could anyone get enough bread for them to eat?" ⁵He asked them, "How many loaves do you have?" They said, "Seven." ⁶He instructed the crowd to take places on the ground. Taking the seven loaves and giving thanks, he broke them and gave them to his disciples to serve. They served them to the crowd. ⁷They had a few small fish. After blessing them, he said that these should be served as well. ⁸They ate and were full. They collected seven baskets of broken pieces that were left over. ⁹The men numbered about four thousand. He sent them on their way.

10 Getting into a boat without delay with his disciples, he went to the region of Dalmanutha. ¹¹Pharisees came out and began to argue with him, insisting that he provide a sign from heaven, to test him. ¹²He sighs deeply in his spirit and says, "Why does this generation

insist on a sign? I assure you, if any sign will be given to this genera-tion...." [13]Leaving them, he again got into the boat and went across to the other side.

14 They neglected to bring any bread. Except for one loaf, they had no bread with them on the boat. [15]Now, he was instructing them, saying, "Be on guard. Look out for the yeast of the Pharisees and the yeast of Herod." [16]So they were saying among themselves that they did not have any loaves. [17]Aware of this, he says to them, "Why are you saying that you do not have any loaves? Do you still fail to see? Do you not understand? Do you have a hardened heart? [18]Do you have eyes and fail to see? Do you have ears and fail to hear? Do you not remember? [19]When I broke the five loaves for the five thousand men, how many hand-baskets full of fragments did you collect?" They tell him, "Twelve." [20]When I again broke the seven loaves for the four thousand men, how many baskets full of fragments did you collect?" They tell him, "Seven." [21]So he said to them, "Do you still not understand?"

22 So they go to Bethsaida. They bring a blind man to him. They beg him to touch him. [23]Taking the blind man by the hand, he brought him out of the village. Spitting upon his eyes and plac-ing his hands upon him, he asked him, "Do you see anything?" [24]Looking up, he said, "I see men, because I see something like trees walking around." [25]Then he again placed his hands on his eyes. He opened his eyes wide. He was restored. He saw everything clearly. [26]He sent him back to his home, saying, "You may not even go into the village."

27 Jesus departed, and his disciples, for the towns of Caesarea Philippi. On the way he asked his disciples, "Who do men say that I am?" [28]They tell him, "John the Baptist. Others say Elias. And others say that you are one of the prophets." [29]So he himself posed the question to them: "But you—who do you say that I am?" Peter

in reply tells him, "You are the Christ." ³⁰So he warned them not to tell anyone about him.

31 He started to teach them that it was necessary for the Son of Man to suffer many sufferings, and to be formally rejected by the elders, chief priests, and scribes, and to be killed, and after three days to rise. ³²He said this with complete directness. So Peter drew him aside and began to criticize him sharply. ³³But turning and looking at his disciples he rebuked Peter sharply. He says, "Get behind me, Satan!—since you are mindful, not of the things of God, but of the things of men."

34 Calling together the crowd, along with his disciples, he told them, "If anyone wants to come after me, let him deny himself. Let him take up his cross. Let him follow me. ³⁵For anyone who wants to save his soul will lose it, and anyone who loses his soul for my sake, and for the sake of the good news, will save it.

36 "After all, what does it profit a man, to gain the whole world and suffer the loss of his soul? ³⁷What, after all, could a man give to get his soul back in the exchange?

38 "For if someone is ashamed of me and my words, in the midst of this adulterous and sinful generation, the Son of Man will be ashamed of him, too, when he comes in the glory of his Father with his holy angels."

Commentary

The Gospel of Mark, we say, presents the viewpoint of Peter, who, as an eyewitness, aims to convey "what it was like to be there." We interpret the selection and grouping of episodes as an expression of Peter's role as universal pastor in the Church. The significance of these episodes is typically complex because they are to be considered both as Peter understood them when they occurred and as he sees them with the advantage of hindsight.

Peter's experiences during his three years or so with Jesus shape the narrative of this Gospel, in which we can discern two phases. In the first, Peter, impressed by the amazing works of Jesus, tries to figure out who he is. Of course, the reality is right in front of him, but often reality is not easy to grasp. He might even state the reality— "You are the Christ"—and not quite understand it. That confession comes at almost exactly the midpoint of Mark's Gospel, as eight chapters are nearly finished, and eight more are to come.

But no sooner does Peter make this confession than Jesus begins to teach that he must suffer many things, be rejected by the authorities, and be killed. And soon events begin to unfold as he said. Indeed, they move rapidly, with a sense of inevitability and, at the same time, with a sense that it could have been different if people had chosen differently.

For Peter, this second phase culminates not in another forthright confession of faith but in his betrayal. As he tells his story, he rises and falls spiritually. What was it like to live with Jesus? It was to be carried away by amazement at great deeds, to love him deeply and need him as a merciful friend, but also to be overturned and shocked by the events of the Passion.

As is well known—we will discuss it in its place—the ending of the Gospel of Mark is different in different manuscript traditions. In one tradition, the Gospel ends with women finding Jesus' tomb empty yet guarded by an angel. That version of the Gospel is almost certainly not complete as an account of the life and mission of the Christ. But in a way, it *is* complete as an account of Peter, for from his point of view, his time with Jesus would have ended in his own failure but for the extraordinary intervention of God in the Resurrection.

Peter's own tale, as it were, ends there, and the story of the Church begins. Indeed, he will be the vicar of Christ and universal pastor, but only after he himself has died a kind of death along with Christ and found himself gratuitously accepted and restored.

1–9

1 he calls his disciples

Mark switches to the historic present again in his transition from background description to present action, suddenly placing us right in the scene.

4 "Where in this remote place...?"

We might criticize the disciples for not remembering what happened the last time Jesus asked about food for the crowd. It is praiseworthy that they do not presume he will do another miracle, though this seems to be a leading question.

5 "How many loaves...?"

He uses similar words as previously because he wants them to see this as a repetition of what was accomplished before and to recognize an element of ritual. These feedings stand for the Eucharist, which he is to institute later.

They said, "Seven."

Their food is depleted also. They have only seven loaves left for Jesus, the twelve apostles, and perhaps other disciples.

6 He instructed the crowd

The disciples would have organized the orderly seating of the people as before, dividing the crowd into groups. But Mark does not say this. He says, rather, that Jesus instructed the crowd to do so, as if what Jesus does through his apostles he does himself.

10–13

10 without delay

Jesus wanted to leave quickly lest the crowd try to keep him there for additional meals.

12 He sighs deeply in his spirit

Apparently, a sigh of sadness or exasperation. Bede contrasts his groan here with the groan he uttered in thanksgiving as he blessed the bread before: "He groans; because, bearing about with him the feelings of human nature, as he rejoices over the salvation of men, so he grieves over their errors."[1]

"if any sign will be given to this generation...."

That is, a sign will never be given.

14–21

16 they were saying among themselves

What must they have been assuming, to respond to Jesus in this way? Presumably, they took him to be referring to yeast used in the baking of bread—bread that was already made. Jesus' language, after all, was suggestive of a present threat: "Be on guard! Look out!" Apparently, then, they supposed him to be telling them to avoid bread baked using yeast supplied by the Pharisees or Herod. Yet if they were out of bread, there would be no immediate threat, so they were saying, in effect, "What is the problem, since we do not have any bread at all except for this loaf?"

17 "Do you not understand?"

Given the miraculous feedings, they should have suspected that what Jesus meant by "bread" was something other than ordinary bread. But they were not searching for the spiritual meaning. Apparently, they did not even suspect that there was such a meaning.

"Do you have a hardened heart?"

Here and elsewhere, Jesus speaks of the heart in the singular—the "heart" of a group of men, not the hearts of individual men. A

---

1 Bede, quoted in Saint Thomas Aquinas, *Catena Aurea: Gospel of Mark*, trans. William Whiston (Grand Rapids, MI: Christian Classics Ethereal Library), p. 118.

group becomes more unified through deliberation and discussion. We speak of a group's being "of one mind." Jesus seems to have thought, instead, of their becoming "of one heart."

18 "Do you have eyes and fail to see?"

Jesus had explained his use of parables in general with similar language (4:11–12). Now he rebukes his disciples for not grasping that his teaching about bread was a parable.

This exchange between Jesus and his disciples seems to operate on three levels: (1) Simply as a concrete reminder: When someone has failed to ponder something important, a good first step is to recall the details. Jesus is inviting his disciples to recover these events interiorly and discover their meaning. (2) He draws attention to the miraculous character of the events they have witnessed. The loaves considered as mere food for the body were wholly insufficient for feeding those thousands with so many baskets left over. The disciples were not to think of them, then, as physical food but as signs of something else. (3) He invites his disciples to reflect on the numbers involved in the miraculous feedings: five and seven (loaves), and seven and twelve (baskets).

Recounting the story later, Peter would have seen it as an invitation to the Church, then and today, to reflect on the meanings of these numbers. One is free to assign meanings to biblical numbers as seems appropriate, and a meaning is "right" insofar as it is appropriate. So let us see what the numbers in this story might mean.

The baskets clearly stand for superabundance. Take them, then, to stand for God's outpouring of grace. Therefore, let the seven baskets stand for the seven sacraments, and let the twelve baskets stand for the twelve offices of the apostles.

On the other hand, the loaves of bread seem to stand for material instruments, which, when offered up to God, become that *through which* grace is poured out. Therefore, let the number five represent the five senses, which we offer up for sanctification, and let the number seven represent these senses together with the powers of imagination and memory.

22–26

23 out of the village

There is a fundamental asymmetry in a blind person's relation to others—they can see him, but he cannot see them. By leading this man out of the village, where his neighbors can no more see him than he can see them, Jesus expresses this man's equal dignity. Also, he can deal with the man more directly and intimately.

Spitting upon his eyes

The Greek says that Jesus spat *into* his eyes rather than *upon* his eyes. Perhaps Mark puts it this way because the man's eyes, being nonfunctional, seemed like inert objects. Yet it seems unlikely that Jesus would spit directly into his eyes, as this would startle the man and be humiliating. It seems likely that Jesus produced spittle and then placed it upon his eyes. In any case, the important point is that spittle that originated with Jesus was placed upon the man's eyes. Because of the incarnation, the spittle would serve as an instrument of divine power.

and placing his hands upon him

Jesus did not place his hands on the man's *eyes*; otherwise Mark would have said so. He must have placed them on the man's head, in the manner of a blessing, or on his shoulders, in the manner of a friend.

"Do you see anything?"

Jesus knew, but he wanted others to hear the man's report. He wanted to show that miraculous help from God sometimes comes in stages, not all at once, and when it does, it has a progressive, subjective character. Miraculous power and grace work objectively, but they are experienced subjectively. In the case of objective, miraculous power applied to the eyes, the imperfect character of the cure is shown in the man's report about how things seem to him.

24 Looking up, he said

We wondered where Jesus placed his hands. This verse is the best evidence that he placed them on the man's head. It is natural to bow your head when someone places his hands on your head to impart a blessing. We can imagine that when Jesus took his hands away and asked the man if he saw anything, he lifted his head and attempted to look around.

"something like trees"

We do not know whether this man was born blind. Had he seen men before? From the manner of his answer it seems probable he was not born blind and remembered what men and trees looked like. When he regains his sight, then, he realizes that it is still unclear. Seeing something like what he remembers trees to look like but which are moving, he infers that they are men.

25 Then he again placed his hands on his eyes.

This verse supports the idea that Jesus produced spittle and placed it on the man's eyes with his hands, since now he does so "again."

He opened his eyes wide.

Opened, restored, saw clearly: a progression evoked by the inscription on Blessed John Henry Newman's tombstone: *ex umbris et imaginibus in veritatem*—"out from the shadows and imaginary scenes into the truth."

Some say there can be no true conversion which is not immediate and complete, as anyone who was obedient to even part of the truth would be obedient to all of it. Others say that conversion can be a slow process in which a man moves gradually from an imperfectly grasped truth to the whole truth. Since sight symbolizes faith, Jesus' arrangement of this healing seems to support the second view.

26 "You may not even go into the village."

Jesus does not *ask* him but *forbids* him. The one who saves us has authority over us; we owe obedience to the Lord for his saving us.

27–30

27 "Who do men say that I am?"

He asks this question to set up the next. St. John Chrysostom writes, "From the manner, however, itself of the question, he leads them to a higher feeling, and to higher thoughts."[2]

28 "John the Baptist"

The disciples indicate that the common view is that Jesus is John the Baptist risen from the dead. As we saw with Herod, it was easy for people to think so. The prevalence of that opinion might even be a reason that Mark starts his Gospel with an account of John the Baptist, a figure prior to and different from Jesus.

29 So he himself posed the question to them: "But you—who do you say that I am?"

Importantly, Mark adds an intensifier, "he himself." When he asked, "Who do men say that I am?" he was asking for a report about others. But when he asks, "Who do you say that I am?" he is asking for a personal pledge and commitment, which originates *from him.*

The disciples have seen many miracles and heard much teaching. They have had time to ponder. Now Jesus provokes a crisis. It is time for them to make a decision.

Peter in reply tells him

Peter speaks, yet Jesus accepts the reply as the pledge of the commitment of the disciples as a whole. Peter therefore speaks for the disciples, even in the sense that he can commit them by his commitment.

---

2 Chrysostom, quoted in *Catena Aurea*, p. 123.

We know from Matthew's Gospel that Jesus went on to say to his chief disciple, "You are Peter, and on this rock I will build my church," and conferred on him the "keys of the kingdom of heaven" (Mt. 16:17–19), but Mark omits that declaration. Some Fathers say this was because Mark also omits the second half of Peter's confession—"You are the Christ, *the son of the living God.*" The conferral of authority on Peter as the rock, they say, corresponds to this second element of his confession: it was because Peter clearly confessed Jesus as God that he became worthy of being appointed the rock.

Alternatively, Mark prefers to emphasize the corporate, rather than the individual, dimension of Peter's confession. The confession had both elements, of course—Mark would be emphasizing the one and Matthew the other.

Alternatively, Peter sees the purpose of this chapter as narrating the events that led up to his confession, "You are the Christ." Jesus' reciprocal recognition of Peter would draw attention to the apostle and would therefore be out of place.

"You are the Christ."

As we saw, this term means anointed one of God. In the Jewish tradition, three types of person were anointed: prophets, priests, and kings. So to confess Jesus as *the* Christ is to confess him as *the* prophet, priest, and king. But what does this mean? Presumably, Jesus immediately begins to teach the disciples openly about his passion and death, because Peter's confession has made it opportune to answer these questions about the implications of his being the Christ.

If Peter did not know that the Christ had to suffer, did Peter fully understand what he was saying when he confessed that Jesus was the Christ? The answer must be no. His confession expressed a basic commitment and principle, giving a specific form to what he took "following Jesus" to be. Henceforth he was following him not because he was a wonderworker but because he was the Christ. Jesus now reveals to him and his fellow apostles what it means to be this Christ.

30 he warned them not to tell

The truth about Jesus would be preached soon enough. But if the people misunderstood what the Christ was supposed to be—expecting him to be a political deliverer—they would try to make him king, which could interfere with his true mission.

31–33

31 the Son of Man

The "necessity" of suffering and death arises from the fact of his incarnation, which is expressed in the title "Son of Man": God became man to pay the penalty of sin on behalf of man.

formally rejected

The Greek term means being subjected to a test, found wanting, and rejected as a result.

32 complete directness

In other words, he did not express this to them in parables. We know he used parables to express the same truth, such as "unless a seed dies and falls into the soil, it yields no fruit." But Mark wishes to emphasize now that Jesus explained these things in much the same language that Mark uses to report it.

The Greek term here is *parrhēsia*, which means the sincerity shown between friends in speech, as when a friend understands that his friend wants to hear the truth, not what is pleasing to hear.

So Peter drew him aside

Peter responds in the way a friend should, in the same spirit of candor, drawing Jesus aside and telling him frankly what he thinks. Our strengths are our weaknesses: his strong and passionate character leads him astray here. He loves Jesus passionately and therefore speaks up for what he regards as Jesus' best interests. He is a natural leader, too, and therefore takes the initiative—even though, admittedly, such sharp criticism of his own leader was out of bounds.

33 turning and looking at his disciples

Jesus is ostensibly correcting Peter, yet he looks away from Peter and at the disciples in doing so. It seems, then, that his correction is stylized. He wants to use Peter's intervention as the occasion for correcting a potential misunderstanding of all the disciples. If so, then "Get behind me, Satan," is addressed to all of them as much as to Peter—and indeed to any follower who would deny the necessity of the cross.

he rebuked Peter sharply

Mark uses the same Greek word for what Jesus does ("sharply criticize,") that he used for Peter's remonstration, indicating the reciprocity. Yet this exchange, although it looks sharp, was an exchange of goodwill. Our Lord's appropriate correction of Peter is directed to his best interests, just as Peter thought he had Our Lord's best interests in view.

"Get behind me"

This means the same as in verse 34, "If anyone wants to come after me." It means following his lead, following his example.

"Satan"

Satan is the highest created being who preferred himself over God. His fundamental sin was the sin of disorder. His nature was very good, and it was right of him to love himself intensely. But he erred by not loving God more. Why, then, does Jesus call Peter "Satan," when Peter had Jesus' best interests in mind, not his own? Because the goods we wish for others are the goods we wish for ourselves. Jesus understood that Peter wished for himself—and therefore for Jesus—human goods over necessary divine goods. He was unintentionally committing the same error as Satan, putting himself over God.

34–38

34 Calling together the crowd

This is a turning point in the Gospel of Mark. Looking ahead now to his Passion, Jesus wants the people to prepare for it as well, so he begins talking about it not only to his disciples but also to the crowd. But his language now lacks the blunt *parrhēsia* of his language with his friends. Admittedly, he says that a follower should "take up his cross," yet the crowd could not easily guess what this means. Jesus must have proposed it as something that would make sense later.

"If anyone wants to come"

He leaves it as a matter of freedom. He proposes but does not impose.

"to come after me"

A principle of ordering. It means, "love me more than himself." The phrase is another example of Jesus' simply presuming that he is God. Just as we are to prefer God over our own good, so we are to prefer Christ over our own good.

"let him deny himself"

The first thing is not to be disordered, as Satan was. A follower of Jesus must be prepared to sacrifice his own good out of love of God.

"Let him take up his cross."

The cross is promised: Jesus does not say, "let him take up a cross, if there happens to be one." His follower should take up the cross that (assuredly) will be assigned to him.

"Let him follow me."

This is slightly different from "come after me," which is a principle of ordering. "Let him follow me" in the context means, "Show your love for me by imitating me, by doing what I do, even when that conflicts with your own good."

We see, then, the logical progression in Jesus's statement: "If anyone wants to come after me, let him deny himself. Let him take up his cross.

Let him follow me." It gives a principle of ordering, what is necessary to attain that ordering, the means or instrument for attaining it, and a consequence of the ordering.

35 "anyone who wants to save his soul"

This next sentence gives the motivation. Why should anyone choose freely to come after him? To save his soul.

36 "suffer the loss of his soul"

The word rendered "soul" (*psychē*) refers to the fundamental cause of the activity of life in a living thing. Sometimes it is used to mean the life itself. Translators must decide whether to translate it as "soul" or "life." Which is best depends upon context and reasoning; only a living being can gain something. So gaining the world but losing one's soul must mean something like losing the ultimate good of the soul (by being headed for hell) or losing control over the soul (by disintegration of one's personality) or losing the good of one's soul (by becoming corrupt).

37 "What, after all, could a man give…?"

This is one of those sayings of the Lord that means many things at the same time. It means that if a man loses his soul, the devil possesses it, but the devil will never take anything in exchange for it because the devil wants the destruction of men more than the possession of any material thing. It also means that if a man has lost his soul, then there is no man left, really, who can do anything. It also means that if a man has lost his soul, the desire to gain his soul back is lost as well. Finally, it means that if someone has lost his soul for the sake of the world, then he failed to appreciate the worth of the soul, and no responsible person will render it back to him.

38 "if someone is ashamed of me"

To be ashamed of something is to regard it as wrong when among those whose opinions one respects. It is to respond to something as though one finds oneself a bad person among the good. The life of

Christ, a dramatic offering for the salvation of others, is romantic and beautiful. It is something good amidst the pervasive evil of the world. So are the words of Christ, which invite us to a similar way of life. It would be perverse to be ashamed of these.

Our own characters are formed, for good or for ill, by how we treat things. We become good by treating what is good as good and by treating what is bad as bad. If we do the opposite, then we become bad. Anyone who is ashamed of Christ and his words—that is, who treats them as bad—becomes bad himself. Christ, the true standard and just judge, will test him and find him to be so.

CHAPTER 9

1 He used to say to them, "I tell you assuredly, that there are some of you standing here who will not taste death until you see, in a work of power, the coming of the Kingdom of God."

2 So six days later, Jesus takes aside Peter and James and John and brings them up a high mountain, just them by themselves. He was changed in appearance in their presence. ³His clothes became an extreme gleaming white, a white such as no launderer on earth can produce by whitening. ⁴Elijah appeared to them, with Moses. They were conversing with Jesus. ⁵So Peter adds his own comment and says to Jesus, "Rabbi, that we are here is excellent. Let us make three tents: one for you, and one for Moses, and one for Elijah"— ⁶he did not know how to respond, since they were overcome with fear. ⁷So a cloud formed, which cast a shadow on them. There was a voice from the cloud: "This is my Son, my beloved. Listen to him." ⁸Then suddenly, as they looked around, they no longer saw anyone with them—only Jesus, by himself.

9 As they were coming down from the mountain, he said to them firmly that they should not tell anyone what they had seen until the Son of Man rose from the dead. ¹⁰They did what he said, though they

could not figure out among themselves what it meant "to rise up from the dead."

11 They posed a question to him: "Why do the scribes say that Elijah must come first?" ¹²He said to them, "Well, Elijah comes first to restore all things—and yet, even then, how is it written of the Son of Man, that he is to suffer many things and be reduced to nothing? ¹³Yet I affirm for you that Elijah did come, and they did to him what they wished, just as was written of him."

14 So they came to the disciples and saw a great crowd around them and scribes arguing with them. ¹⁵The moment the crowd saw him, as a group, they were astonished. They ran to greet him. ¹⁶He asked them, "What are you arguing about with them?" ¹⁷A man from out of the crowd replied, "Teacher, I brought my son to you, because he has a dumb devil. ¹⁸Whenever it gets hold of him, it throws him to the ground. He foams at the mouth and gnashes his teeth. He is wasting away. I spoke with your disciples, for them to cast it out, and they couldn't." ¹⁹So he says to him in reply, "Faithless generation! How long shall I be with you? How long shall I endure you? Bring him to me, will you!" ²⁰So they brought him to him. Then, the moment the spirit saw him, it convulsed him. Falling to the ground, he began to roll around, foaming at the mouth. ²¹He questioned the father, "How many years has he been like this?" He said, "Since he was a child. ²²Many times, it even throws him into fire or into water, to destroy him. But if you can do anything... have mercy on us and help us!" ²³Jesus said to him, "'If you can'?! Everything is possible for a man who believes." ²⁴Without missing a beat, the father of that little boy cried out and said, "I believe! Help my unbelief!" ²⁵But Jesus, when he saw that a crowd was running toward them, rebuked the unclean spirit, saying to it, "Dumb and deaf spirit, I command you, come out of him and enter into him no longer!" ²⁶Crying out and convulsing him with great convulsions, it came out. He became as

if a corpse, so that many were saying, "He is dead." ²⁷But Jesus took his hand to lift him up. And he rose up again. ²⁸After he went into his house, his disciples in private asked him, "Why couldn't we cast it out?" ²⁹He told them, "It is not possible for this kind to come out other than by prayer."

30 Departing from there, they traveled throughout Galilee. He did not want anyone to know, ³¹because he was teaching his disciples. He was telling them, "The Son of Man is betrayed into the hands of men. They will kill him. Once he is dead, after three days, he will rise up." ³²But they did not understand this language. They were afraid to ask him.

33 They came to Capernaum. Once he was in the house, he asked them, "What were you discussing on the way?" ³⁴But they kept quiet. Why? Because on the way they had been arguing among themselves who was greater. ³⁵So after he sat down, he called the Twelve by name. He tells them, "If anyone wants to be first, he will be last of all and servant of all." ³⁶He took a little child and stood it in the middle of them. He enfolded the little child in his arms and told them, ³⁷"Whoever receives one of these little children in my name, receives me. Whoever receives me, does not receive me, but the one who sent me."

38 John said to him, "Teacher, we saw someone expelling devils in your name who is not following us. We stopped him because he is not following us." ³⁹But Jesus said, "Do not stop him: there isn't anyone who does a work of power in my name who will soon speak ill of me. ⁴⁰Whoever is not against us is for us. ⁴¹If anyone gives you a cup of water to drink because he counts you as belonging to Christ—I tell you solemnly that he will not lose his reward.

42 "It is better that a heavy millstone is placed around someone's neck and he is cast into the sea than that he should lead one of these little ones who believe in me to sin.

43 "If your hand leads you to sin, chop it off. It is better to enter into life as a deformed man than to go off with two hands into Gehenna, into the unquenchable fire.

45 "If your foot leads you to sin, chop it off. It is better to enter into life as a crippled man than with two feet to be thrown into Gehenna.

47 "If your eye leads you into sin, pluck it out. It is better to enter into the Kingdom of God as a one-eyed man than with two eyes to be thrown into Gehenna, [48]where their worm does not die, and the fire is not quenched.

49 "For everyone will be salted by fire. [50]Salt is good. But if salt becomes saltless, how will you concoct it? Have salt in yourselves. Be at peace with one another."

Commentary

This chapter has three parts: the "Transfiguration" (verses 1–13), an exorcism (14–29), and teachings on authority and discipleship in the kingdom of God (30–50).

The Transfiguration looks back to Peter's profession and confirms it, and it looks forward to Christ's passion, revealing the sort of being who will freely accept suffering. The exorcism is remarkable on its own, but as Peter looks back on it, he recognizes that it is also an image of the resurrection.

The final part of this chapter seems to fit with the teachings in chapter 10. Both sets of teaching are given while Jesus is traveling from Galilee to Jerusalem by way of Perea, the region to the east of the Jordan between the Sea of Galilee and the Dead Sea—his so-called "Perean ministry."

1 He used to say to them

Jesus would deliberately speak of things to come, presumably because (1) only God knows the future, so doing so would give his disciples more reason to believe that he was God; (2) with an advance warning, the disciples would feel secure, believing that all was proceeding according to their Teacher's intention; and (3) the disciples needed to learn how to recognize the fulfillment of a prophecy. After all, the Transfiguration—a "work of power" pointing to the "coming of the kingdom of God"—was the fulfillment of Jesus' prophecy in verse 1 of this chapter, yet no one could have guessed in advance what form that fulfillment would take.

"in a work of power"

Again, "work of power" renders the Greek word *dunamis*, which Mark uses for Christ's miracles. Mark does not call them "miracles," which means, strictly speaking, things to be marveled at. Jesus will accomplish some *work of divine power* that will make clear to the witnesses that the kingdom of God has arrived.

2–8

2 six days later

It is unusual for Mark to give the number of days between episodes. Why does he do so here? Some thoughts:

- These days represent the time from the day Jesus first began to teach plainly about his passion (Mk. 8:31–35). Peter remembered that day and dated later events in reference to it.
- Luke says it was eight days, the figure one gets counting "inclusively," including both this day and that one. Six is

the result of "exclusively" counting only the intervening days. By either count, Jesus' revelation of his coming passion and the Transfiguration both took place on the same day of the week.

- But why might Jesus have deliberately timed the Transfiguration to take place exactly one week after he revealed his coming passion? In Jewish culture, a week stood for God's work of creation. Jesus wanted to convey that his suffering and death would bring about a new creation in the resurrection. The Transfiguration ought to be interpreted, then, in light of the coming passion, and the passion in light of the Transfiguration.

- The Transfiguration prefigures Christ's resurrection, so we may speculate that it took place on a Sunday, as would be fitting.

just them by themselves

Mark apparently thought that simply writing "Jesus took Peter and James and John" would leave open the possibility that others joined them, so he clarifies that the four were "just them by themselves." Generally we must take care not to attribute more exactness to a Gospel text than is strictly required. For example, if the evangelist gives a list, we are not justified in inferring that the list is exhaustive.

changed in appearance

In Greek, *metamorphosed*. The word implies that he stayed the same but changed in appearance. Here it also implies that Jesus always *is* this glorified being, even if he does not *appear* to be so. What changes is how he appears as a man. When the God-man is metamorphosed, his humanity appears glorified.

3 an extreme gleaming white

Jesus' metamorphosis is not limited to the change in his clothes. He was so changed in bodily appearance that even his clothes appeared changed.

In the ancient mind, clothes were more closely connected with a person's bodily "showing" before society than we take them to be today. Clothing was a "habit," a characteristic mode of presentation of a person.

The word for "gleaming," which might describe the shining coat of a horse in the sun, the reflection of light on moving water, or the twinkling of a star, conveys two effects: a shimmering of light and extreme whiteness. Peter is using comparisons to describe something he had never seen before.

4 Elijah appeared to them, with Moses.

Elijah and Moses stand for the prophets and the law, and we might have expected Mark to write, "Elijah and Moses appeared to them." Phrasing this as he does, Mark seems to accord some sort of primacy to Elijah.

But how did Peter know who these two figures were? Perhaps Jesus paused to tell Peter and his companions who they were. Or perhaps Peter simply knew by an interior intimation.

They were conversing with Jesus.

The term means a discussion with back and forth. What were they conversing about? It is difficult to say. In any case, there are three important implications for Christians:

- The appearance of Elijah and Moses, both obviously alive in heaven, indicates that there are saints other than Christian saints
- The saying "no salvation outside the Church" could not mean that only baptized Christians who are visibly

members of the Church can be saved, but rather something like "anyone who is saved will be, and will see himself to be, saved through Christ"

- It is right to pray to departed holy men and women—after all, Elijah and Moses were the great holy men of the Old Testament, and prayer is conversation

5 Peter adds his own comment and says to Jesus

It is difficult to guess what Jesus said to provoke Peter's reply, but we at least see that Peter was not speaking on his own initiative. Mark, following Peter's own sense of the matter, presumes that it would have been importunate for him to address these great men without an invitation. Peter's remark, although humorous in retrospect, was not out of order.

"Rabbi, that we are here is excellent."

This is typically interpreted to mean it is good that we are *here*—rather than somewhere else. Yet it would seem presumptuous for Peter to group himself (by implication) with the two prophets. It seems more likely that he was commenting on the presence of himself, James, and John—it is good that *we* are here. The next line, then, would show why Peter might have thought that.

"Let us make three tents"

So now we understand Peter to be saying, "It is good we are here because each of us can erect a tent for each of you."

Let us suppose Peter was replying to a question from Jesus, such as, "Do you understand why I brought you here?" He suggested erecting tents because he thought that Jesus, Elijah, and Moses would somehow establish themselves as teachers on that mountaintop for a while.

7 a voice from the cloud

It was not an interior intimation but a physical sound, although of itself, it might have been mistaken for thunder.

"This is my Son, my beloved."

An allusion to Psalm 2, the declaration from heaven recalls the voice from the cloud at the baptism of Our Lord. It is another divine confession, confirming Peter's own confession of Jesus as the Christ.

"Listen to him."

A confession is not genuine unless confirmed by obedience.

9–10

9 not tell anyone

A warning against the distortion of motives when people say or do things to be admired by others rather than to please God.

10 they could not figure out

In the previous chapter, Jesus posed a puzzle—What was the meaning of the miraculous feedings?—which the disciples could not solve until Peter solved it with his confession near the end of the chapter. Here, Jesus poses another puzzle for his disciples—What does it mean to rise from the dead?—which the exorcism that follows helps to solve. Posing a problem and then moving to its resolution, Peter displays his skill as a storyteller in chapters 8 and 9.

11–13

11 "Elijah must come first"

Has the appearance of Elijah on the mountain refuted the scribes' objection that Jesus cannot not be the Messiah because the Messiah is to be preceded by Elijah? This raises another question: What should the arrival of Elijah, and of the Messiah, look like, so we can tell whether they "have come"?

12 "he is to suffer many things"

The Son of Man will accomplish what he intends, and yet he will appear to be utterly crushed, as Jesus continues to try to impress upon his disciples. If his victory entails his being "reduced to nothing"—annihilated—then Elijah's return may well take an unexpected form.

13 "Elijah did come"

He was here, and yet the scribes did not see him.

"and they did to him what they wished"

John the Baptist was a success, accomplishing perfectly what God asked of him. That included pointing the way to the Christ, even in his manner of death.

The word "passion" means being subject to the action of another, even being pushed around, abused, humiliated. The Baptist was ridiculed and put to death on a whim. Those who could "see" that John the Baptist was nonetheless a success might also be able to "see" that the Son of Man's success would be similar.

14–18

14 a great crowd around them

Mark, following Peter, clearly represents the Transfiguration as a preparation for the passion. Our hypothesis is that Peter, in retrospect, did not think it was merely a matter of chance that this exorcism came immediately after the Transfiguration. He saw it as a providential sign of Christ's mission. Jesus' descent from the mountaintop stands for his coming from heaven to take on human nature to save us from eternal death. The astonishment of the crowd running to him and the argumentativeness (not love) of the religious leaders stand for humanity as he finds it. The possessed boy stands for the human race enslaved by sin.

15 They ran to greet him.

The crowd did, but the scribes were aloof.

16 "What are you arguing about . . . ?"

We might speculate that the scribes were contending that the inability of the disciples to expel this devil showed that Jesus was not the Christ or that the reports that the disciples had expelled devils previously were fabrications.

17 A man from out of the crowd

Peter is narrating what it was like to hear this in the moment; he does not yet identify this man as the child's father. But since Peter also regards the scene as standing for something, this "man from the crowd" represents humanity. He could be any one of us.

"a dumb devil"

A "dumb devil" is not a stupid one but a spirit that renders a person unable to speak. The phrase in Greek seems to have been an idiomatic expression. The devil's silencing of this boy is like the effect of sin in us: it keeps us from seeking fellowship with God, especially in prayer.

19–24

19 "Faithless generation!"

Jesus's purposeful exclamation explains why the boy was not helped, contrary to the argument of the scribes.

At the same time, in the allegorical dimension that Peter now recognizes, Jesus' complaint—"How long shall I be with you? How long shall I endure you?"—reveals how the Incarnate Lord sees the human condition and the genuine difficulty of the "emptying of himself" (*kenōsis*) that was necessary for the Son of God to take on flesh. The Greek verb "to endure" implies being "subject to": there is already a "passion" in the fact of the Incarnation.

"Bring him to me, will you!"

Perhaps, in the allegorical dimension of the healing, this stands for the Lord's appointing disciples to bring him a humanity oppressed by sin.

20 it convulsed him

Continuing the allegory, our response to the Lord's presence is a violent reaction induced by our domination by sin.

21 "Since he was a child."

Peter, looking back, sees the son's possession since childhood as a symbol for the human race's domination by sin since the beginning.

22 "to destroy him"

The father says this literally of his boy, but in the allegorical dimension, it means the devil's desire to destroy man by serious sin.

"have mercy on us and help us!"

The father's use of the plural supports the allegorical dimension of this episode: he represents humankind wondering whether God has any means for rescuing it from slavery to sin.

23 "Everything is possible for a man who believes."

We are meant to supply the object of the belief: everything is possible for a man who believes in God, for whom everything is possible (Lk. 1:37).

24 "I believe! Help my unbelief!"

An expression of imperfect faith moving toward perfect faith, which fits perfectly Aristotle's definition of motion as the actualization of that which is in potential, insofar as it is in potential. The man expresses his faith as the actualization of possible faith, but with respect to a remaining unrealized faith. There is no time, however, for the man's movement toward faith to reach completeness.

25–29

25 a crowd was running toward them

Jesus does not expel the unclean spirit simply in view of the imperfect faith of the man. (This is suggested in the adversative language, "*But* Jesus. . . .") He does so, rather, in view of the imminent arrival of the crowd, which makes quick action necessary—given the Lord's practice of avoiding flashy public displays of power.

In the allegorical dimension, the man's profession stands for all imperfect devotion—routine prayers, signs and symbols we take for granted—which God nonetheless frequently honors.

26 convulsing him

If we understand the exorcism to stand for the healing of the human race by Christ, take this second convulsion to stand for the suffering of the Christ, who becomes our sin, to save us (2 Cor. 5:21).

He became as if a corpse

These lines provide the chief clue that Peter attributes to this healing the allegorical meaning we have been developing. The boy appears to be a *corpse*; he looks dead, but then he is raised up. The disciples had wondered what it might be to rise from the dead, and Jesus here provides a picture.

28 "Why couldn't we cast it out?"

Significantly, the disciples had expected that they could cast out the devil. Their failure was not from lack of faith.

29 "other than by prayer"

Another instance of Jesus' presuming that he is God. After all, *he* did not pray. If this kind does not come out except through prayer, the man's petition to Jesus must have been the prayer, in which case he is God.

In the allegorical interpretation, the inability of the disciples to expel the devil points to the ineffectiveness of even the best means unless they are instruments of the Christ. The disciples, after all, were such instruments. By going to the disciples, the boy was brought to the Lord, who saved him.

30–32

30 they traveled throughout Galilee

Recall that their purpose at this time was not to preach but to allow Jesus to instruct his closest followers. Presumably, they kept on the move so his location could not be guessed.

31 "The Son of Man is betrayed"

The assertion is placed in the present tense. Plans for his betrayal are already under way.

"They will kill him."

The Greek is as brutally direct as this English sentence. Jesus speaks of himself in the third person because his death is the fulfillment of the role of Redeemer and Son.

33–37

34 But they kept quiet.

A charming detail: they were embarrassed, so like little children, they avoided answering. Perhaps they busied themselves with chores or tried to change the subject. Jesus does not force the matter. He allows them—for their own good—to stew in their embarrassment. Note once more the presupposition that Jesus is God. He knows what they were discussing, and as Peter relates it, it is not the least bit surprising.

who was greater

Apparently they were arguing over their ranking, not just who had the top spot. After all, Jesus himself drew distinctions: Peter, James, John, and Andrew were often set apart from the rest. Of those, the first three seemed to have some kind of priority. And of those three, Peter seemed preeminent.

35 he called the Twelve by name

Literally, "he called the twelve," but the verb connotes a direct and individualized calling—a reaffirmation of their original calling as apostles. Jesus calls them specifically in virtue of their "apostolic office."

"he will be last of all"

Note the future tense. Jesus does not say that if anyone wants to be first he *should* be last but that he *will* be last. The Lord leaves room for human freedom. He prefers that we respond to him because we *want* to rather than because we *have* to. The future tense depicts how someone *will* act out of love.

36 a little child

In Greek, as in German, the word for "child" is neuter, since children are innocent and have not taken on the bodily characteristics of mature men or women; thus "he stood *it*."

This child can stand for any child and therefore for any vulnerable or frail member of humanity. By placing the child in the middle of the apostles, who represent the hierarchy of the Church, Jesus composes a picture of the Church as it should be—in the service of such as these. The same idea is represented by Bernini's colonnade, which enfolds the faithful in St. Peter's Square.

37 "Whoever receives one of these..."

Through his love for the child, Jesus has become identified with the child.

Because of the universal scope of this "whoever," we can understand the passage to mean that if anyone—not necessarily a Christian—receives a child in need, to "save" that child, he has done so "in the name of Jesus," since the name Jesus means "Savior," and he came to save wrecked human nature. On the other hand, the saying is fulfilled with greatest clarity when a Christian, specifically out of love of Christ, receives a child as standing for Christ.

"the one who sent me"

Here we see the great beauty of Christianity as a revelation of God. The Lord is inviting us to see that his Father in heaven embraces him at the same time he is embracing this child, thus forming a chain of love for neighbor, leading through Christ to love of God. This is intensely beautiful.

We must note with astonishment how Jesus, through a subtle and refined correction of his disciples, who were disputing so vainly along the way, has turned an incident of folly into a demonstration of profound wisdom.

38–50

These final verses have the character of a miscellaneous collection of teachings, inserted here because of their connection with the two episodes that followed the Transfiguration and through association. Recall that one indication that Mark's Gospel is an "interpretation" of the teachings of Peter is that some material seems to be added in the way we add things when we speak, in digressions, because they are associated with the subject we are speaking about.

Consider, too, that sometimes writing in the ancient world was adjusted to the length of a scroll. If in a certain scroll Mark found that the two stories he planned on recording, the Transfiguration and the exorcism, took up only two-thirds of the scroll, then to make good use of the expensive writing material he might well have resourcefully filled up the rest with related teachings.

38–40

38 "expelling devils in your name"

Jesus had explicitly given his disciples the power to expel devils. John's statement implies that this power could in turn be conferred by the disciples upon others who became followers, perhaps through an already established ritual. And yet this person clearly acts outside of that channel. What should those with official authority do about it?

John's report also implies that the name of Jesus itself has power—another example of the presupposition, always at work in Mark's Gospel, that Jesus is God.

"We stopped him"

Presumably they stopped him by a command, as authorized representatives of Jesus. And he seems to have accepted their authority and obeyed their command, since John does not say merely that they *tried* to stop this man.

39 "Do not stop him"

Jesus' statement implies that they have the authority to stop him. Otherwise, he would have said something like "You cannot stop him" or "You have no right to stop him."

"will soon speak ill of me"

When someone has the authority to do something, he should use that authority in view of the common good and for the purpose for which it was granted. The apostles are given their authority for the good order of the Church, which is for the salvation of souls. What promotes that end can vary according to circumstance. In the immediate context, the salvation of souls depends upon the spread of the good news. Jesus therefore gives a prudential reason, related to the need for the good news to spread rapidly: anyone who invokes the name of Jesus and finds the name to have power will be keen to say good things about him and thus propagate the good news.

The Lord's correction—in using their authority they should be servants of all—has not affected their status as apostles or touched upon their genuine authority but has recast that authority as an authority of service.

40 "Whoever is not against us is for us."

Elsewhere Jesus says, "He who is not with me, is against me" (Mt. 12:30). Does he contradict himself? But both statements say the same thing: people divide into those for and those against, with no one in between.

41–42

41 "a cup of water to drink"

Jesus means a simple gesture of kindness, of the sort one would make to anyone, simply in view of his humanity.

"he will not lose his reward"

A reward is given to a deed that merits a reward. By implication, then, deeds can be meritorious or not, and they can also be more or less meritorious.

Significantly, Jesus does not spurn a Christian's acting for a reward, but he *wants* us to act with fortified motives. These form a sequence: to give the cup of water to that person because *he is a fellow human being*, to give it because he *holds himself out as a Christian*, to give it because *one wants the reward that Christ will give.*

42 "a heavy millstone"

Jesus' use of the present tense here shows that the millstone is a preventive, not a punishment. If someone were about to lead a little one astray, it would be better for him if, in order that the contemplated evil not come to pass, he were tied to a millstone and dropped into the depth of the sea. Jesus speaks as if the prevention of evil were effected by another person. But it follows that the would-be malefactor should take measures to stop himself.

There follow several other verses in which Jesus emphasizes the lengths we should go to avoid sin.

43–48

Saying something three times, in Jewish as in other cultures, is a way of asserting it solemnly. Because it is rare for Jesus to assert something with this pattern of three, we can infer that what he says here is of the highest importance.

The three sentences employ the main technique of Jewish poetry—repetition with deliberate variation. The first variations take the form of a progression from hand to foot to eye. The phrases that express this progression are exactly alike, except for the change in the main term:

If your *hand* leads you to sin..."
If your *foot*..."
If your *eye*..."

The phrase "leads you to sin" is "scandalizes you," which means, literally, "causes you to stumble."

Then there follow variations in what one should do—(chop, chop, pluck), dictated by the nature of the thing to be separated from the rest of the body—and variations in what one enters into (life, life, the kingdom):

to go off into Gehenna, into the unquenchable fire
to be thrown into Gehenna
to be thrown into Gehenna, where their worm does not die and the fire is not quenched

Gehenna was a fire pit for garbage outside the city walls of Jerusalem. The place Jesus has in mind is like that, but the fire is never extinguished and those who are thrown into it are never consumed—"their worm does not die," a detail that makes it clear that these souls suffer forever.

In this carefully crafted, emphatic triad of warnings, the emphasis on Gehenna is clear from its placement at the end of each assertion and the frightening description.

49–50

In the preceding teaching, Jesus referred to an eternal corruption resulting from sin. In the ancient world, meat and fish were preserved mainly by curing them with salt. We should therefore understand salt here not as a flavoring but as *that which preserves from corruption*.

49 "everyone will be salted by fire"

Is "everyone" the entire human race or only Jesus' disciples? It seems the latter, for all of these teachings are addressed to them. So construed, the saying looks like a prophecy of Pentecost, when flames appeared above the heads of the disciples. The "salting" would be their receiving the Holy Spirit. If so, then the preservation from corruption attained by this salt of the Holy Spirit would be twofold: the preservation from error of the Church in its teaching and the preservation from sin of any Christian who holds fast to the life of grace.

50 "Salt is good."

Salt is good, but not inherently good: it is good *with* something. Its value consists in its preservative properties.

"... how will you concoct it?"

There is no need here to take "if salt becomes saltless" to refer to a physical transformation of salt (there is no such thing) because Jesus is speaking in a parable about the disciples themselves.

"Be at peace with one another."

The same agent of grace that preserves them from the corruption of false teaching and sin likewise preserves their fellowship with one another. So we are fittingly brought back to the argument along the way about "who is greater." That kind of contention was a sign that they were at risk of losing their saltiness: false ambition puts one at risk of corruption by sin.

CHAPTER 10

1 From there they went up into the regions of Judea, and those across the Jordan. Once more, crowds gathered to be with him. So once more, as was his custom, he taught them.

2 Pharisees came up and posed the question, as a test, whether a man is permitted to divorce his wife. ³He said to them in reply, "What did Moses command you?" ⁴They said, "Moses made a provision for a man to write a certificate of separation and divorce her." ⁵But Jesus said to them, "It was with a view to the hardness of your hearts that he wrote this commandment for you. ⁶But from the beginning of creation 'he made them male and female': ⁷for this reason, 'man will leave his father and mother and be joined to a wife, ⁸and the two will become one flesh.' So they are no longer two but one flesh. ⁹Therefore, what God has joined, man may not divide."

10 The disciples raised a question with him about this, once more, when they were in the house. ¹¹So he tells them, "Anyone who divorces his wife and marries another woman commits adultery with her. ¹²And if she, after divorcing her husband, should marry another man, she commits adultery."

13 So they were bringing little children to him for him to touch them. The disciples rebuked them. ¹⁴But Jesus, when he saw this, was visibly upset. He told them, "Let the little children come to me—do not stop them! The kingdom of God is for precisely those who are like that. ¹⁵Yes, I assure you, whoever does not welcome the kingdom of God in the manner of a little child will not enter into it." ¹⁶So he goes on to hug each of those children, and placing his hands on each one he gives them his blessing.

17 As he was leaving for the main road, a man just on his own ran up and fell to his knees in front of him to ask him a question: "Good teacher, what shall I do to inherit eternal life?" ¹⁸Jesus said to him, "Why do you call me good? No one is good except one—God. ¹⁹The commandments—you know them? You shall not murder. You shall not commit adultery. You shall not steal. You shall not bear false witness. You shall not defraud. Honor your father and your mother." ²⁰He said to him, "Teacher, all these I have taken care to keep from my youth." ²¹Jesus looked at him and loved him, and he said to him, "There is one thing that you lack. Go, and sell what you have. Give it to the poor—you will have treasure in heaven—and come, follow me!" ²²And yet he was downcast by what Jesus said and left in sadness. And why was that? Because he had many possessions.

23 So Jesus then looks around at his disciples and says to them, "How difficult it will be for those who have possessions to enter into the kingdom of God!" ²⁴The disciples were taken aback by his words. Yet Jesus in response says to them again, "Children, how difficult it is to enter into the kingdom of God! ²⁵It is easier for a camel to pass through the eye of a needle than for a wealthy man to enter into the kingdom of God." ²⁶They were beside themselves with astonishment and were saying to one another, "Who can be saved, then?" ²⁷Jesus looks at them intently and says, "With men, it is impossible, but not with God, because everything is possible with God."

28 Peter began to say to him, "As you see, we have left everything and have followed you.... " ²⁹But Jesus said, "Yes, I assure all of you, there is no one who has left home, or brothers and sisters, or mother and father, or children, or fields, for my sake, and for the sake of the good news, ³⁰who will not receive, now in this present age, a hundred times as many homes, and brothers and sisters, and mothers and fathers, and fields—though with persecutions!—and in the coming age, eternal life! ³¹Yet many who are first will be last, and many last will be first."

32 They were traveling on the road up to Jerusalem. Jesus was going before them. They were feeling elated, but some of the men following him were filled with apprehension. It was at that point that he took the Twelve aside once more and told them what was about to happen to him: ³³"As you see, we are going up to Jerusalem. The Son of Man will be betrayed to the chief priests and scribes. They will condemn him to death. They will betray him to the Gentiles. ³⁴The Gentiles will mock him. They will spit on him. They will have him scourged. They will kill him. After three days, he will rise up."

35 So James and John, the sons of Zebedee, approach him and say to him, "Teacher, there is something we want to ask you, which we would like you to do for us." ³⁶He said to them, "What is it that you want me to do for you?" ³⁷They said to him, "Grant that we should sit one on your right and the other on your left in your glory." ³⁸Jesus said to them, "But you do not know what you are asking. Can you drink the cup that I am drinking? Or can you be baptized with the baptism with which I am being baptized?" ³⁹They said to him, "We can." Jesus said to them, "The cup that I am drinking, you shall drink. The baptism with which I am being baptized, you shall be baptized with. ⁴⁰But to sit on my right or on my left is not mine to give, but it is for those for whom it is prepared."

41 When the ten got wind of this, they became indignant over James and John. ⁴²So Jesus calls them over and says to them, "You know that the men who are held to rule over the Gentiles lord it over them. Their great ones get their way over them. ⁴³But that is not how it is to be among you. Rather, anyone who wants to become great among you will be your servant. ⁴⁴Anyone among you who wants to be first will be a slave to all. ⁴⁵And why is that? Because the Son of Man has come not to be served but to serve, and to give his life as a ransom to purchase many."

46 So they come to Jericho. And as he was leaving Jericho—his disciples too, and a substantial crowd—Bartimaeus, the son of Timaeus, a blind beggar, was sitting by the side of the road. ⁴⁷When he heard that it was Jesus of Nazareth, he started crying out, "Son of David, Jesus, have mercy on me!" ⁴⁸Many of the men there were telling him to be quiet. Yet he cried out all the more, "Son of David, Jesus, have mercy on me!" ⁴⁹Jesus stopped and said, "Call for him." So they call out to the blind man and tell him, "Have courage! Get up! He is calling for you!" ⁵⁰Throwing his cloak to the side and getting on his feet, he went to Jesus. ⁵¹Jesus said to him then, "What do you want me to do for you?" The blind man said to him, "Rabbi...that I might see..." ⁵²So Jesus said to him, "Go on your way. Your faith has saved you." Right then and there, he gained his sight. He did follow him on the road.

Commentary

This tenth chapter is the first that could be said to convey Christ's "moral teachings" in any prolonged way. The chapter divides into two parts. In the first, Jesus teaches "the crowd" and deals with domestic matters, namely, marriage and openness to children. In the second, beginning at verse 17, Jesus sets out on the road to Jerusalem. He teaches his disciples, and his theme is how love of money and love of power interfere with discipleship.

In its consideration of discipleship, the chapter draws a contrast between the rich young man who turns down Jesus' invitation to follow him because he loves his wealth (verse 22) and the blind beggar Bartimaeus, who follows Jesus once his sight is restored (verse 52).

How does the choice of material in the chapter reflect Peter's concerns? First, it shows us that as a pastor, he views Christians as taking one of two broad paths in serving Christ: either they do so as married, in a family, immersed in the ordinary world of daily work, within a neighborhood and under civil authority, or they do so through apostolic work, detached from family and material goods. The former path requires fidelity to marriage and a proper love of children; the latter, separation from marriage, children, and wealth. These modes of Christian life complement each other, and each teaches something important about the other. One can see these same pastoral concerns reflected in the First Letter of Peter (3:1–7, 1:3–9).

Second, the material in this chapter shows how Peter, looking back on himself and the other disciples, detects the seeds of their later abandonment of Christ. His concern, then, is with motives that interfere with loyalty to Christ.

1

Now Jesus is turning toward Jerusalem, where he will be betrayed and put to death. All of the teachings of this chapter should be understood in that light. They represent various ways in which his followers will imitate him and "take up their cross daily."

Since the feeding of the four thousand, Jesus has mainly been instructing his disciples privately. Mark wishes to indicate that now he is resuming a public ministry. His ministry has previously been centered in Galilee; now he teaches in Judaea and Perea.

2–9

2 as a test

The Pharisees were not interested in the answer to the question they posed to Jesus. They simply wanted to get evidence against him, hoping to embarrass him no matter how he answered. On the one hand, since the sister of Herod the Great had set down a law permitting divorce (according to the Jewish historian Josephus), if Jesus said that divorce was permitted, he would seem to be agreeing with the court of Herod against John the Baptist. On the other hand, if Jesus affirmed that divorce and remarriage were wrong, he would appear to be contradicting Moses.

3 "What did Moses command you?"

As he often does, Jesus answers a trick question with another question. His question, too, is something of a trick because he asks what Moses "commanded." A law can command, forbid, or permit, and in this matter Moses had only *permitted*. Jesus' question is designed to lead the Pharisees, in deference to Moses, to commit to a definite policy.

Note that Jesus does not ask, "What did Moses command *us*?" He does not regard himself, the highest lawgiver, as bound by Moses.

4 "Moses made a provision"

Their reply is that there is a lawful procedure, which involves drafting a certificate, and that someone who follows this procedure is blameless. They do not think about the substance of the law or the persons involved. They are taking refuge in the procedure.

Note that they do not refer the procedure to themselves—"Moses made a provision *for us*", that is, for the Jewish people—but reply as if it had general application.

5 "hardness of your hearts"

Jesus now corrects them, supplying the qualification they had omitted: "... he wrote this commandment *for you*." He implies that the Pharisees are presented with a choice in the matter. The provision for divorce was a concession Moses made for a particular people because of an incapacity to follow the proper and better law. The Pharisees, then, can choose to regard that authority as final, taking refuge in the established legal process, or look to the substance of the question, which might reveal a higher authority with a different mandate.

As we have seen, Peter regards "hardness of heart" as Jesus' favorite way of describing a settled resistance on our part to God's love.

6 "from the beginning of creation"

What is found in the beginning of creation expresses the intention of the Creator, and Jesus presumes he has authority to state and interpret this intention.

"'male and female'"

No male on his own or female on her own possesses the good of human nature in its fullness. To love this good, then, without a hardened heart is to desire its completion as intended by the Creator.

7–8 "and the two will become one flesh"

This sentence reveals that the reason for the distinction between male and female is the one-flesh unity. This unity is greater even than the unity of parent and child, for a man leaves his parents to be joined to a wife. If the one relationship cannot be severed, then neither can the other. Or, to put the point differently, to affirm the possibility of divorce is to attack also the weaker tie between children and parents.

9 "what God has joined, man may not divide"

The Pharisees had hoped to set Jesus against John the Baptist or Moses. Now they appear, by their own intention, to be set against God.

10–12

Explaining why divorce is impermissible, Jesus has declared, "What God has joined man may not divide." But suppose man *does* divide—what then? Is God's intention negated? No. The instruction "what God has joined man may not divide" means not simply that man is *not allowed* to divide, but also that man *cannot* divide. The original one-flesh unity between husband and wife persists, no matter what man says and how man acts.

In particular, if man divides, and a separated spouse purports to marry someone else, there is no new marriage. That separated spouse belongs to another in a one-flesh unity, and adultery is absolutely forbidden. Jesus thus shows how the question is governed by the Ten Commandments. Divorce is contrary to God's intention in creation, and purported remarriage is contrary to God's intention expressed in the Commandments. Creation is on a par with the Commandments as an authority: both are "natural law."

11 "commits adultery with her"

The Greek is literally "commits adultery *upon* her." Does "her" in this context refer to the man's original wife or to the woman to whom he is purportedly remarried? Almost all modern translators interpret the phrase in the first sense, rendering the Greek as "commits adultery *against* her." The Fathers and St. Thomas Aquinas, however, took the phrase in the second sense, which I follow. Adultery is wrong for two reasons: It is an injustice, a betrayal of one's spouse, and it contradicts the one-flesh unity of the spouses intended by God. The injustice to the betrayed spouse should not be downplayed, but in this discussion with the Pharisees, Jesus' concern has clearly been the inviolability of the one-flesh unity. From that perspective, the sin at issue is the adultery "with" this second woman.

13–16

The text of Mark is the product of five "collaborators": (1) God, by whose providence the events portrayed occur in such a way as to convey lessons; (2) Jesus, the Son of God sent into the world, whose actions and words respond to their immediate context but also transcend it, offering timeless instruction; (3) the Holy Spirit, who inspires Mark's selection of material and his way of expressing it; (4) Mark himself, whose own insights and creativity are at work in his writing; and (5) Peter, on whose recollections Mark relies and whose purposes shape his composition. The activity of one collaborator does not imply the absence of activity by another. For example, a particular emphasis might reflect Mark's own insight, but it does not follow that it was not inspired by the Holy Spirit or that Jesus did not intend for the act or teaching to be aptly emphasized.

We should note, too, that rarely does any author compose anything with just one meaning. From our own reading, we know that deep and interesting works have layers of meaning, and the meaning we perceive varies with the context.

I apply these observations to the present text. The human author, Mark, has chosen to place a teaching on welcoming children immediately after a teaching on marriage. He had multiple purposes in doing so, *and* he was inspired by the Holy Spirit. Moreover, it might well have happened that the one episode followed immediately upon the other because the God of history arranged it so.

There appear to be two links between these teachings on marriage and children. The first is that, as marriage is an institution for founding a family through having children, the Lord's words "do not stop the little children from coming to me" include the meaning that a married couple should be open to life and not stop up the sources of their fecundity. After all, in the same passage from Genesis to which Our Lord refers, the Creator God says, "be fruitful and multiply." The second link is that, while "hardness of heart" leads some to divorce, becoming as a little child can overcome this hardness of heart, enabling a couple to live together faithfully in love for life.

13 they were bringing little children to him

We should suppose that it was common for people to bring children to Jesus for a blessing and that, ordinarily, the disciples did not prevent them. Why, then, did they try to do so now? Perhaps the seriousness of Jesus' teaching on his own suffering and death led them to conclude he would not want to be interrupted by children.

14 was visibly upset

Jesus was not a stoic. Elsewhere Mark describes him as angry, astonished, and compassionate. Here he is indignant. There is no sin in an emotion itself. The sin is in acting on an emotion against reason—directing it to the wrong object, following it beyond the bounds of temperance, and so on.

As we are attributing to this episode a meaning beyond its immediate context, we may take Jesus' emotion as a sign of the importance of the teaching that is to follow.

"Let the little children come to me—do not stop them!"

Jesus repeats himself for emphasis, which Mark hardly ever shows him doing. But the repetition also broadens the teaching. The first statement—"Let the children come"—is passive. The second—"Do not stop them"—is active. If we are to allow, we certainly are not to hinder.

"The kingdom of God is for precisely those who are like that."

This phrase is usually translated "for of such is the kingdom of God." But that phrase, besides being archaic, is indefinite. It could mean that the kingdom of God *belongs* to such as these or that it is *composed of* such as these. The second sense seems more plausible because it comports with the verse that follows.

15 "whoever does not welcome the kingdom of God in the manner of a little child will not enter into it"

That is, the only ones in the kingdom of God are those who welcome or receive it as do children.

17–22

17 a man just on his own

That is, the man who runs up to Jesus is not part of a crowd, and he acts on his own initiative. We must understand the ensuing exchange, therefore, as a confidential conversation between himself and the Lord. Waiting until the last minute to ask his question—he runs to catch Jesus on his way out of town—the man seems hesitant or fearful, but his sole purpose must be to find an answer to his question.

Though Mark offers no description of this man other than that he was wealthy, Matthew tells us that he was "young" (19:22), so he is traditionally called the "rich young man."

"Good teacher, what shall I do to inherit eternal life?"

The phrase "Good teacher" carries the suggestion of flattery. There is something patronizing about it, as if he were evaluating Jesus.

Yet the question itself at first looks admirable enough. The great medieval commentator Theophylact, for example, marvelled "at this young man, who, when all others come to Christ to be healed of their infirmities, begs of him the possession of everlasting life." Yet he does not outright ask Jesus for eternal life. After all, the people Jesus healed did not say, "What must I do to be healed?" but simply, "Please heal me!" Hence, he might have said, "Lord, have mercy on me and grant me eternal life!" So on second thought, the way this man addresses Jesus and the question he asks appear mixed and problematic.

18 "Why do you call me good? No one is good except one—God."

Jesus seems to assume here—it was a truism in the classical world—that to call something good is to say that it is loveable. He is therefore asking the man, "Do you love me, and if so, on what basis?" By declaring that no one is good but God, he requires the man to consider how his love for Jesus relates to his love for God.

19 "The commandments—you know them?"

As so often happens, what Jesus says in response to a question becomes a test of the person who posed the question.

The young man assumes that Jesus means that if he has kept the commandments, then he has done what is necessary to inherit eternal life. But Jesus does not say this. Indeed, from the context, it is clear that Jesus is asking whether he has kept the commandments out of love of God. The commandments are fundamental laws that a person must follow to belong to the community that God forms with men.[1] Love of God is therefore their ultimate purpose.

"You shall not murder," etc.

As a preliminary observation, note that "you" here, as in the Mosaic law, is second person singular. ("Thou shalt not...," as it was translated when English still had a distinct second person singular pronoun.) Imagine the Lord looking into this young man's eyes and stating each of these commandments to him personally, as a father might state his will for his son. The Lord is not reciting the law; he is reaffirming it for him.

Jesus cites only the commandments that pertain to love of our fellow man—the so-called "second tablet"—not those that pertain

---

1 Saint Thomas Aquinas writes, "The precepts of the Divine law direct man in his relations to a community or commonwealth of men under God." *Summa theologiae*, Ia-IIae, q. 100, a. 5, s.c.

to love of God. The reason seems to be, as we have said, that Jesus is, in effect, asking the young man whether he loves God sufficiently. Is he content to follow the second tablet but omit the first?

20 "Teacher, all these I have taken care to keep from my youth."

The young man does not ask about the missing commandments, though someone who takes care to keep the law usually wants to know and keep the law in its completeness. And he seems to over-state his adherence to the law. What would it mean to be constantly on guard against murder and adultery even from childhood?

21 Jesus looked at him and loved him.

An extraordinary statement, without parallel in the Gospels. The Greek word for "loved him" has a threefold connotation: (1) being "well pleased" with someone, especially after some kind of trial or choice, (2) having special esteem for someone, even amounting to a preference for that person over others, and (3) an appreciation for someone's preciousness and worth. Whatever the man's shortcomings, Jesus loved him with great love.

"There is one thing that you lack."

Jesus speaks with considerable understatement. The one thing he lacks is everything. Compare a famous prayer of Blessed John Henry Newman: "... if I gain the whole world and lose you, in the end I have lost everything; whereas if I lose the whole world and gain you, in the end I have lost nothing."

"Go, and sell what you have."

Knowing this man's attachment to his riches, Jesus appeals to him with an image that will make an impression on his heart: *you will have treasure in heaven.* Let us look at some phrases within this sequence.

"Sell what you have": Jesus does not say "sell the wealth you have" or even "sell all that you have." He states the principle in a way that can apply to everyone.

"Give it to the poor": The man is to convert what he has to money, or something useful to the poor, and then give it to the poor. The underlying logic here is that because the poor are incapable of repaying him, the transaction is not merely earthly but reaches up to heaven.

"Come, follow me": The expectation is that if the man were keeping the commandments in the right spirit and were not hindered by love of money, he would naturally accept the invitation.

22 left in sadness

Why did the rich young man leave in sadness if he was returning to that which he loved? Wouldn't he be joyful not to give them up? He must have wanted to accept the invitation to follow Jesus but was unable to do so because of his love of his possessions. In the end, he left knowing the answer to his question—*what he needed to do* to inherit eternal life—but also knowing that *he was unable to do it*.

23–27

23 "for those who have possessions"

To understand the statements that follow, it is necessary to realize that Jesus means "for those who have any goods at all."

"How difficult it will be"

This statement admits of two interpretations. It might mean (1) that those who possess goods now will hardly be able to enter the kingdom of God later or (2) that those who possess goods later, when it is time to enter the kingdom of God, will hardly be able to enter it. The disciples understand the words in the first sense, but it seems that Jesus means them in the second. The first sense implies that entering the kingdom of God will hardly be possible for anyone, since nearly everyone possesses some goods. The second sense implies that each person must somehow divest himself of his goods by the time he is to enter the kingdom of God—a challenge that may be daunting but is not surprising.

24 says to them again

When we say that someone said something "again," we usually mean that he repeated the same words. But here Mark is referring to two different statements, and they do not even say the same thing in different words. The second statement omits an important qualification contained in the first ("those who have possessions"). Perhaps one could say that the two statements are the same in the basic or rough sense that they are intended to have a similar effect on the disciples.

If Mark is correct that Jesus intended to say the same thing "again," and yet in doing so Jesus varied his words markedly, then we should assume that when Jesus stated his teachings on different occasions, he might vary what he said in interesting ways. We should not be surprised, therefore, if two Gospel writers give different formulations of a saying, since each writer might be reporting a different variation of the "same" teaching.

"Children"

The Greek *tekna* was a term of affection.[2] The only other time it appears in Mark's Gospel is when Jesus addresses the paralytic let down through the roof on a pallet (2:5). But there are several affectionate terms of address in Greek. Why does Mark use this one here? Perhaps because he has just recorded Jesus' teaching that it is necessary to welcome the kingdom of God as a child, and children typically have a carefree attitude toward worldly goods. (St. John in his epistles likes to address his readers as "little children," perhaps in deliberate imitation of Christ.)

25 "It is easier for a camel to pass through the eye of a needle than for a wealthy man to enter into the kingdom of God."

Commentators wanting to explain away the apparent absurdity in the comparison have come up with two main theories.

---

2 Julius Caesar used it in his famous last words. They were not *Et tu, Brute?* in Latin, but affectionately, in Greek, *kai su, teknon*—"You too, child?"

One is that there was a very narrow gate into Jerusalem called the "Eye of the Needle," which a camel could pass through only if one removed everything it was carrying and pushed it through. But there is no evidence from archeology or ancient literature that such a gate ever existed.

Another interpretation is that Jesus used the word *kamilos* (rope) rather than *kamelos* (camel). It is incredible, however, that both Peter and Matthew (19:24) would mishear Jesus in the same way,[3] and the notion of a rope's passing through the eye of a needle is hardly less absurd. It is better, then, to favor the more vivid image. The disciples' response, moreover, supports the choice of "camel."

26 "Who can be saved, then?"

They understand Jesus to be teaching that it is impossible for anyone with any goods at all—not just wealthy men, of whom there were few—to enter the kingdom of God.

27 Jesus looks at them intently

Peter is recollecting this moment, conveying to us how Jesus looked at them when he gave them the way out of the difficulty.

"everything is possible with God"

The word rendered as "with" (*para*) appears in the prologue of the Gospel of John—"the Word was with God." It means alongside and in the presence of. It can also mean "with the help of those who are alongside you," and that seems to be its meaning here. Human power is inadequate to enable someone who has possessions to enter the kingdom of God. The rich young man is a case in point. Relying only on his own powers, he was unable to choose what he recognized as the better path. And yet suppose that instead of walking away sad, he asked Jesus to help him? Would he have been given the strength

---

3 Theophylact suggests, more plausibly, that Jesus intended both meanings, making a play on words.

to leave his possessions and follow the Lord? Divine power can achieve what is impossible for men on their own.

The contrast "with men...with God..." points to the difference between human devices and God's devices. Human devices, such as legislation and punishments, have proved ineffective in releasing men's attachment to their possessions. God's devices, however, include the suffering that everyone must face in life. Material possessions lose their luster for someone who has lost a loved one, is gravely ill, or is on his deathbed.

With grace, moreover, a wealthy person can attain to an impressive detachment, living as if he had no possessions, placing his goods at the service of others. Such detachment has been evident in many Christian saints who were also wealthy or powerful.

28–31
28 "we have left everything"
Peter is in effect asking, "Unlike that rich man, we have abandoned our possessions and have followed you. Do we, then, enter into eternal life?" As is common, Peter, first among the apostles, speaks for them all. (Note that Peter does not say that he sold his possessions and gave them to the poor—because he had relatives whom he had to support.)
29 "home, or brothers and sisters"
The list explains what Jesus meant by "possessions"—not luxuries or conveniences but the most basic and estimable of human goods. He evidently regards a familiar place—"home"—and relatives as the most valuable of earthly goods.
"for my sake, and for the sake of the good news"
This fascinating phrase is clearly set down with a view to the future. To abandon these goods "for his sake" is to leave them and follow him on the road. To abandon them "for the sake of the good

news" is to leave them and go out into the world as an apostle, as these men did after his death. Or Jesus is referring simply to the sacrifices they made in going throughout the towns, preaching and healing.

30 "now in this present age"

These are not "treasures in heaven," since they are "in this present age." Jesus represents them as similar to one's family but more numerous.

These words seem to have no intelligible reference except to those men and women in the future who, like the disciples, would leave the goods of ordinary life to become missionaries or to found religious communities, counting as relatives all the members of their congregation or community. And because the houses of these congregations and communities would be possessed by all—so that a Dominican, for example, today might travel anywhere in the world and regard as "his own" the houses of his fellow Dominicans everywhere—there are "a hundred times as many homes...and fields."

"though with persecutions!"

This addition is characteristic of the genius of Jesus in spiritual matters. He adds the qualification to avoid giving the impression that one receives the hundredfold to be able to settle down in even greater tranquility and comfort.

"and in the coming age, eternal life!"

Jesus finally answers Peter's implicit question: Yes, he and the others will inherit eternal life because they left everything out of love of him and love of the Gospel.

31 "Yet many who are first will be last"

Many of the things Jesus says about the kingdom of God are relevant in various contexts. This is one of them. Its application here is that many who are wealthy in earthly goods are poor in heavenly goods, and vice versa. But in context, another natural interpretation of this statement is that it is a warning about Judas, who will not share in the general assurance just given to Peter and, through him, to the apostles.

32–34

32 They were feeling elated

Mark offers no reason for their elation, but perhaps some of them believed that their journey would end with Jesus' assuming an earthly Messianic kingship.

some of the men following him were filled with apprehension

We can imagine that the fearful men included both those who were aware of the plots of the religious authorities and those who had some dim understanding of what Jesus was telling them earlier. Both groups would be afraid that this journey to Jerusalem would lead to some kind of destructive confrontation.

33 "The Son of Man will be betrayed"

To betray is to hand over one's own to an enemy. The Lord mentions both betrayals—by his friends and by his nation.

34 "mock him ... spit on him ... have him scourged"

Jesus includes these details so that when they occur, his disciples, remembering these words, will understand that he freely accepted this suffering, which was taking place by the will of God.

35–40

There are two levels of meaning in this episode: what the apostles meant and said in the moment and their unintentionally prophetic utterance on behalf of other Christians.

35 "Teacher"

With this title, Mark signals that this episode is to be understood as parallel to that of the rich young man, who, we noted, asked what he should do to inherit eternal life instead of simply asking directly for the gift of eternal life. Here the apostles James and John ask Our Lord straight up for positions of glory, yet they do not ask what they must do to be given them.

38 "you do not know what you are asking"

There is a kind of hierarchy of goods which is recognized in the two episodes, from highest to lowest:

1.   Heavenly glory.
2.   Treasure in heaven.
3.   Earthly goods gained in the kingdom (the "hundredfold").
4.   Earthly goods.

The rich young man had plenty of the lowest sort of goods, which made him incapable of acting to attain the higher. Leaving behind these lowest goods, the apostles gained a hundredfold of similar but transformed goods in the kingdom, and treasure in heaven besides.

When James and John ask to be seated next to Our Lord in glory, they think they are asking for goods on level 3. They believe that when the Lord arrives in Jerusalem, he is going to assume kingship in the kingdom of God, and they are asking to take places next to him. This is the literal meaning of their request. But because Christ's kingship is of a different order, they are really asking for goods on level 1. That is why Jesus says, "You do not know what you are asking." Their request has a deeper meaning that they do not recognize, but it can and shall be granted. Their literal request, however, will not be granted because Jesus is not going to attain earthly glory as they imagine.

"Can you drink the cup...?"

Jesus uses the present tense, "that I am drinking" and "with which I am being baptized," presumably to refer to his passion. Believing that Jesus' going up to Jerusalem is the inauguration of his earthly kingdom, the apostles think the Lord is asking whether they can share in the earthly glory he is about to receive, since in Jewish culture, one's "cup" was one's lot in life.[4] And they seem to have mistaken the "baptism" to which he refers as some kind of ritual cleansing.

The "cup" is instead an offering cup, which will be revealed in its full significance at the Last Supper as the Eucharistic Cup. The "baptism" is suffering unto death, an image they could not have understood until later, when Jesus instituted Christian baptism and declared it to be a way of dying with him. The Lord, then, is asking of his idealistic followers, represented by James and John, are you able to accept suffering unto death, as co-redeemers with me?

39 "We can."

The apostles answer, "We can," by which they mean "We would love to share in the glory you are about to assume." But they are actually saying that they are able to accept suffering unto death. Such is the nature of Christ's kingdom.

It turns out that this deeper meaning—understood as their speaking prophetically on behalf of all Christians—is also a truthful reply. They speak for young persons of all times who, with childlike hearts, have responded "We can!" to Christ's call, whose youthful idealism opened them to the grace that allowed them to persevere through many serious difficulties.

"We can" proves true also in the sense that James and John have left everything to follow Jesus. Unlike the rich young man, they are unhindered in carrying out what they want to attain in their zeal, answering on behalf of those Christians throughout history who have voluntarily accepted poverty to follow the Lord and setting an example for all Christians of the acceptance of suffering as co-redeemers.

---

4 See Psalm 16:5, "You, O Lord, are my portion and cup."

"The cup that I am drinking, you shall drink."

Our Lord's use of the future tense here expresses not a prediction but a promise. With these words, he grants their request—albeit, as we have said, not in the way they meant it. Through them, he grants this also to the Church.

40 "to sit on my right or on my left is not mine to give"

Sitting at the right hand or left hand of the Lord is presumably close to the highest honor that can be attained in the universe. Of course, it is not the Lord's to bestow this honor in response to a request without regard for the common good and history of the Church. It is "for those for whom it is prepared," and how it is bestowed will depend on the future deeds of Christian still to come.

41–45

41 the ten

The number of the Twelve is so significant that when two are considered in separation, Mark (presumably representing Peter's idiom) nonetheless refers to the others as "the ten"—further confirmation that the Lord, in appointing the Twelve, established twelve "offices."

43 "that is not how it is to be among you"

Speaking in the future tense, the Lord is not only instructing these particular men but also prescribing the behavior of the future pastors in the Church.

44 "will be a slave to all"

Why this change from "servant" to "slave"? Perhaps because Jesus was at first describing the relationship of the apostles and their successors, the bishops, to the rest of the Church—"servants." But here he describes the relationship of a leader among those servants, and so he needs a term that connotes even more dedicated service.

It is implied, then, that if Peter is first among the apostles, he must be "slave of the servants."

45 "to purchase"

Literally, "in exchange for many," but it seems fitting to bring out more vividly the meaning of the Greek, which is that the payment of the ransom purchases the freedom of those who are ransomed. Typically, a ransom was paid in money, but here Jesus says he pays the ransom by substitution, taking the place of the ransomed. Someone who is prepared to give up his life for others must be prepared to give up his freedom, and his own will, for others in serving them. Christian service, therefore, is underwritten by a fundamental act of charity by which one wills to give up one's life for the good of others.

"to purchase many"

Jesus does not say "to purchase all," which is all the more striking because he has just used the expression "slave to all." The reason seems to be that the scope of service is a matter of the intention of the servant only. Someone who *wishes* to serve all is *ipso facto* the servant of all, even if some reject his service. But ransoming, in contrast, implies success in ransoming. If someone paid a ransom for all the captives in prison, but some captives refused to leave, all would not be ransomed, even though it would be true that *sufficient ransom* had been paid for all.

46–52

46 and a substantial crowd

Mark's unusual description of the procession conveys that it was a big group and that Jesus was in a circle within a circle. The convoluted description shows us that for practical purposes, Jesus was inaccessible to the beggar.

Bartimaeus, the son of Timaeus

Mark gives his name and patronymic because he joins the disciples (verse 52) and becomes known to the Christian community in this way. This is the story of how he became a disciple. There is also an implied contrast with the unnamed rich young man, who did not follow Our Lord. This blind beggar, who had nothing, did. So we are introduced to him personally.

47 "Son of David, Jesus"

Not the patronizing "Good teacher" but "Son of David," an acknowledgment of Jesus as the Messiah and acceptance of his authority.

48 "Son of David, Jesus, have mercy on me!"

By dropping the name "Jesus" now, this beggar refers to the Lord solely by his role. He is professing his faith as much as crying for help.

49 "Call for him."

The Greek verb means literally "make a sound." That is how one gets the attention of a blind man. The term comes to be used to mean "call him by name." The first thing the blind man heard in response to his crying out was, beautifully enough, his own name: *Bartimaeus!*

49 "He is calling for you!"

There is a certain urgency here, as if they are saying, this is your chance, and you must act now.

50 Throwing his cloak to the side

Here is another of Mark's memorable "picture details," showing that this beggar, unlike the rich young man, immediately leaves behind everything that he has. He leaves his cloak behind without a thought.

51 "Rabbi...that I might see..."

"Rabbi" means "teacher," but Mark, writing from Peter's eyewitness perspective, puts the word in its Hebrew transliteration rather than the Greek, sharing with his readers the very sound of this request. When Jesus was far off, the blind man called out to him as to the Messiah, but now that he is in the immediate personal presence of Our Lord, he calls him simply "Rabbi," which is how his disciples probably addressed him most commonly.

52 "Your faith has saved you."

The word rendered "saved you" has a double meaning. On the one hand, it can mean healing. In this sense, it refers to Bartimaeus' regaining sight. On the other hand, it can mean being rescued from danger. In this sense it refers, we presume, to the forgiveness of his sins. The Lord sent him away with his sins forgiven and his sight restored, just as he sent the paralytic away with his sins forgiven and his mobility restored.

He did follow him

Why did he not "go on his way" as Jesus told him to do? Probably because this statement, "go on your way," when said idiomatically as to a friend, means "you may go." Jesus was not commanding him to return home.

CHAPTER 11

1 So when they are approaching Jerusalem, near Bethpage and Bethany, by the Mount of Olives, he sends out two of his disciples on a task. ²He tells them, "Go into the village ahead of you. As soon as you enter it, you will find a foal which is tied up, upon which no man has ever sat. Untie it and bring it. ³If anyone should say to you, 'Why are you doing this?' say, 'The Lord needs it. He will send it back shortly.'" ⁴So they left. They did find a foal tied up outside near a doorway, by the street. So they untie it. ⁵Some of the men standing there said to them, "What are you doing untying the foal?" ⁶But they told them what Jesus said, and they let them untie it. ⁷So they lead the foal to Jesus. They throw their garments over it. And he sat on it.

8 Many spread their garments on the road, and others, rushes which they cut from the fields. ⁹As they went before him and followed behind him they cried out, "Hosanna! Blessed is he who comes in the name of the Lord! ¹⁰Blessed is the coming kingdom of our father, David! Hosanna in the highest!" ¹¹So he entered into Jerusalem, into the temple. He looked around at everything, but given that the hour was already late, he left for Bethany with the Twelve.

12 The next day, as they were leaving Bethany, he was hungry. ¹³He saw a leafy fig tree from a distance and went to see if, therefore, he would find any fruit on it. When he got to it, he found that it had nothing but leaves—it was not the season for figs, after all— ¹⁴so he reacted by saying to it, "May no one eat fruit from you again, until the end of time!" His disciples could hear him.

15 So they go into Jerusalem. He went into the temple and commenced throwing out those who were selling goods and those who were shopping in the temple. He turned over the tables of the money-changers and the chairs of the dove merchants. ¹⁶He would not so much as allow anyone to walk through the temple carrying a vessel. ¹⁷He began to teach. He was saying to them, "Is it not written, 'My house shall be called a house of prayer by all the nations'? But you have made it a den of thieves!" ¹⁸The chief priests and scribes could hear. So they started looking for a way to destroy him. Why was that? Because they were afraid of him. Because the entire crowd of people was amazed by his teaching. ¹⁹So when evening came, they exited from the city.

20 Early next morning, as they were passing by, they saw the fig tree, withered from its roots up. ²¹So Peter remembers and says to him, "Rabbi, look! The fig tree that you cursed—it is withered up!"

22 So Jesus tells them, "Have faith in God. ²³I give you my assurance, if anyone should say to this mountain, 'Be taken up and be cast into the sea!' and he does not doubt in his heart, but he has faith that what he says happens, it will be so for him. ²⁴This is why I am telling you, in connection with everything that you pray for and ask—have faith that you receive it, and it will be so for you."

25 "Whenever you stand up to pray, if you have any claim against anyone, remit it, so that your Father in heaven, too, will remit you your transgressions. ²⁶But if you do not remit it, neither will your father in heaven remit your transgressions."

27 So they go into Jerusalem again. As he is walking around in the temple, the chief priests, the scribes, and the elders approach him. ²⁸So they were saying to him, "By what authority do you do these things? Or who gave you the authority to do these things?" ²⁹So Jesus said to them, "I will ask you a single question. Answer it for me, and I will tell you by what authority I do these things. ³⁰The baptism of John—was it from heaven, or from men? Give me your answer." ³¹They then held a discussion among themselves and said, "If we should say, 'From heaven,' he will say, 'Then why did you not believe him?' ³²And yet if we should say, 'From men'…"—they were afraid of the crowd because everyone held that John was a genuine prophet. ³³So giving their answer they say to Jesus, "We do not know." ³⁴So Jesus says to them, "And neither do I tell you by what authority I do these things."

Commentary

Conveying Peter's view of what it was like to live with Christ during his public ministry, Mark holds a magnifying glass up to events, giving greater attention to shorter spans of time as his narrative proceeds:

Chapters 1–9: in and around Galilee (months or years)

Chapter 10: journey to Jerusalem (several days)

Chapters 11–15: in Jerusalem (a week)

Peter lived with Jesus about 150 weeks, but the last third of Mark's narrative deals with the last week alone. And strangely enough, with more space devoted to smaller lengths of time, the story accelerates.

According to John's Gospel, Jesus made several other trips to Jerusalem. Mark's simplifying narrative omits those, making Peter's life with Jesus look like a single prolonged action terminating in the Cross.

1-7

One-fifth of this chapter is devoted to how the foal was found! Why should Mark have devoted so much space to such a small detail? Good storytellers embellish their accounts with curiosities, and Peter begins his account of Christ's last week with this strange incident. People love stories about animals, and since a dumb beast can add a slightly comical touch, the procurement of the foal lightens the tale of great suffering that follows.

The prediction of accidental particulars is proof of direct knowledge of the future. Jesus' foreknowledge of where the disciples would find the foal and how bystanders would react to their taking it assures his disciples (and us) that he also knows what will happen to him in Jerusalem. Everything that follows is in accordance with God's plan.

The manner in which the disciples acquire the foal establishes that it is not simply a beast of burden but also a symbol. The Fathers stress this last point: "Not indeed that He was compelled by necessity to ride on a colt from the mount of Olives to Jerusalem, for He had gone over Judaea and all Galilee on foot, but this action of His is typical," that is, a "type" or symbol of something else.[1]

Having left everything to follow Jesus, the disciples would not have owned any animals. This story explains how they got one— like a simple mendicant friar today explaining how he providentially obtained a pickup truck for a necessary job.

The many reasons for this small detail confirm the presupposition of this commentary that there is a "logic" to Mark's Gospel, which we can uncover by thinking about it carefully.

---

1 Chrysostom, quoted in Saint Thomas Aquinas, *Catena Aurea: Gospel of Mark*, trans. William Whiston (Grand Rapids, MI: Christian Classics Ethereal Library), p. 173.

1 he sends out two of his disciples

Matthew writes that the disciples were sent to get both a foal and an ass. Assume this is true. If Mark had decided to include this story for the reasons mentioned above, he might have sensed, rightly, that it was a complication of his main narrative, so he kept it as clean and simple as possible.

2 "As soon as you enter it"

The detail is important because it would not be strange if they wandered around the town and *eventually* found an animal tied up.

"Untie it and bring it."

To untie an animal was to assert the right to take possession of it. It was a significant act, like entering a house. If one did not have authority to untie the animal, this act would amount to theft.

3 "'The Lord needs it.'"

Was this a "password," agreed on in advance by Jesus and cooperators in Bethany? But Jesus does not add, "which friends have offered for our use." The cooperation seems to be miraculous: "They would not have allowed this, if the Divine power had not been upon them, to compel them, especially, as they were country people and farmers...."[2]

8–11

8 Many spread their garments on the road

Suppose that the few, the disciples, spread their garments so that he might rest directly on them; the crowd, who could not do this, did the best they could do in imitation, spreading their garments on the road.

Those two actions are in turn connected with "others spread branches"—those, that is, who were too poor to spread garments—and so they got rushes, in a further imitation.

---

2 Theophylact, ibid., p. 173.

Apparently, the crowd's celebration of the Lord's entrance into Jerusalem was not, as we might like to imagine, spontaneous, sweeping up the disciples with it. Mark depicts it instead as the radiation of the affection and faith of the disciples, which the crowd shares in.

9 "Hosanna!"

A transliteration of an abbreviation of a phrase from Psalm 118:25 meaning "Save us right now!" The root of the word, *yeshua*, is the same as in the name Jesus. Originally the word was a plea for help. Somehow over time it got changed—no one understands precisely how—into a celebratory cry meaning essentially "glory and praise."

"Blessed is he who comes in the name of the Lord!"

The people exclaim the one verse from Psalm 118, but Peter understands an allusion to entire psalm: you might wish to read it at this point.

12–14

12 he was hungry

This clause provides the key to the proper interpretation of this episode, which can seem problematic. Why was he hungry immediately after the time for a morning meal? Presumably because he fasted instead of eating. He wanted to be hungry, as his hunger would be an occasion for him to teach the disciples something.

In Mark, many episodes in the life of Christ have both a literal and symbolic meaning. When the disciples saw that the Lord deliberately made himself hungry, expressed that hunger (unusual for a man who was accustomed to severe ascetic practices), and said aloud, as we may imagine, that he was going to look for figs—at a time when everyone knew there would be no figs—they understood him to be communicating another meaning. It was for them a living parable: "Just in the same way as He speaks parables, so also His deeds are parables."[3]

14 he reacted by saying to it

We must imagine this as deliberately spoken so that the disciples could overhear; it was not an outburst of anger.

"May no one eat fruit from you again"

According to Matthew (21:19), Jesus said, "May fruit not come from you again until the end of time!" Mark mentions eating; Matthew does not. Let us use this difference as an exercise in harmonizing. Our hypothesis is that both Mark and Matthew are accurate, and we ask whether and how we can reconcile the two.

There are two approaches to such a reconciliation. With the first, we hold that the actual words are important and postulate words that Jesus might have spoken that make both reports correct. For example, if Jesus' actual words expressed both ideas—"May no one eat fruit from you, and may you not even bear fruit until the end of time!"—then both Mark and Matthew are accurate in selecting different parts of that sentence to recount.

With the second approach, it is enough if the sense is correct. So St. Augustine, who often followed this approach, says that the Holy Spirit sometimes inspires the evangelists with different words to teach us that the meaning is important, not the words themselves.

The approach of Claude Tresmontant—assuming a common original Hebrew text—would not help us here. The difference between the words in Matthew and Mark is too great to say they are different translations of a single Hebrew original.

Suppose that the cursing of the fig tree is an acted-out parable. Its most common interpretation among the Fathers was that Jesus has the

---

3 Bede, ibid., p. 178.

power to "wither up" those who do not receive him, and even those who persecute him. He would undergo the Passion only because he freely accepted it. He taught this lesson using a tree rather than harming a human being: He wished "to shew His disciples that if He chose He could in a moment exterminate those who were about to crucify Him."[4]

Recall that not every component of a parable needs to be meaningful—the detail that it was not the time for figs, for example. It might be simply an explanation for the availability, at that time and for purposes of teaching, of a fig tree that had leaves but no fruit. On the other hand, it is possible to attribute meaning to that detail. If we do, then simply bearing fruit by natural processes—natural virtue, natural goodness, natural achievement—is not sufficient from Christ's point of view. "We may also say...that the Lord sought for fruit on the fig tree before its time, and not finding it, cursed it, because all who fulfil the commandments of the Law, are said to bear fruit in their own time, as, for instance, that commandment, *Thou shalt not commit adultery*; but he who not only abstains from adultery but remains a virgin, which is a greater thing, excels them in virtue. But the Lord exacts from the perfect not only the observance of virtue, but also that they bear fruit over and above the commandments."[5] On this interpretation, the cursing of the fig tree illuminates Jesus' encounter with the rich young man of the preceding chapter.

15–19

15 So they go into Jerusalem.

Here as elsewhere, the historical present throws us into the scene.

he...commenced throwing out

In his simplified life of Christ, Mark omits other trips by Jesus to Jerusalem. But John tells us that on one such trip, Jesus

---

4 Theophylact, ibid., p. 178.
5 Chrysostom, ibid., p. 178.

expelled the money-changers and merchants. If so, then this episode recounts an additional cleansing of the temple. And indeed, it may have been his practice, whenever he went into the temple, to cleanse it in this way.

16 He would not so much as allow anyone to walk through the temple carrying a vessel.

How did Jesus succeed in driving out the money-changers and merchants? There were temple guards who could be summoned to deal with violent people. It is unlikely that the money-changers suffered from a bad conscience.

The word "allow" is the clue, since it implies authority. What is depicted here is hardly possible for someone who does not have an aura of authority. The temple had its established practices and hierarchy of authority. What Mark describes is as if a civilian walked into the Pentagon and took command of the army by the force of his personality, or a layman walked into a convention of physicians and was quickly regarded as the chief medical authority in the hall. The best explanation of the cleansing of the temple is that Jesus was sensed to have the authority to act as he did.

17 He began to teach.

After the merchants had been expelled, a hush would have come over the temple, and those who remained would have watched expectantly as Jesus began to teach.

"'My house shall be called a house of prayer by all the nations'"

Jesus quotes Isaiah 56:7, in which the prophet foretells the reception of the Gospel by the Gentiles.

18 The chief priests and scribes could hear.

The newfound silence in the temple made it possible for them to overhear, even though they kept their distance.

for a way to destroy him

Not just antiseptically kill him. The core sense of the Greek is to destroy utterly.

Because they were afraid of him.

Even the chief priests and the scribes recognized that Jesus had authority. But they did not acknowledge it for themselves, so to speak: they saw it reflected and verified in the crowd. This frightened them, because it suggested his authority was greater than theirs.

The Lord has just arrived in the holy city and is preaching in the temple that he has quieted. But the religious authorities react by wanting to destroy him. Searching for an explanation, Peter attributes their behavior to the very human motive of fear, which will affect Peter himself: from "fear of the crowd" he will deny Jesus.

20 Early next morning

Matthew writes about the fig tree:

> [18]In the morning, as he was returning to the city, he was hungry. [19]And seeing a fig tree by the wayside he went to it, and found nothing on it but leaves only. And he said to it, "May no fruit ever come from you again!" And the fig tree withered at once. [20]When the disciples saw it they marveled, saying, "How did the fig tree wither at once?" (KJV)

Let us assume that Matthew's and Mark's accounts are both correct. Can they be reconciled? They differ in four details:

1. Matthew says that the fig tree withered "at once," but Mark does not.
2. Matthew says the disciples commented that the fig tree withered "at once," but in Mark the disciples see the tree withered the day after.
3. Matthew says the disciples marveled at the withered tree, but Mark describes only Peter as doing so.
4. Mark assigns the curse and the disciples' wonderment to different days, but Matthew does not.

Can a single story encompass both of these accounts and explain the difference in details? Detail 3 is easily dealt with: postulate that all the disciples wondered at the withered tree, but Peter spoke on behalf of them. Detail 1 is next easiest: say the fig tree began withering the moment Jesus cursed it, but the disciples didn't notice; Matthew adds "at once" to underline that it was miraculous, whereas Mark adds "from the roots up." Detail 2 can be dealt with by saying that the disciples, when they saw the withered tree, inferred (correctly) that it had begun withering immediately. Finally, detail 4 can be taken care of by saying that Matthew telescopes into one moment two incidents—the curse of the tree and the disciples' noticing that it had withered—that were in fact separated by a day. His phrase "When the disciples saw it" leaves open that they saw it at some other time than when it was cursed.

It is good to engage occasionally in "harmonization" of the Gospels to test their truthfulness. I assume in this commentary, however, that each Gospel is meant to stand on its own. So in general, I avoid "harmonization" and prefer to read the Gospel of Mark on its own terms.

22–24

We wondered about the meaning of the episode of the withered fig tree. The contiguity of this text with that episode would suggest that, whatever else it was meant to convey, it points to the power of faith.

23 "...he has faith that what he says happens, it will be so for him."

Jesus uses the present not the future tense. Other translations alternate between giving a past tense ("have faith that you have received it") or the future ("have faith that you will receive it"). But the present tense seems important as revealing the nature of faith in God. It seems Jesus is teaching about the genuine dialogue that should take place between a believer and God. This "living in the presence of God" will affect what a Christian believes he can and should ask for. It also can tell him with assurance—not always, but sometimes—that God will do something for him if he asks for it and believes upon it. Jesus is *not* teaching that faith is an interior conviction that, if we make it firm enough, has the power to alter the world. Rather, God, who can do anything, lives in an eternal present. In the context of a relationship with God, if the Lord intimates to the believer that something will be done, it "is" done.

25–26

Pseudo-Jerome makes a remarkable comment about this passage: "Mark has, as he is wont, expressed seven verses of the Lord's prayer in one prayer."[6] The Lord's Prayer is found only in Matthew and Luke. But consider whether Mark regarded the parts of the Lord's Prayer in the teaching here:

Have faith in God.... Your Father in heaven	Our Father, who art in heaven, hallowed be thy name.
as regards everything that you pray for and ask, have faith that you receive it, and it will be so for you	Thy kingdom come, thy will be done, on earth as it is in heaven.
?	Give us this day our daily bread.
Whenever you stand in prayer, if you have any claim against anyone, remit it, so that your Father in heaven, too, will remit you your transgressions.	Forgive us our trespasses, as we forgive those who trespass against us.
?	Lead us not into temptation, but deliver us from evil.

6 Jerome, quoted in *Catena Aurea*, p. 183. The earliest commentary on the Gospel of Mark, now dated to the seventh century, was thought in the Middle Ages to have been written by St. Jerome. In the Renaissance, scholars rejected that identification, and since then the author of the commentary has been called "Pseudo-Jerome." A leading theory today holds that the commentator was an Irish monk.

Perhaps because of the prominence in Mark's Gospel of the two feedings of the multitudes and the various exorcisms performed by Jesus, the remaining two petitions are present too, as continuing background suppositions of Mark's narrative.

27–34

28 "By what authority do you do these things? Or who gave you the authority to do these things?"

These are two different questions. The first supposes that Jesus takes himself to have no authority and therefore must invoke the authority of another. The second supposes that he has authority but that it is received from another.

The two questions seem to arise from the chief priests, the scribes, and the elders' prior rejection of John. They did not oppose John openly, but if they had spoken their minds, they would have challenged him in a similar way.

32 "if we should say, 'From men'.... "

Mark breaks off in mid-sentence, conveying something actually overheard by Peter. Someone merely describing, not remembering, the scene would complete the thought and the sentence.

33 "We do not know."

The Lord knows that they believe it was not from heaven. What they really mean is, "We are not going to tell you."

34 "And neither do I tell you.... "

People who "do not know" look for the truth and are happy when they find it, but these men never continued to look into the question of whether John was a prophet.

The chapter and the episode end here—an expression of Peter's unabashed pride in how Jesus so cleverly dealt with this trap.

Chapter 12

1 Then, using comparisons, he spoke to them:

"So a man planted a vineyard. He placed a fence around it. He dug a wine vat. He built a tower. He rented it out to some gardeners. Then he left the country.

2 "He sent a servant to the gardeners, when the time was right, to get some of the vineyard's yield from the gardeners. ³They got hold of him—and they gave him a beating. They sent him back empty-handed.

4 "Once again, he sent another servant to them. They threw rocks at this one, hitting him on the head. They treated him with disgrace.

5 "So he sent yet another servant. This one they killed.

"Many others he sent—some they beat, others they killed.

6 "Still, he had one other, his beloved son. At the very last, he sent him to them, saying, 'They will show my son some respect.' ⁷But those gardeners said to themselves, 'This man is the heir. Come, let's kill him, and so the inheritance will be ours.' ⁸So they took him and killed him. They threw him out—outside the vineyard.

9 "So what will the master of the vineyard do? He will come and destroy those gardeners. And he will give the vineyard to others. ¹⁰You

have at least read this verse, haven't you, 'The stone which the builders rejected is the very stone that has become the chief corner stone. [11]By the Lord this was done and it is marvelous in our eyes.'"

12 So they were looking for a way to capture him. Yet they were afraid of the crowd—because, of course, the crowd realized that he directed this comparison at them. So they did nothing and just left.

13 So they send a group of Pharisees and Herodians to catch him with words. [14]They come and say to him, "Teacher, we know that you are true. You do not care what anyone thinks, because you do not look for human approval, but you teach the way of God based on truth: Is it permissible to pay tribute to Caesar or not? Should we pay, or should we not pay?" [15]He saw their hypocrisy and said to them, "Why are you testing me? Bring me a denarius, so that I can look at it." [16]They brought one. So he says to them, "Whose likeness is this? Whose inscription?" They told him, "Caesar's," [17]to which Jesus said, "Give back to Caesar what belongs to Caesar, and to God what belongs to God." They found him astonishing.

18 So Sadducees come to him—these are men who deny a resurrection. They posed him a question: [19]"Teacher, Moses wrote it down for us, that if someone's brother should die and leave a wife and not leave a child, his brother should take the wife and 'raise up seed' for his brother. [20]Now there were seven brothers. The first took a wife. When he died, he did not leave 'seed.' [21]So the second took her. And he died not leaving 'seed.' The same with the third. [22]And all seven failed to leave 'seed.' Finally, the woman died too. [23]Now, in the resurrection, when they are raised, to which of these brothers will she belong as his wife? After all, all seven possessed her as a wife." [24]To which Jesus said, "Isn't this the reason you've lost your way—that you do not know the scriptures or the power of God? [25]Since, when men rise from the dead, they neither marry nor are given in marriage but are like angels in heaven. [26]As for the dead, that they do rise, have you

not read in the book of Moses how God in the burning bush addressed him saying, 'I am the God of Abraham and the God of Isaac and the God of Jacob'? [27]He is not a God of dead men, but a God of living men. You have very much lost your way."

28 So one of the scribes came up to him, who had heard them disputing, and who had seen that he answered them so well, and he asked him, "Which commandment is first of all?" [29]Jesus replied, "First is, 'Hear, O Israel, the Lord our God is one Lord, [30]and you shall love the Lord your God with all your heart and with all your soul and with all your reason and with all your strength.' [31]This is second: 'You shall love your neighbor as yourself.' There is no other commandment greater than these." [32]The scribe said to him, "Rightly, teacher, do you say in truth that he is one and that there is no other except him, [33]and that to love him with one's whole heart and with one's whole understanding and with one's whole strength, and that to love one's neighbor as oneself, exceeds all burnt offerings and sacrifices." [34]So when Jesus saw that he replied so discerningly, he said to him, "You are not far from the kingdom of God." And no one dared to question him any longer.

35 So Jesus spoke out in reply and taught in the temple: "How can the scribes say that the Messiah is the son of David? [36]David himself said, in the Holy Spirit, 'The Lord said to my Lord, "Sit on my right until I place your enemies beneath your feet."' [37]David himself calls him Lord. How can he be his son?" And the immense crowd that was there listened to him with pleasure.

38 He would also say when he taught, "Look out for the scribes, whose goal is to go around in robes and be given signs of respect in the marketplace [39]and noteworthy seats in synagogues and places of honor at banquets— [40]the ones who devour the houses of widows while uttering lengthy prayers as a pretext. These men will receive an overflow of judgment."

41 So he took a seat opposite the treasury and was watching how the crowd of people put coins into the treasury. And many wealthy men gave many coins. [42]So one poor widow came along who gave two lepta, the equivalent of a kodrantes. [43]He summoned his disciples and said to them, "I tell you with assurance that this poor widow gave more than everyone who gave to the treasury. [44]And why is that? Because they all gave out of their abundance. But she out of her destitution gave everything she had, the whole of her life."

Commentary

In chapter 11, Mark presented Jesus as assuming the position of authority in the temple that belongs to him by right. In this chapter, Jesus exercises that position: he reveals his standing as the Son of God, confounds his critics, and begins teaching fundamental truths. The crowd is astounded and listens to him eagerly (verse 37). He begins to gain supporters even among the religious establishment (verse 32). The chapter seems to reflect Peter's bittersweet sense of what could have been, what *should* have been, "if only you and I had recognized the day of the Lord."[1]

The chapter is carefully constructed. It begins with a parable in which the Lord shows clearly that he understands his enemies and knows what they are about to do to him (verses 1–12). Through the parable, he also warns these men. The parable, in effect, provokes a crisis. They do not accept the warning but instead plot against him.

There follow three episodes in which Jesus is shown to be a sublime teacher whose wisdom soars above that of merely clever men: he foils a trap about paying tribute to Caesar (13–17), he resolves the

---

1 St. Josemaría Escrivá, *The Way of the Cross*, (Cleveland, OH: Scepter Publishers, 2004), p. 1.

puzzle about the resurrection (18–27), and he reveals the foundation of the Law and the Prophets (28–34).

1–12

1 "So a man planted a vineyard...."

I have translated these statements as separate sentences because I understand Jesus to have spoken this parable by pausing after each statement, allowing his listeners to visualize each point, perhaps gesturing for emphasis.

What do the elements of the comparison stand for? A suggestion: "God the Father is called a man by a human conception. The vineyard is the house of Israel; the hedge is the guardianship of Angels; the wine vat is the law, the tower is the temple, and the husbandmen the priests."[2]

"Then he left the country."

People wonder, "Where is God?"—and this phrase is God's own description of how he allows room for human freedom. While he is "out of the country," those deemed his servants, and his own son too, are abused, beaten, and murdered. He knows this; he permits it; he takes it into account.

2 "He sent a servant to the gardeners"

There are five sendings: a first servant (beaten), a second servant (wounded in the head), a third servant (killed), "many others" (some beaten, some killed), and finally the son. St. Bede says that the first servant represents Moses, against whom the Israelites rebelled in the wilderness. The second servant, he says, represents "David and the other Psalmists;" while the third servant and those who followed him represent the "band of the prophets."[3] According to Theophylact, on

---

2 Jerome, quoted in Saint Thomas Aquinas, *Catena Aurea: Gospel of Mark*, trans. William Whiston (Grand Rapids, MI: Christian Classics Ethereal Library), p. 185.
3 Bede, ibid., p. 186.

the other hand, the first servant represents the prophets of the time of Elijah, the second servant represents the prophets of the time of Hosea and Isaiah, and the third servant represents the prophets of the time of Daniel and Ezekiel.[4]

"get some of the vineyard's yield"

Pseudo-Jerome says the yield of the vineyard stands for obedience.[5]

6 "his beloved son"

As the master of the vineyard represents God, and the son in the story represents Jesus, Jesus is plainly declaring himself to be the Son of God.

"At the very last"

This language implies that the son is the last one to be sent, that is, that prophecy and revelation will come to an end with the son.

"'They will show my son some respect'"

The Fathers struggle over how the man could have thought this, given how badly his servants had been treated. Pseudo-Jerome says that he is speaking ironically.[6] St. Bede says that he speaks not firmly but doubting, indicating the room God leaves for human freedom.[7] Theophylact says, "He said this not as though He were ignorant of what was to happen, but to shew what it was right and fitting for them to do."[8]

7 "'This man is the heir.'"

There are many theories as to why Jesus was crucified. Some say it was because he was perceived as a threat to Roman power. Others say it was a test, to see if he would extricate himself and establish the

---

4 Theophylact, ibid., p. 186.
5 Jerome, ibid., p. 186.
6 Jerome, ibid., p. 186.
7 Bede, ibid., p. 186.
8 Theophylact, ibid., p. 186.

kingdom. Jesus' own explanation, implicit here, is that he was put to death out of envy.

The "gardeners"—the priests and scribes—sensed that he had a legitimate claim on the authority they enjoyed. But to deal with the Son in this way, they had to believe that God could be defeated or that the Son would return to the "distant country" and God would never make things right.

8 "outside the vineyard"

The son is the only one of those sent whose body is cast out of the vineyard. Jesus will be crucified outside the walls of Jerusalem, and Mark's inclusion of this detail suggests that Jesus was especially hurt by this token of rejection.

9 "So what will the master of the vineyard do?"

Previously described simply as a "man," the owner of the vineyard is now called the "master" or "Lord" (Greek *kyrios*). The personal name of God, regarded as too holy to pronounce, was rendered in Greek versions of the Jewish scriptures as *Kyrios* (customarily indicated in English translations of the Old Testament as "LORD"). Calling the owner of the vineyard *kyrios* is therefore an evocation of God, and Jesus' question amounts to "What will God the Father do after his Son is treated in this way?"

"He will come and destroy those gardeners."

Matthew, in contrast, depicts Jesus as asking a crowd what the master of the vineyard will do. They answer him, "He will put those wretches to a miserable death, and let out the vineyard to other tenants..." (21:40–41). How are these two accounts best harmonized?

First, it is possible that Matthew and Mark are not recounting the same recitation of the parable. The temple was a large place, and as Jesus walked around it teaching, he might have told the same parable more than once.

But if Jesus did tell the parable only once, the two versions can be harmonized by assuming that Jesus first asked the crowd what the master of the vineyard would do, and when they replied, he affirmed their answer, saying something like, "That's right. He will come and destroy those vinedressers."

(This kind of harmonization is typically not difficult to achieve. Once it is worked through, it typically adds nothing interesting, which is why we have tended to avoid it.)

"destroy"

Not "he will kill those gardeners" but "he will destroy" them, as if to imply that the offices, not merely the persons, are destroyed.

"he will give the vineyard to others"

"[T]he vineyard is given to others, that is, to those who come from the east, and from the west, and from the south, and from the north, and who sit down with Abraham, Isaac, and Jacob in the kingdom of heaven."[9]

10 "You have at least read this verse"

He says "at least" presumably because he regards the meaning of the verse as so plain that simply reading it is enough. Yet why should its meaning be so plain? From the events of the days before, especially the entry of Jesus into the holy city with hosannas, it ought to have been obvious that Psalm 118 was then being fulfilled.

13–17

13 So they send a group of Pharisees and Herodians to catch him with words.

The change to the historical present throws us into the scene and makes it seem that this next encounter follows immediately upon the last.

---

9 Jerome, ibid., p. 187.

Herodians

No one knows for sure who these people were. There are two plausible opinions: (1) they were members of a contrarian religious sect that held that Herod was the Messiah, or, more plausibly, (2) they were supporters of Herod who, strongly favoring the payment of tribute to Caesar, were brought along in part to pressure Jesus into giving a certain answer and in part as witnesses.

to catch him with words

The word for "catch" is taken from hunting. These men set out to ensnare Jesus, like a hunter going after prey. Extremely clever, they were dangerous to him.

14 "You do not care what anyone thinks"

Literally, "no one causes you concern."

"you do not look for human approval"

Literally, "you do not look toward the face of men," that is, you do not search for their approving or disapproving looks.

"you teach the way of God based on truth"

The Pharisees and Herodians do not themselves believe any of these things, but they are attempting to flatter him. Assuming that he will somehow make it plain to the crowd that he is pleased, they hope that his self-satisfaction will lure him into the trap and make it more obvious and laughable to everyone when he has been caught.

These men are cleverly laying multiple traps. The first is in the very way the question is posed. To appreciate its seriousness, recall that the Herodians are there, ready to report to the authorities any seemingly rebellious statement. Jesus can either say what he thinks, without regard to the authorities, or he can say what the authorities want him to say. If he were to choose the former ("the way of God based on truth"), then if he did not say what was true without any defect—a high standard to attain—he would be discredited. If the latter, he would be seen as caring about what people think, like everyone else—and so again he would be discredited.

"Is it permissible to pay tribute to Caesar...?"

Note the deceptive way the question is phrased. The Pharisees and Herodians first ask if it is *permissible* to pay tribute to Caesar, but then they immediately rephrase the question, asking if they are *obliged* to pay. These are two different ideas. By "permissible," they mean permissible according to *God's* law, and by "obligatory," they mean obligatory according to *Caesar's* law. They assume that if God's law permits paying, then because of Caesar's law they should pay.

But here is a second trap. If Jesus says they *ought* to pay tribute, he will seem to support the Roman occupation of Israel and alienate his audience. But if he says they *need not* pay, he will seem to foment lawlessness and rebellion, and as there are witnesses who will report him to the authorities, the crowd will distance themselves from him out of fear of reprisals.

15 "Bring me a denarius"

Jesus responds immediately, needing no time to ponder their question. Simply from a human point of view, the Lord's response is a display of great genius. Imagine that you had never heard this story before, and that you found yourself in the same trap. How would you get out of it?

16 "Whose likeness is this? Whose inscription?"

A denarius was roughly a day's wage for people who had no money to spend on luxuries. It can be taken to represent "wealth" in general, as the world knows it.

By asking "Whose *likeness* is this?" Jesus poses for us the questions, "Where do you find the likeness of God?" and "Where do you find his inscription?" Those questions might not occur to us if he had asked whose *picture* was on the coin. Because he phrases the question as he does, we are prompted to recall that God's likeness is found in man, who is created in his image and likeness, and God's name is inscribed on any person calling himself after God, a Christian.

17 "Give back to Caesar what belongs to Caesar"

This statement frees Jesus from the trap and confounds his questioners because it establishes an important principle, one that prudent statesmen and citizens have meditated on for centuries. Jesus' answer is so vivid, transparent, and convincing that everyone who heard it was instantly persuaded.

The principle Jesus establishes here is that of the distinctness, separate legitimacy, and coordination of political and religious authority. Each makes a legitimate claim; to each something must be rendered. Neither is reducible to the other, and neither can be subsumed under the other. And yet political authority is *ordered to* religious authority: that with which political authority is directly concerned—money and everything connected with it—is for the sake of that with which religious authority is directly concerned—the human heart in its relationship to God.

Using a coin to make this point was ingenious. Money is the universal stand-in for any good traded on the market, and the market is the original source of social unity in a society. That is to say, the diversity of talents, resources, and interests produces a natural division of labor, and the market is where those who specialize in providing one good or service can exchange it, through the instrument of money, for the other goods and services needed for daily life. The denarius stands for the main good that political administration provides: oversight of the economy and the confirmation of social unity provided by the market. Anyone who enjoys these goods is obliged to "make repayment to Caesar" from that money.

We should also contemplate the nature of our repayment to Caesar and to God. The money we render to Caesar is an instrumental good. But to God we render inherent goods, such as obedience and our heart.

They found him astonishing.

Even these men had to acknowledge the genius and perfect acceptability of his reply.

18–27

18 So Sadducees come to him. . . . They posed him a question

This question is not a trap. The Sadducees pose a stock objection to the doctrine of the resurrection, which they have probably used many times before. Their fault is not deviousness or hypocrisy.

these are men who deny a resurrection

Mark must assume that the Sadducees are less well known than the Pharisees. Acts 23:8 tells us the Sadducees also deny the existence of angels and the spiritual nature of man.

19 "if someone's brother should die"

The relevant law is found at Deuteronomy 25:5–6. The Sadducees omit the detail that for the law to be binding, the brothers must be living together. Jesus could have quibbled with them about that point, but he chooses not to.

25 "they neither marry nor are given in marriage"

The Sadducees suppose that the resurrection is a reprise of this life and possession of the same kind of body as one had before death.

26 "'I am the God of Abraham'"

This implies that Abraham, Isaac, and Jacob still exist. Someone might object, Theophylact notes, that God's declaration shows only that the souls of these patriarchs still exist; it does not show that their bodies are raised. But in response he says that Abraham is not his soul; thus, it is improper to refer to the soul of Abraham by the name "Abraham." The name "Abraham" must denote the body also, and, although the resurrected body of Abraham will not exist in fact until the general resurrection, it does even now exist, virtually, "in God's ordinances."[10]

28–34

28 one of the scribes came up to him

There is a progression in the questioners. The Pharisees and Herodians aim simply to entrap him. The Sadducees show some openness to the truth in wondering how he will reply to their stock objection. Now a scribe approaches, who is genuinely searching for the truth—indeed, Our Lord's excellent answers inspired the scribe to ask his question. This progression shows how Jesus sealed his authority through his teachings that day. Everyone was astonished, no one dared to challenge him, and even some of the religious leaders moved toward accepting him.

"Which commandment is first of all?"

All the commandments were regarded as equally binding. This question is about undergirding principles. The first principle informs all the others: that is why it is "greatest." Contrast this scribe's question with that of the rich young man, whose question was purely pragmatic and self-centered.

29 "First is, 'Hear, O Israel,'"

Jesus quotes Deuteronomy 6:4, which reads, "YHWH our God is one YHWH." The statement is often explained as a strong assertion of the unity of God. But "one" modifies "YHWH," not God. The verse seems, then, to assert the unity of Israel's *relationship* with YHWH. That is, it says that the "object" to which Israel is related in a covenant is singular. That is why this verse is inseparable from the one that follows, making a single commandment based on the complete personal

---

10 Theophylact, ibid., p. 192.

unity and totality by which the people of Israel are to be related to this one YHWH.

30 "you shall love the Lord your God with all your heart"

A quotation from the next verse in Deuteronomy, to which Our Lord has added "with all your reason." He apparently felt free to elaborate on the first and most basic of all the commandments! And yet note that this elaboration is not a matter of addition but of unfolding, because *reason* is one of the powers of the *soul*.

But why does he add "with all your reason"? Perhaps because this is what the scribe exemplifies as he inquires of Jesus about the ordering of the commandments. His reason is leading him to Jesus and thus leading him to God.

31 "There is no other commandment greater than these."

With this language, Jesus leaves it open that there may be other commandments *as great*. Perhaps he wanted to suggest that all the commandments were "great," even apparently small or slight commandments, though one commandment came first and the other was second.

32 "Rightly, teacher, do you say"

In the scribe's reformulation of the Lord's reply, it becomes clear that the first commandment is not free-standing but based upon a truth: "He is one and there is no other except him" is not, after all, a commandment.

Not "there is no other God except him" but "there is no other except him." This is the language of love: it is a profession of the extreme goodness and worth of one's beloved.

35-37

35 "the Messiah is the son of David"

Now Jesus offers his own test. Of course, he does not disagree that the Messiah is the Son of David; he accepted that description of himself and was a descendant of David. The puzzle is that descendants are meant to honor ancestors, as children honor parents, not the reverse, and yet David calls the Messiah "Lord," an obvious sign of respect and honor.

36 "David himself said, in the Holy Spirit"

That is, what David said in Psalm 110 represents God's viewpoint, not simply David's opinion. Jesus adds this qualification because many things that David thought and did were not true. But this statement, he says, has divine authority.

37 "How can he be his son?"

The solution is that Jesus is the son of David by the flesh but Son of God in his divine nature, as the parable of the vineyard implies. Mark's Gospel thus affirms the same truth that is presented in the infancy narratives in the Gospels of Matthew and Luke. The implied conclusion is that David would honor the Messiah in this way only if the Messiah were God. Indeed, Psalm 110 goes on to assert the divine sonship of the Messiah (verse 3) and his eternal priesthood (verse 4).

38–40

38 "whose goal is"

There is nothing wrong with wanting honor that is bestowed for the sake of God, as when a father rightly expects honor from his children. But Jesus is warning against scribes who take for themselves the honor due to God.

40 "These men will receive an overflow of judgment."

The term rendered here as "overflow," *perissoteron*, is the same word the scribe used when he said that keeping the first two commandments exceeds all the others, *perissoteron*. The connection seems deliberate: those scribes who want for themselves the "excess" of love and respect due to God will receive in the end an "excess" of punishment instead.

41–44

41 he took a seat opposite the treasury

To take a seat is to assume the posture of a teacher. This episode, presenting an image of love of God and neighbor, sums up the Lord's teaching of the chapter.

42 two lepta

Lepton, a Greek word meaning "lightweight," was the name of a Jewish coin. Mark gives its exchange value in terms of the Roman coin the *quadrans*. That Mark takes pains to give the Roman equivalent is regarded by scholars as additional evidence that the Gospel was based on Peter's narratives presented in Rome.

43 He summoned his disciples

The widow and her gift are so extraordinary to him that he calls his disciples over to share his admiration.

44 "out of their abundance"

If you give out of your abundance, you give only the exchange value of the money. If you give "out of your destitution," that is, you give up what would meet one of your basic needs, you give, in contrast, something of yourself.

"gave everything she had"

That is, she loved God with her whole heart, soul, mind, and strength. She is an image of the fulfillment of the two great commandments.

This chapter can be called "the chapter of first principles." Jesus has assumed the position of authoritative teacher in the temple for one day, and he uses this opportunity to set down first principles for the life of his followers:

- government in the Church—it is for the sake of the "fruit of the vineyard"

- the relationship between Church and state ("render unto Caesar")
- doctrine in the Church—it requires knowledge of both the Scriptures and the power of God
- the moral life of the Church—to love God with one's whole self and one's neighbor as oneself
- the spiritual life of the Church—to give to God of one's own life, as the poor widow did

As we have noted, Peter's recollection of that day of teaching is bittersweet. But we might also say that, providentially, the development of this teaching would be left to the apostles and their successors under the sure guidance of the Holy Spirit. In this way, God takes a great evil—the betrayal and destruction of the Christ—and turns it into the great good: the development of the Christ's teachings with surety over time by his followers.

CHAPTER 13

1 So as he is leaving the temple, one of his disciples says to him, "Teacher, just look at these stones and buildings!" ²Jesus said to him, "Do you see these great buildings? There is not a stone here that will be left upon another and not thrown down."

3 So when he had sat down on the Mount of Olives, across from the temple, Peter, James, John, and Andrew asked him privately, ⁴"Tell us when these things will take place. What is the sign that all these things are about to be accomplished?"

5 Jesus said to them at first, "Watch out that no one leads you astray. ⁶Many men will come in my name, claiming 'I am.' They will lead many astray. ⁷When you hear reports of wars and of rumors of wars, do not be disturbed. It is necessary that this take place, but the end is not yet. ⁸Because nation will rise up against nation, and kingdom against kingdom. There will be earthquakes all over. There will be famines. These are only the beginning of the birth pangs.

9 "You must watch out for yourselves. They will betray you to councils. You will be beaten in assemblies. You will stand before governors and kings, for the sake of my name, to witness to them: ¹⁰to be sure, it is necessary, first, that the good news should be proclaimed to

all the nations. [11]If they happen to lead you away in betrayal, do not worry beforehand what you will say. But simply speak what is given to you at that hour. Because it will not be you who are speaking but the Holy Spirit.

12 "Brother will betray brother to death, and father child. Children will rise up against their parents and have them put to death. [13]You will be hated by everyone because of my name. The man who perseveres to the end will be saved.

14 "When you see the Abomination of Desolation set up where it should not be (you who are reading this, understand!), that is when the inhabitants of Judea should flee to the mountains. [15]A man on his housetop should not come down or take anything from his house. [16]A man in the fields should not turn back to take his garment. [17]It will be trouble, much trouble, for pregnant women or mothers nursing infants in those days! [18]Pray that it does not take place in wintertime. [19]Because those days will be a tribulation such as has not taken place from the beginning of the creation which God has created until now—and never shall be. [20]Indeed, if the Lord did not cut short those days, no fleshly thing would have survived. But because of the chosen ones, the ones he selected out, he cut short those days.

21 "At that time, if someone should say to you, 'Look, here is the Christ!' 'Look, he is there!' do not believe it! [22]Because false Christs will arise and false prophets. They will give signs and work wonders to deceive even the chosen ones, if that were possible. [23]As for you— watch out! I have told you everything in advance.

24 "But in those days, after that tribulation, the sun will be darkened. The moon will not give its light. [25]The stars will be falling from the heavens. The powers which are in the heavens will be shaken. [26]Then they will see the Son of Man coming in clouds, with much power and glory. [27]Then he will send angels. He will gather up the

chosen ones out of the four winds, from the farthest point on earth to the farthest reaches of heaven.

28 "Learn this parable, taken from a fig tree: When its branch becomes tender, and it puts forth leaves, you know that summer is near. [29]You also, when you see these things taking place, should know that he is at the door.

30 "I tell you solemnly that this generation will not have passed away before all these things have taken place. [31]Heaven and earth will pass away, but my words will not pass away.

32 "But as to the day or hour, no one knows, not even the angels in heaven, nor the Son, but only the Father. [33]Watch out! Stay awake!— because you do not know the crucial time. [34]It is just as when a man goes away on a journey, leaving his household, and assigning responsibilities to his servants, each having his own work to do: To the doorkeeper, he assigns the task of keeping watch. [35]Keep watch, then, because you do not know when the Lord of the household is coming, whether in the evening, or at midnight, or at dawn when the cock crows, or in the morning. [36]May he not come and find you sleeping.

37 "But what I say to you I say to everyone: Stay awake."

Commentary

Mark devotes this chapter entirely to Jesus' teachings about the destruction of Jerusalem, which would take place at the hands of the Romans in A.D. 70, and the end of the world—evidently an important pastoral concern of Peter, whose first epistle also emphasizes the end times: "The end of all things is at hand; therefore keep sane and sober for your prayers. Above all hold unfailing your love for one another, since love covers a multitude of sins." (4:7–8) And: "Beloved, do not be surprised at the fiery ordeal which comes upon you to prove you, as though something strange were happening to you. But rejoice in so far as you share Christ's sufferings, that you may also rejoice and be glad when his glory is revealed." (4:12–13) These verses show that, for Peter, a Christian who lives with an awareness that the end is near will be more fervent in charity and identify more closely with Christ.

This chapter, then, looks both backward and forward. It looks backward to Jesus' teaching about love of God and neighbor in the previous chapter, adding both urgency and a reinforcing motive. It looks forward to Jesus' rejection and betrayal in the next two chapters, making clear to Christian readers that what they see happening to the Christ is what they should expect to share in as his followers.

The chapter probably also includes Peter's personal reflections. We said that he viewed the betrayal and death of Christ as an incomprehensible reversal. What happens to the world after it rejects and expels its Creator, the Lord of life? There must be consequences. From now on, it must have built into it somehow a judgment of its own destruction.

Peter's own experience of abandoning and denying his friend must have led him to reflect also on the mystery of human freedom. As we have seen, Christ's parables allow room for human freedom, so the question arises how men will use that freedom. Will they turn toward God or against him? In this chapter, Jesus teaches that the human race, in its freedom, will harden its heart and turn against God. But once these teachings are stated, might they change from prophecies to warnings—at least for those who follow Jesus? This question would be of pastoral as well as personal interest for Peter.

Other pastoral questions arise from Peter's role as the chief representative of Christ among the apostles and governor of the Church. Many Jewish people were expecting the Messiah to usher in an earthly kingdom of dominion and glory. So the question would arise whether and in what way that expectation will be fulfilled.

As St. Augustine comments, Jesus tells his disciples about three things that are to come: "[1] the destruction of Jerusalem which occasioned their question, … [2] His own coming through the Church, (in which He ever comes even unto the end, for we know that He comes in His own, when His members are born day by day,) … [and 3] the end itself, in which He will appear to judge the quick and the dead."[1]

In sum, the chapter sets down the outlook on the world that the new Church would adopt. It was not simply that utopianism had to be rejected; the power of the prince of this world had to be recognized. We find in this chapter the same outlook that Peter emphasized at the conclusion of his first epistle (RSV 5:8–11):

> Be sober, be watchful. Your adversary the devil prowls around like a roaring lion, seeking someone to devour. Resist him, firm in your faith, knowing that the same experience of suffering is required of your brotherhood throughout the world. And after you have suffered a little while, the God of all grace, who has called you to his eternal glory in Christ, will himself restore, establish, and strengthen you. To him be the dominion for ever and ever. Amen.

1–2

1 as he is leaving the temple

The phrase signals the end of his tenure in the temple—his glorification and revelation as the authoritative teacher of the things of God. In Mark's account, he will not return to the temple, and his next two days will be filled with betrayal, suffering, and death by crucifixion.

---

1 Augustine, Epistle 199.9, quoted in Saint Thomas Aquinas, *Catena Aurea: Gospel of Mark*, trans. William Whiston (Grand Rapids, MI: Christian Classics Ethereal Library), p. 200.

one of his disciples says to him

Once again, the historical present shifts us quickly into this new scene.

It seems likely that Peter (and Mark) knew which disciple this was but declined to name him, perhaps to avoid embarrassing him but perhaps also because all the disciples shared such thoughts that day. Remember that the disciples would have been exulting in their teacher's complete victory over his opponents.

Mark was not a follower of Jesus in Galilee, but his mother had a house in Jerusalem, and he might have begun following him in this final week. If so, it is possible that the disciple quoted is Mark himself.

2 "Do you see these great buildings?"

The Lord does not deny their greatness—an acknowledgement of the objectivity, in the eyes of God, of differences in scale relative to human nature and human size.

"not a stone here that will be left"

This temple is passing: it will be replaced by a building of "human stones," the indestructible Church of God, built on a rock, against which the gates of Hell will not prevail. As Peter writes, "like living stones be yourselves built into a spiritual house, to be a holy priesthood, to offer spiritual sacrifices acceptable to God through Jesus Christ." (RSV 1 Peter 2:5)

3-4

3 when he had sat down

His sitting down indicates, again, that he is teaching authoritatively. They are looking at the temple from a distance, and also at the city of Jerusalem, which represents the community of God. "The Lord sits upon the mount of Olives, over against the temple, when He discourses upon the ruin and destruction of the temple, so that even His bodily position may be in accordance with the words which

He speaks, pointing out mystically that, abiding in peace with the saints, He hates the madness of the proud. For the mount of Olives marks the fruitful sublimity of the Holy Church."[2]

asked him privately

Peter is mentioned first, as always. That these four ask privately implies that the answer will be direct, not in parables.

4 "Tell us when these things will take place."

The first question is about ordering; the second is about how to infer from signs that the order is underway. Since they say "all these things," it seems that Jesus has referred to them before, or perhaps they interpret the destruction of the temple as the culmination of many other calamities. They may sense that the Lord's time on earth is coming to an end, and they think that this may be their last chance to get a definitive account. Since they are asking about the future, and only God knows the future, they are presupposing that Jesus is God.

5–8

6 "claiming 'I am.'"

The simplest way to interpret this statement is to assume that the word "Christ" is implicit—"Many men will come in my name claiming 'I am Christ.'" To come in his name and to claim to be the Christ are the same. But another way of interpreting the statement is to say that many will come calling themselves Christian (that is, in the name of Christ) and claiming divine warrant for their teaching, as if they invoked the name of God, "I am." Of these two interpretations, the latter seems most plausible since men claiming to be Christ have been rare, while false teachers calling themselves Christians and leading many astray have been plentiful.

---

2 Bede, quoted in *Catena Aurea*, p. 200.

8 "nation will rise up against nation"

It is not that armies will fight against armies, but whole nations will be mobilized against other whole nations.

"beginning of the birth pangs"

Birth pangs can be prolonged, and there can be false labor.

9–11

9 "You must watch out for yourselves."

Reliable authorities have always held that Christians should prudently avoid being persecuted if possible. Peter as pastor conveys that sensible prudence here.

"They will betray you to councils."

We can apply to these statements the principle of interpretation of St. Augustine: (1) this statement was true of the apostles themselves, as is evident in the Acts of the Apostles, (2) it has been true throughout the history of the Church, and presumably (3) it will be verified in a striking way at the end of the world.

10 "the good news should be proclaimed to all the nations"

That is, God in his providence will use such persecution to spread the good news.

11 "speak what is given to you"

Divinely granted simplicity rather than human craftiness will be most effective. If they try to craft what they are to say, their own motives will inevitably show through and potentially obscure the good news.

The Lord presumes that these betrayed and persecuted followers will be praying constantly. It is not that they are to be thoughtless.

12–13

12 "Brother will betray brother"

Hatred of the Gospel is so diabolical that it overrides even the deepest natural affections. The Lord expresses the point through examples of increasingly strong natural piety, the piety of children to parents being the strongest.

13 "You will be hated by everyone"

In the persecutions in the Roman Empire, Christians were called "enemies of the human race."

"who perseveres to the end"

There are three "ends" here, if we apply St. Augustine's principle of interpretation: (1) the end of the apostolic age, when the Church was being established; (2) the end of one's life, for any Christian at any time in the Church; and (3) the end of time, for those who undergo trials close to the end of the world.

14–20

14 "the Abomination of Desolation"

What is this? "When we are challenged to understand what is said, we may conclude that it is mystical. But it may either be said simply of Antichrist, or of the statue of Caesar, which Pilate put into the temple, or of the equestrian statue of Adrian, which for a long time stood in the holy of holies itself. An idol is also called an 'abomination' according to the Old Testament, and He has added 'of desolation' because it was placed in the temple when desolate and deserted."[3] "He means by 'the abomination of desolation' the entrance of enemies into the city by violence."[4]

Neither of these interpretations, which pertain to the impending destruction of Jerusalem, is exhaustive, because Mark appeals to

---

3 Bede, ibid., p. 203.
4 Theophylact, ibid., p. 203.

"you who are reading this," and he wrote it to endure over time. So following St. Augustine's threefold principle of interpretation, we should understand the warning about the "Abomination of Desolation" as also pertaining to the ongoing history of the Church and to the last days.

19 "a tribulation such as has not taken place"

Obviously, this phrase applies principally to the tribulations of the last days, for the destruction of Jerusalem by the Roman army was not the worst tribulation in the history of the world. The twentieth century has so far been the century of the greatest tribulations endured by humankind.

20 "he cut short those days"

What is spoken about takes place in the future, but it is phrased in the past, because the decision of the Lord to cut short those days is from eternity and has "already" been made. From his seat overlooking the temple and Jerusalem, Jesus sees the future as though it is past.

Modern scholars of the New Testament who rule out the possibility of prophecy assume that this chapter from the Gospel of Mark, with its accurate and detailed description of the destruction of Jerusalem, had to have been composed after the event. But if Mark wrote after A.D. 70 and wanted to depict Jesus as forecasting the city's destruction, it is unlikely that he would have been so clumsy as to put the prophetic words in the past tense here.

21–23

22 "false Christs will arise"

Here the subject of the Lord's predictions seems to shift. No longer is he talking primarily about apostolic times and secondarily about the centuries that would follow. Now he is talking primarily about the end times. The Fathers interpret this passage in particular as foretelling the Antichrist.

"They will give signs and work wonders"

Jesus noticeably does not use the word *dunameis* ("works of power"), which as we have seen, Mark prefers for denoting the miracles of the Lord. That is to say, these "signs and wonders" will not be miracles, and they may not even look like miracles: consider the "wonders" of modern science and technology.

Newman writes in his treatise on the Antichrist, "that by Antichrist is meant some one person, is made probable by the anticipations which, as I have said, have already occurred in history, of the fulfilment of the prophecy. Individual men have arisen actually answering in a great measure to [the Lord's] descriptions; and this circumstance creates a probability, that the absolute and entire fulfilment which is to come will be in an individual also."[5]

23 "I have told you everything in advance."

That is, everything important and necessary. Other particular details might be held to have been revealed by Mary in some of her apparitions and by private revelations to some saints.

24–27

25 "stars will be falling from the heavens"

The stars are not lamps in the vault of the sky, as was commonly believed in ancient times, and so they cannot fall from the heavens. As if to recognize this, the Lord literally says, "the stars will be stars-falling-from-heaven," suggesting that they will look *as if* they are falling.

---

5 John Henry Newman, *Discussions and Arguments on Various Subjects* (London: Longmans and Green, 1899), p. 53.

"powers which are in the heavens will be shaken"

In the light of modern cosmology, we are likely to see in this prediction some visible change in the basic laws governing the universe. We might speculate that cosmological phenomena such as anti-matter, dark matter, and dark energy, which we know almost nothing about, could cause the sudden annihilation of the universe. The Fathers, in contrast, take these powers to be angels.

28–30

28 "Learn this parable"

The end of the world has already been likened to childbirth. Here it is likened to the rejuvenation of a fig tree in springtime, leading to its full growth in the summer. Both processes are natural rather than mechanical and unfold according to their own internal principles. Unless there is interference from the outside, the process can be slowed but will not be stopped.

30 "this generation will not have passed away"

Again, this statement should be understood as holding for all three interpretations of the word "generation." Jesus' words (1) were fulfilled in the generation living then, (2) have been fulfilled in the "generation" of Christians throughout history, and (3) will be fulfilled in the "generation" that is the human race in the end times.

32–37

32 "nor the Son, but only the Father"

By "only the Father knows," the Fathers understand "only the Father knows so as to share this knowledge, which he has done with the Son," whereas "no one knows...nor the Son" means "the Son knows but not so as to share it with anyone." St. Hilary comments, "[L]et common sense decide whether it is credible that He, who is the cause that all things are, and are to be, should be ignorant of any out of all these things."[6] The statement, then, is a discreet way by which the Lord tells his disciples that it is hopeless for them to try to acquire from him any direct, particular knowledge of the day. The necessary attitude is that of watchfulness.

33 "you do not know the crucial time"

Nor will you ever be able to find it out. It is forever outside your knowledge, until it is too late to plan for it, when it is upon you already.

34 "each having his own work to do"

A beautiful image, which means three things, depending on how we interpret the parable. If we take the different types of servants to be Christians with different roles, it means that the bishops, as successors of the apostles, are the "doorkeepers," with the primary responsibility for keeping watch in the Church. If we take the different types of servants to be different members of the human race, then the "doorkeepers" are Christians, who, among humanity, have the task of keeping watch for the Lord. If the different servants represent the different virtues of a Christian, the "doorkeeper" stands for the virtue of prudence, which encompasses detachment, sobriety, expectation, and hope.

37 "Stay awake"

The closing paragraph from Newman's treatise on the Antichrist offers a compelling gloss on these words:

> Such meditations as these may be turned to good account.
> It will act as a curb upon our self-willed, selfish hearts, to
> believe that a persecution is in store for the Church, whether
> or not it comes in our days. Surely, with this prospect before
> us, we cannot bear to give ourselves up to thoughts of ease

---

6 St. Hilary, quoted in *Catena Aurea*, pp. 210–211.

and comfort, of making money, settling well, or rising in the world. Surely, with this prospect before us, we cannot but feel that we are, what all Christians really are in the best estate (nay, rather would wish to be, had they their will, if they be Christians in heart), pilgrims, watchers waiting for the morning, waiting for the light, eagerly straining our eyes for the first dawn of day—looking out for our Lord's coming, His glorious advent, when He will end the reign of sin and wickedness, accomplish the number of His elect, and perfect those who at present struggle with infirmity, yet in their hearts love and obey Him.[7]

7 John Henry Newman, *Discussions and Arguments on Various Subjects* (London: Longmans, Green and Co., 1891), p. 106.

CHAPTER 14

1 In two days it was the Passover and festival of Unleavened Bread. The chief priests and the scribes were looking for a way to capture him and put him to death by stealth, ²as they were saying, "Not during the festival, or else there will be a riot among the people."

3 When he was in Bethany, at the house of Simon the leper, while he was reclining at table, a woman came with an alabaster flask of very expensive genuine myrrh nard. Breaking the flask, she poured it on his head. ⁴Some were expressing among themselves their irritation over this: "What is the point of this waste of myrrh? ⁵This myrrh could have been sold for more than thirty denarii and given to the poor." They were incensed at her. ⁶But Jesus said, "Leave her alone. Why are you giving her trouble? She has done an admirable service for me. ⁷You have the poor with you always, after all. Whenever you wish, you can do good for them. But you do not always have me. ⁸What was open for her to do, she did: she has taken care to anoint my body in advance for its burial. ⁹I give you my assurance that, wherever the Gospel is proclaimed, anywhere in the world, what this woman has done will also be recounted, as a testament to her."

10 So Judas Iscariot, one of the Twelve, departed to go to the chief priests, to betray him. ¹¹When they learned of this, they were delighted. They agreed to give him a payment in silver. He in turn began to look for how he might betray him at an opportune time.

12 On the first day of the festival of Unleavened Bread, the time when they would sacrifice the paschal lamb, his disciples say to him, "Where do you want us to go and make preparations for you to eat the Passover meal?" ¹³So he sends two of his disciples on a task. He tells them, "Go into the city. A man will chance upon you who is carrying a pitcher of water. Follow him. ¹⁴In the place that he enters, tell the chief steward there, 'The teacher says, "Where is the apartment where I may eat the Passover meal with my disciples?"' ¹⁵He will show you a large room on an upper floor, furnished and ready. There make preparations for us." ¹⁶So the disciples left. They went into the city. They found everything just as he had told them. They made preparations for the Passover meal.

17 So when it is evening, he arrives with the Twelve. ¹⁸When they were reclining at table and eating, Jesus said, "I tell you solemnly that one of you eating with me will betray me." ¹⁹They were pained and began to say to him, one by one, "It is not I?" ²⁰But he said to them, "One of the Twelve—someone who dips his bread in the bowl with me. ²¹The Son of Man goes just as it is written of him. But woe to that man by whom the Son of Man is betrayed. It would have been better for that man if he hadn't been born."

22 When they were at supper, taking bread, after saying a blessing, he broke it. He gave it to them. He told them, "Take. This is my body." ²³Then, taking a cup and giving thanks, he gave it to them. Everyone drank from it. ²⁴He said to them, "This is my blood, of the covenant, which is poured out for many. ²⁵I tell you with assurance that I will drink no longer from the fruit of the vine, until that day when I drink it new in the kingdom of God."

26 After singing a hymn, they went outside, to the Mount of Olives. [27]Jesus said, "All of you will find me offensive and abandon me, as it is written, 'I will strike the shepherd, and the sheep will be scattered.' [28]But after I have risen, I will go before you to Galilee." [29]But Peter said to him, "Even if everyone takes offense and abandons you, I nevertheless will not." [30]So Jesus says to him, "I tell you with assurance that today, this very night, before a cock crows twice, you will deny me three times." [31]But he insisted all the more, "Even if I have to die along with you, I will not deny you." But everyone spoke in this way.

32 So they go to the area which has the name Gethsemane. He says to his disciples, "Have a seat here while I pray." [33]He takes along with him Peter, James, and John. Then he began to be bewildered and in deep distress. [34]So he tells them, "My soul is beset with sorrow to the point of death. Stay here and keep watch." [35]Going a bit farther he fell to the ground. He prayed that if it were possible, the hour would pass from him. [36]He said, in fact, "Abba, Father! All things are possible for you. Take this cup away from me. But not what I will, but what you will." [37]So he comes and finds them sleeping. He says to Peter, "Simon, do you sleep? Do you lack strength to keep watch for one hour? [38]Keep watch and pray, that you may not enter into temptation. The spirit is eager, but the flesh is weak." [39]Again he left them and prayed, saying the same thing. [40]Again coming to them he found them sleeping, as their eyes were heavy. They did not know what to say to him in reply. [41]So he comes back a third time and says to them, "Still sleeping and taking your rest? It is enough. The hour has come. Look, the Son of Man is betrayed into the hands of sinful men. [42]Get up! Let's go! Look, the man who is betraying me is near."

43 And right then, while he was still speaking, Judas shows up, one of the Twelve, and with him a crowd with swords and clubs, along with the chief priests and scribes and elders. [44]The man betraying him had proposed a sign to them and said, "The one that I shall kiss is he.

Capture him and lead him away securely." ⁴⁵So when he arrives, he straightway comes up to him and says, "Rabbi!" He kissed him! ⁴⁶They placed their hands on him and took him into custody. ⁴⁷(One man, among those standing there, drawing his sword, struck the servant of the chief priest and cut off his ear.) ⁴⁸To which Jesus said: "So you come out to capture me with swords and clubs, as if I were a thief? ⁴⁹I was with you day after day, teaching in the temple, and you did not capture me. But so that the scriptures may be fulfilled...." ⁵⁰And they abandoned him and fled—all of them. ⁵¹(A certain young man was one of his followers. He had clothed himself with a fine linen garment wrapped around his naked body. So they capture him. ⁵²But he just left his garment behind and got away, naked!) ⁵³They led Jesus away to see the chief priest.

So all the chief priests and the elders and scribes assemble in a meeting. ⁵⁴Peter followed him from a distance, as far as going into the courtyard of the chief priest. He was sitting with the officers and warming himself by the fire. ⁵⁵The chief priests and the whole council were looking for testimony against Jesus sufficient to put him to death. They could not find any. ⁵⁶Many men were giving false testimony against him. Their testimonies did not agree. ⁵⁷So certain men stood up and gave false testimony against him saying, ⁵⁸"We heard him say, 'I will destroy this temple made with hands, and in three days I will build another temple, not made with hands.'" ⁵⁹And yet their testimony was not even consistent as to this. ⁶⁰So the chief priest got up in the center and posed a question to Jesus, "You say nothing in reply? Consider the charges these men are making against you." ⁶¹But he kept silent. He did not say anything in response. So again the chief priest posed a question to him. He says to him, "Are you are the Christ, the Son of the Blessed One?" ⁶²To which Jesus said: "I am. You will see the Son of Man seated at the right hand of Power and coming with the clouds of heaven." ⁶³So the chief priest tears his garments and says,

"Why do we still need witnesses? ⁶⁴You have heard the blasphemy. How does it look to you?" At which the whole of them judged him as worthy of death. ⁶⁵Some even began to spit on him. They covered his face, they struck him, and they said to him, "Prophesy!" The officers hit him repeatedly on the face as they took him into custody.

66 So while Peter is below in the courtyard, one of the servant girls of the chief priest comes up. ⁶⁷Seeing Peter warming himself, she looked right at him and then says, "You too were with Jesus the Nazarene." ⁶⁸But he denied it and says, "I neither know nor even understand what you are saying." So he left to go outside the courtyard, to the anteroom. Then a cock crowed. ⁶⁹So the servant girl, watching him, started saying again to men standing there, "This man is one of them." ⁷⁰But he denied it again. So, after a little while, again, the men standing there said to Peter, "You are definitely one of them. You are a Galilean. You speak like a Galilean." ⁷¹He began to curse and swear, "I do not know this man you are talking about." ⁷²Right then and there, a cock crowed for a second time. Peter remembered the statement Jesus had spoken to him, "Before a cock crows twice, you will deny me three times." And he broke down crying.

Commentary

This chapter, like chapter 12, is devoted to a single day, the day before his passion, when he is betrayed, abandoned, rejected by the priests and scribes, and beaten. We can feel Peter's amazement that these events unfolded as they did and so quickly.

1–2

1 the Passover and festival of Unleavened Bread
The Passover meal had been celebrated for more than a thousand years since the Exodus in the time of Moses. God had commanded

each Israelite household to sacrifice a lamb and share it as a meal to mark their protection from the final plague against the Egyptians and their delivery from bondage. The blood of a lamb sprinkled on their lintels protected the Israelites—but why? Indeed, why should there be a sacrifice of a lamb at all? Did their slavery and deliverance stand for something else? On this Passover, the meaning of that tradition is going to be revealed.

a way to capture him and put him to death by stealth

They wanted Jesus to disappear so that the crowd would not know what had happened to him. But the disciples, they thought, would hardly cause them problems.

3–9

3 When he was in Bethany

Bethany is for Jesus a village of friendship, repose, and refreshment. He would stay there at the house of his friends Lazarus, Mary, and Martha, who took care of his needs.

Simon the leper

Perhaps he is the leper by the wayside who was healed and who followed Jesus. If so, he might continue to be called "the leper" in commemoration of his healing—a leper but for the grace of Christ.

a woman came

Her name was known, but Mark omits it, even though the event is recounted "as a testament to her" (verse 9). Why? Her name is irrelevant—because she is alive now, she exists now, and what she did is credited to her, regardless of whether you or I can identify her, which is mere fame.

This woman, or someone she knew, had procured the myrrh at great expense—and at some risk as well, for she might have been turned away from the house where Jesus was a guest. Despite the human uncertainty, she had faith, perhaps acting on an intimation or inspiration that she received in prayer. Her unusual gesture might expose her to ridicule, for it was completely novel and creative, and her timing had to be just right, when the Lord nearby and at rest. Finally, she showed remarkable courage, boldly intruding on this assemblage of men, who could be expected to rebuff a lowly woman.

very expensive genuine myrrh nard

Peter piles on the descriptive words in the manner of a simple man who rarely sees such fine things.

Breaking the flask, she poured it on his head.

A woman would first use this fine myrrh to perfume her hair, and she deals with Jesus as she would with herself. Tellingly, she is not said to "anoint" his head. She poured it out liberally, and he received it fully.

4 Some were expressing among themselves their irritation over this

They speak loudly enough to be overheard. They might have been opposed to the woman's even coming into the meal, and when she starts pouring out expensive myrrh, their original judgment seems to be confirmed. The woman's entrance and actions no doubt made everyone feel awkward. They could have kept silent. But they were hardly discreet: they introduce contentiousness into an already delicate situation, not caring if they embarrass her.

4–5 "What is the point of this waste of myrrh? This myrrh could have been sold for more than thirty denarii and given to the poor."

Mark captures the spirit of their grumbling with the emphatic language "this waste" and "this myrrh."

Something can be wasted only if it has a proper use. If the dinner guests want to accuse her of wasting the myrrh, then they have to be prepared to say what such expensive myrrh is good for. And what is that?

They were incensed at her.

Mark wants to emphasize the overbearing manner of these men who supposed they had a right to govern her because she was a woman. Hence the Lord rebukes them doubly:

6 "Leave her alone. Why are you giving her trouble? She has done an admirable service for me."

But the Lord goes on to give a patient threefold defense of the woman, tailored to her critics. First, he explains that the myrrh was not "wasted," since anointing a body for burial is a proper use. Second, he sets down a principle for deeds done out of love— namely, it is enough "to do what is open to us to do." When the object of our deed is holy—and above all when it is the body of Christ—a certain extravagant adornment and precious treatment are fitting. Finally, he explains why the woman was without fault: she seized her opportunity to show her love for God, and it was a passing opportunity. After the Lord's death and burial, the poor would still be there to help.

9 "what this woman has done will also be recounted, as a testament to her."

The fact that we are reading this passage now is evidence that Jesus insured that her act would be remembered. But why? Because of his gratitude for its nobility and greatness. And yet we remember this woman because her deed was recorded in Peter's memoirs and presumably made normative in the preaching of the early Church. The Church's remembrance of this woman did not arise spontaneously. Peter heard the Lord say that she would be remembered, and he deliberately took steps to see that she would be remembered.

10–11

10 So Judas Iscariot, one of the Twelve, departed

From another Gospel (Jn. 12:6), we know that Judas was one of the woman's critics and that he was incensed because he was a hypocrite: he stole from the common fund for his own purposes and would have liked to use the money himself. But Mark omits these details. Perhaps he does not want to suggest that this temporary dispute was the reason Judas betrayed Jesus, or even that it was in some way understandable that Judas betrayed Jesus.

People feel compelled to explain Judas' betrayal. Some think he intended to force Jesus' hand in establishing his earthly kingdom. Some think he was afraid that Jesus would provoke a Roman reprisal. Some think that when Judas grasped that Jesus was claiming to be God, he thought he should be tested or punished with death. And others think that Judas, knowing that Jesus was aware of his sinfulness, was moved by guilt to eliminate him. But it is striking that Mark offers no theory at all of Judas' motivation, as if Peter regarded Judas' actions as evil because they had no reason.

11 When they learned of this

They had no prior expectation. Judas played into their hands.

They agreed to give him a payment in silver.

In another Gospel (Mt. 26:15), we are told that it was thirty pieces of silver, which fulfilled a prophecy from the prophets. Peter and Mark must know this but decline to give that detail, perhaps because it might be confusing, given the thirty denarii just mentioned.

12–16

12 the time when they would sacrifice the paschal lamb

Mark's circumlocution to describe the feast emphasizes that the occurrence of the Lord's sacrifice during that festival was the result of providence, not a human plan. Judas didn't "have to" betray him then, or at all, and the plotting of the chief priests and scribes was indeterminate. It surely caught Peter by surprise when everything came together as it did at that time.

"for you to eat the Passover meal"

Not "for *us* to eat the Passover meal." The disciples view themselves as, so to speak, witnesses of the Lord's actions, not as equals. They are even prone to see him as priestly in offering the lamb.

13 So he sends two of his disciples

His practice is to send his disciples two by two for safety, for support, for encouragement, and for the good of friendship. Luke tells us that these disciples were Peter and John. Peter and Mark knew that detail but omitted it—why? Presumably, Peter does not want to draw attention to himself here.

"A man will chance upon you who is carrying a pitcher of water."

There was no prior agreement. If there were, Jesus would have to tell the disciples where and when to meet this man. This statement is another proof of Our Lord's divinity, since only God knows the future. It is also proof that he could have avoided his coming passion if he had willed. As God, he has power over men's acts even when they act freely!

14 "In the place that he enters, tell the chief steward there..."

Disciples are sent who encounter a man who leads them to a steward who points to a room. The intricate arrangements show that this meal transcended ordinary meals and human conventions. It could not be covered by, contained within, or underwritten by any human authority, choice, or tradition. It was a manifestation of the priesthood of Melchizedek, without lineage.

17–21

17 he arrives with the Twelve

Not "arrives with the ten," so Peter and John made the preparations and returned.

18 reclining at table and eating

The Passover meal was supposed to be eaten standing (Exod. 12:11). Theophylact comments: "It is probable that they had first fulfilled the legal Passover, and had reclined, when He began to give them His own Passover."[1]

"I tell you solemnly that one of you eating with me will betray me."

Let us suppose that these words did not necessitate that Judas betray him and that he continued to have freedom. Then what was the purpose of this statement? It was a warning. "The Lord who had foretold His Passion, prophesied also of the traitor, in order to give him room for repentance, that understanding that his thoughts were known, he might repent."[2] It is a mystery: Jesus knew that Judas would betray him, and yet he earnestly appealed to Judas' freedom to repent.

19 They were pained and began to say to him, one by one, "It is not I?"

Each of the Twelve besides Judas was aware that he had no purpose or plans to betray Jesus, but he was also aware that he had freedom and that he was weak, and he believed that Jesus did know the future.

They were pained

Not "each was pained." They were pained not simply individually but also sympathetically and corporately.

one by one

Judas, we may suppose, spoke first, deliberately, as a subterfuge. Then one or two others said it spontaneously, and the thought occurred to each, "I believe it is not I, but he is God, and I may lack knowledge about myself," and they began to go around in a circle, deliberately, almost as a ritual.

21 "The Son of Man goes just as it is written of him."

What does it mean that he "goes"—not "is taken"? The verb Jesus chooses indicates that his death "was not forced, but voluntary," says Theophylact.[3]

---

1 Theophylact, qouted in Saint Thomas Aquinas, *Catena Aurea: Gospel of Mark*, trans. William Whiston (Grand Rapids, MI: Christian Classics Ethereal Library), p. 221.
2 Bede, ibid., pp. 220–221.
3 Theopahylact, ibid., p. 221.

"It would have been better for that man if he hadn't been born."

The phrase "hadn't been born" could mean either "hadn't come to be" or "had come to be in his mother's womb, but died before birth." The Fathers almost uniformly take it in the first sense, as meaning it would be better not to exist at all than to exist as an evil man. They did not understand Jesus to be saying that not existing is better than being damned to hell. They think that doing evil is bad enough, and hell does not need to be brought in to validate the comparison.

22–25

The ritual that Jesus initiates must have come at the end of the meal because the next thing Mark mentions is their departure. The ritual has two parts. In each part there is a taking, a blessing, a giving, an affirmation, and a consumption:

Taking bread	Taking a cup
Saying a blessing	Giving thanks
He gave it to them.	He gave it to them.
"Take. This is my body."	"This is my blood."
[They eat the bread.]	Everyone drank from it.

"Saying a blessing" and "giving thanks" probably refer to the traditional Jewish blessings said over bread and over wine:

> *Blessed are You, Lord our God, King of the Universe, Who brings forth bread from the earth.*
> *Blessed are You, Lord our God, King of the Universe, Who creates the fruit of the vine.*

That the bread and the wine are first "taken" by the Lord and then given to his disciples shows that this is not an exercise in conviviality but a ritual carried out by the Lord for them. The disciples' obedience to his command to take and eat is essential to it.

The words "Do this in remembrance of me" are not found here or in Matthew's account but only in Luke (22:19) and in First Corinthians (11:24). But the Lord does say that the blood "is" poured out for many (not "will be poured out"), as if timelessly. A ritual, by definition, is to be repeated, and this ritual, moreover, takes place within the Passover meal, which was repeated. It would be misleading to place something that was intended to be singular in the context of a repeated ritual.

22 "This is my body."

Not "This stands for my body" or "This is like my body" or "This means my body." The Lord does not utter these words in the context of a parable. Mark does not use the word "parable" to explain them or in any way indicate that they were a parable. The teller of a parable uses the word "is" only to explain the parable, not to present the parable itself. If anything, Jesus at the Last Supper provides the interpretation of the Cross understood as a parable, but it is an interpretation which gives an instance, not a sign. That is to say, the last supper is a participation prospectively in the sacrifice of the Cross, just as the Mass is today retrospectively. It's as if a child hears the president announce a tax cut and asks his father what that means. The father pulls out his wallet and, knowing that he will have extra money, gives the child five dollars and says, "This is what it means." He is showing the child the meaning by giving him an instance of it.

23 Everyone drank from it.

The cup represents a sharing or commitment, as the Lord had already indicated, and here Peter emphasizes that *everyone* shared in the commitment. Looking back as he tells the story to Mark, he sees here a pledge that the faithful apostles, *without exception*, would suffer a passion similar to Our Lord's.

The word "everyone" raises the question whether Judas was still present, but the Gospels do not say with certainty. St. John

Chrysostom, who believes that the Lord was attempting to provoke Judas to repentance, says that "Christ offered His Blood to him who betrayed Him, that he might have remission of his sins, if he had chosen to cease to be wicked."[4]

24 "This is my blood."

Not "This represents my blood" or "This is like my blood." Jesus uses the same form of words in the consecration of both the bread and the wine, indicating that the form of words matters. Otherwise, he would have altered the form to indicate that the meaning, not the form, was important.

The word translated as "covenant" means literally a disposition of goods, a testament, as in "last will and testament." The Lord, who is about to die, is transferring certain goods to others as an inheritance.

"poured out for many"

Not "for all." And yet, if Judas was there among those for whom Christ's blood was poured out, it must have been poured out for everyone! "Many" suggests that, although the gift is for everyone, we are free not to accept it.

25 "I will drink no longer from the fruit of the vine"

Calling wine "fruit of the vine," Jesus refers back to the prayer of blessing with which the meal began while avoiding a reference to the cup that was just passed to his disciples, which is now his blood.

"until that day when I drink it new in the kingdom of God"

"Drink it new" means "in a new and strange manner, for He had not a body subject to suffering, and requiring food, but immortal and incorruptible."[5] When Peter eats and drinks with Jesus after the resurrection, he recalls this strange turn of phrase from the Last Supper.

---

4 Chrysostom, ibid., p. 224.
5 Theophylact, ibid., p. 224.

26–31

27 "as it is written, 'I will strike the shepherd, and the sheep will be scattered.'"

These words are from Zechariah 13:7, where both the Hebrew and Septuagint put them on the lips of God and in the imperative—"Strike the shepherd, that the sheep may be scattered." Jesus converts this statement to the first person future and treats it as prophecy about himself. Pseudo-Jerome, noticing the change, comments: "For the Prophet prays for the Passion of the Lord, and the Father answers, *I will smite the shepherd*, according to the prayers of those below. The Son is sent and smitten by the Father, that is, He is made incarnate and suffers."[6]

29 "Even if everyone takes offense and abandons you, I nevertheless will not."

What Peter says is, strictly speaking, a contradiction, as he is included among the "everyone"; he does not say "everyone else." Peter recognizes that Our Lord knows the future, but he astutely sees that he has freedom nevertheless. In that freedom he affirms his fidelity.

30 "today, this very night, before a cock crows twice, you will deny me three times"

Understand this as said matter-of-factly, not expressing disappointment. These words are not a warning.

"today, this very night"

That is, right at the start of the day, as the Jewish day began at dusk.

There is no contradiction here with the other Gospel writers' accounts of Jesus words, "Before a cock crows, you will deny me three times" (Mt. 26:34, Jn. 13:38). The three denials occurred prior to the crowing of a cock, and that crowing, as Mark adds, was the second crowing, in the course of the denials, of that particular cock.

---

6 Jerome, ibid., p. 226.

We might ask why Mark, whose narrative is usually simple and clear, adds this complicating detail that the other evangelists omit. An answer suggests itself if we recall that this passage involves Peter personally, who, we have seen, emphasizes his own foibles. His threefold denial of the Lord is bad enough, but in the account he has given to Mark, it is even worse, since the first crowing of the cock should have been a warning to him.

31 "Even if I have to die along with you"

This emphatic assertion shows that Peter has been pondering the Lord's predictions of his coming death. He no longer has to be rebuked ("Get behind me, Satan") but now leads the way. Because of his example, "everyone spoke in the same way."

For the rest of the Gospel, Mark makes frequent use of the historical present to lend a "real-time" character to this narrative and to jar us into realizing that this really did happen.

32–42

Keep in mind that the Passover begins on a full moon, so although it was night, the disciples would be able to see the Lord by moonlight.

33 He takes along with him Peter, James, and John.

The same apostles who were invited to witness the revelation of his divine glory on the mount of the Transfiguration are invited to witness the wrenching proof of his humanity in his suffering on the mount of Gethsemane.

Then he began to be bewildered and in deep distress.

The word rendered "bewildered" can also mean *astonished, amazed, aghast, overcome*. Although the word does not imply that Our Lord lost his reason or control over his actions, it does suggest an unbalance, a staggering, a severe oppression, even a kind of panic.

34 "My soul is beset with sorrow to the point of death."

St. Thomas Aquinas appeals to this verse as proof that the Lord had a human soul, since he not only refers to his soul but is beset with sorrow that is characteristically human. See Psalm 54: 2–6.

This verse is also cited as proof that someone can be virtuous and yet overcome with sorrow. As St. Thomas More writes, "Whereby it appeareth that to fear death and torment is none offence, but a great and grievous pain, which Christ came not to avoid but patiently to suffer."

But is "to the point of death" a figure of speech or literally true? People are said to die of heartbreak or to lose the will to live; sorrow can so weaken them that sickness gets a foothold and progresses rapidly. But could a healthy man in his prime just give up his life from an extreme of sorrow? Or was it that his sorrow was close to causing something like a heart attack or a stroke?

"Stay here and keep watch."

If the disciples had succeeded in keeping watch, would they have been given the grace to follow through with their resolution to die with him if necessary? Verse 38 seems to imply so. But Jesus asks them to keep watch for his sake also, showing that a man who is suffering is weak and needs to be supported by the solidarity of others.

35 Going a bit farther he fell to the ground.

He taught his disciples to pray in secret, and therefore he went to be on his own. Yet he wanted them to know what his prayer was like at this moment of his passion. Therefore, he goes no farther away than a voice carries in the still of the night.

35–36 He prayed that if it were possible, the hour would pass from him. He said, in fact, "Abba, Father! All things are possible for you. Take this cup away from me. But not what I will, but what you will."

Mark first summarizes the prayer then gives four sentences that the Lord actually uttered in that prayer. This is the only time that

Mark provides both his own summary of events and a direct quotation of Jesus, which is how someone would describe something he heard from a distance, getting a general sense of what was said while being able to repeat with precision only a few statements. These verses have exactly the character we would expect to find in an account that someone (Peter) was giving from memory.

if it were possible

St. Augustine points out that this means not "if it is in your power," because it clearly is, but rather "if it is what you might will."

"Abba, Father!"

"Abba" is simply Aramaic for "father." Did the Lord say only "Abba," and Mark gives the translation as well, or did he call upon the Father both in Aramaic and in Greek? Against the former, we should observe that, in earlier instances in Mark's Gospel, when Mark gives a translation of an Aramaic word or phrase, he introduces it with the words "which is to say" or "which means," but these words are absent here. St. Augustine therefore favors the latter. He suspects that both words were used, bringing together in the manner of a sacrament (that is, words or deeds which do what they signify) the two peoples that originally constituted the Church, the Jews and the Gentiles: "And perhaps," he writes, "the Lord said both words, on account of some sacrament contained in them; wishing to shew that He had taken upon Himself that sorrow in the person of His body, the Church, to which He was made the chief corner stone, and which came to Him, partly from the Hebrews, who are represented by the word *Abba*, partly from the Gentiles, to whom *Father* belongs."[7]

---

7 Augustine, ibid., p. 229.

"But not what I will, but what you will."

This prayer implies the presence here of three distinct wills: one will of the Father and two wills of Christ, that is, what he wills considered on its own, and what he wills because the Father wills it. The two wills of Christ are not different wills at different times, as though he underwent a change, becoming convinced, or convincing himself, that he should now want something that previously he did not want. Rather, they are two "wills" within human nature—one by which a man wishes to avoid anything harmful to the body, as he is viscerally repulsed by it, and one by which he wills what rationally appears good. As St. Augustine writes, "When Christ says 'Not what I will, but what Thou wilt' He shows Himself to have willed something else than did His Father; and this could only have been by His human heart, since He did not transfigure our weakness into His Divine but into His human will."[8]

37 "Do you lack strength to keep watch for one hour?"

He speaks primarily to Peter, the one who said he would die with Jesus if necessary.

The Lord gives the length of time, "one hour," to reassure them, because those who fall asleep have no idea how much time has passed.

38 "The spirit is eager, but the flesh is weak."

The word rendered "eager" is *prothumon* in Greek—spiritedness, zeal, enthusiasm, energy. Using that word, Jesus appeals to characteristic strengths of Peter. The word rendered "flesh" is *sarx*, which means the body as enlivened by vegetative and animal functions. Writing against Apollinarius, St. Athanasius understands the contrast here to

---

8 *Contra Maxim.*, ii., 20, quoted by St. Thomas Aquinas in his acute discussion of this question, *Summa theologiae*, III.18.5c.

be exactly the same as the two "wills" in Christ, sensual and rational. If that is correct, then Christ is exhorting Peter to conform his sensual to his rational will, just as Christ did and illustrated in his own prayer.

41–42 "Still sleeping and taking your rest? It is enough. The hour has come. Look, the Son of Man is betrayed into the hands of sinful men. Get up! Let's go! Look, the man who is betraying me is near."

This is one of Mark's longest quotations of Jesus outside his accounts of Christ's preaching. Jesus has just roused Peter from sleep. Things we hear before we are fully awake remain present in our consciousness for a long time, and we can usually remember them vividly. When Peter recounted this story to Mark, he could again hear the Lord waking him up with these words.

43–53

43 And right then, while he was still speaking, Judas shows up, one of the Twelve, and with him a crowd with swords and clubs, along with the chief priests and scribes and elders.

This sentence seems to be a continuation of the previous sentence, a vivid memory of a disorienting moment—Peter woken by Jesus just as Judas and a jumble of people appear—reported just as it was experienced.

one of the Twelve

Mark's readers already know that Judas is one of the Twelve, so why does he include this detail? Because when Judas and his companions arrive at Gethsemane, there is a division between the followers of Christ (including, it appears from verse 51 below, some who are not apostles) and his enemies. In those circumstances, it would be natural to identify the betrayer by the striking feature of having been numbered among the Twelve. The detail, then, reflects the phenomenology of Peter's memory: when he sees Judas among the crowd of enemies, he still sees him as one of the Twelve.

44 The man betraying him

Mark has written verses 44–51 such that only one person's name is mentioned, Jesus, and that is right in the middle, at verse 48. None of the others—"the man betraying him;" "one man among those standing there;" "the servant of the chief priest;" "a certain young man"—is identified by name, although their names were known. Now that "the hour has come," Mark thus focuses our attention on Jesus.

46 They placed their hands on him and took him into custody.

Mark emphasizes that "they placed their hands on him," a violation of the command of Psalm 105:15, "Do not touch my Christ!"

51 A certain young man

It seems that this young man is Mark himself. It is a detail too small to include otherwise, and it seems unlikely that anyone else would have noticed it in the darkness and confusion. The telling of the incident has a humorous tone of self-congratulation, which is difficult to account for if it is about someone other than Mark.

a fine linen garment

Sindon in Greek, a fine linen or muslin cloth, long and broad enough to wrap around oneself, worn usually in the summer, the way we might use a light robe, or worn to sleep in. The shroud in which the body of the Lord was wrapped was a *sindon*.

52 But he just left his garment behind and got away, naked!

This detail is humorous, and if written by Mark, self-depreciating. Jesus likewise escaped "capture" by death, leaving his *sindon* behind in the tomb and "getting away" naked.

53-65

In the remainder of the chapter, Mark writes almost nothing in the historic present, conveying a sense that these events took place secretly, out of common view. Except for Peter's denial, they are not directly witnessed by Peter.

54 Peter followed him from a distance, as far as going into the courtyard of the chief priest.

This sentence depicts Peter as a mix of fearfulness and boldness. Bede speculates that he kept his distance because "he could not have denied Christ, if he had remained close to Him."[9]

58 "'I will destroy this temple'"

According to John (2:19), Jesus had actually said, "Destroy this temple, and in three days I will raise it up." If so, then his actual statement differed from this testimony in two ways. First, he did not say that he himself would destroy anything. Second, he referred not to a project of construction ("I will build") but of resurrection ("I will raise up").

61 "Are you are the Christ, the Son of the Blessed One?"

Here Mark uses the historical present to jar us into seeing that this is the crucial moment. The chief priest poses this question—with an oath, as Matthew adds (26:63)—in the setting of an authoritative council about his identity as Messiah, which merits an answer.

62 "I am."

The chief priest makes a statement in the form of a question, "You are...?" and Jesus correspondingly affirms that statement, "I am...." But in saying this, Jesus invokes the name of God, (YHWH = "I am"), asserting that he is divine, the Son of God as well as the Son of Man and Messiah.

63 So the chief priest tears his garments

---

9 Bede, quoted in *Catena Aurea*, p. 234.

Leo the Great says that by tearing his garments, Caiaphas disqualified himself as priest: "But Caiaphas, to increase the odiousness of what they had heard, *rent his clothes*, and without knowing what his frantic action meant, by his madness deprived himself of the honour of the priesthood, forgetting that command, by which it is said of the High Priest, *He shall not uncover his head or rend his clothes* [Lev. 21:10]."[10] On this theory, the chief priest's finding of blasphemy and the agreement of the council are deprived of any legal basis.

"Why do we still need witnesses?"

A telling question. They were looking for witnesses to get a result, not to get at the truth. Under no circumstances would any statement by or about Our Lord, related to any possible claim of his to be the Messiah, be entertained as anything other than grounds for putting him to death.

64 At which the whole of them judged him as worthy of death.

Making it clear that it was a corporate decision, Mark leaves open the possibility that some did not agree and abstained from voting. (See Lk. 23:51.)

65 Some even began to spit on him.

To be spat upon, mocked, and slapped was regarded as highly shameful. If that happened to your friend, you might try to protect his reputation by keeping these things secret. So it is extraordinary that these details are included at all.

66–72

66 one of the servant girls of the chief priest comes up

John tells us that she assisted the doorkeeper (18:16–17), so she would have carried a lamp, which would have given her a glimpse

---

10 Leo the Great, Sermon 5, ibid., p. 236.

of Peter's face as he came in. And she would have been able to see
him clearly again, as he stood by the fire toward the light, warming
himself.

67 "You too were with Jesus the Nazarene."

It was a servant girl making the accusation, one of the lowest and
least powerful members of society. Yet he cowers before her. "Peter
when he had not the Spirit yielded and lost courage at the voice of a
girl," writes Pseudo-Jerome, "though with the Spirit he was not afraid
before princes and kings."[11]

68 Then a cock crowed.

Did Peter notice? He must have—otherwise, who else would have
remembered it? But did he connect the cock's crowing to what the
Lord said earlier? Presumably not, because we are not told that he
heard it as a warning, and he is not represented as acting as though
he did. When he remembers the Lord's words at the second crowing
(verse 72), he buckles under the weight of the realization of what he
has done.

If the cock's crow could be heard only in the anteroom, we would
have an explanation of why the other evangelists do not mention two
crowings. Peter heard two crowings, but those inside the courtyard,
including John, heard only the second.

"I neither know nor even understand what you are saying."

This striking formulation has the ring of truth. We can easily
imagine its being relayed by Peter. Matthew (27:70) has a shortened
version, "I do not know what you are saying." Luke (22:57) adds what
seems to be a characteristic of Peter's speech when angry—a scorn-
ful "woman" (or "man," as the case may be): "I do not know him,
woman!" John (18:17, 25) gives only the upshot or essence of what
Peter said, "I am not [one of his disciples]." It is easy to harmonize

---

11 Jerome, ibid., p. 238.

these by supposing that the woman stared at him for some time, during which he first denied he was a follower (John), then strengthened his denial (Mark, abbreviated by Matthew), then summed it up (Luke).

69 "This man is one of them."

She must have followed him. Presumably his annoyance at her first question confirmed her suspicions and made her want to upset him even more.

Matthew (26:71) says "another servant girl" called out Peter to the men there. That can be reconciled by saying that the first servant girl took a friend with her, who made the second accusation.

John (18:25–26) says that a man directed this second accusation at Peter. This is easily reconciled by supposing that after the girl made the accusation, one of the men standing there joined in. Luke has Peter replying sharply, "Man, I am not!" (22:54). All of this is perfectly consistent with how male and female acquaintances in the servant class might have behaved when they were bored and found it interesting to taunt and torment someone.

70 after a little while

Luke says it was about an hour (22:59). Mark, it seems, wants to emphasize how quickly the denials followed one another, as if such swiftness magnifies their seriousness—a single denial, as it were, but tripled in seriousness.

72 And he broke down crying.

Matthew (26:75) and Luke (22:62) say that he wept *bitterly*. Mark, reflecting Peter's viewpoint here, does not give Peter that much credit, and he omits that detail.

Chapter 15

1 As soon as it was morning, after taking counsel, the chief priests, with the elders and the scribes, and the entire council, after binding Jesus, brought him out and gave him over to Pilate.

2 So Pilate questioned him: "You are the king of the Jews?" To which he says, "You say."

3 The chief priests made vehement accusations. ⁴Pilate again questioned him and said, "You make no answer? Look at their vehemence in accusing you." ⁵To which Jesus said nothing, which surprised Pilate.

6 Each festival he would release one prisoner they asked for. ⁷There was someone called Barabbas, who had been imprisoned with revolutionaries who had committed murder in an uprising. ⁸A crowd formed and began to demand that he keep to his custom. ⁹To which Pilate said, "Is it your wish that I release for you the king of the Jews?" ¹⁰He said this because he realized that the chief priests had handed him over out of envy. ¹¹But the chief priests had stirred the crowd up for him to release Barabbas to them instead. ¹²To which Pilate said, "So then, what do you want me to do with the man you call the king of the Jews?" ¹³They cried out another time, "Put him on a cross!"

[14]Pilate said to them, "On what basis? What evil has he done?" But they cried out even more strenuously, "Put him on a cross!" [15]Pilate, because he wanted to appease the crowd, released Barabbas to them. He handed over Jesus to be scourged and affixed to a cross.

16 The soldiers led him away into the hall, that is, the praetorium. They called for all of the cohort. [17]They clothed him in purple. They placed upon him a crown that they braided from thorns. [18]They started saluting him, "Hail, king of the Jews!" [19]They kept hitting his head with a stick. They kept spitting upon him. Falling on their knees, they would offer him homage. [20]When they were done with mocking him, they took off the purple and put him in his own clothing.

So now they are leading him out to affix him to a cross. [21]They press into service a certain man who is passing by, coming in from the country, Simon of Cyrene, the father of Alexander and Rufus, to take his cross. [22]They lead him to the Golgotha area, which means "Area of the Skull." [23](They gave him wine mixed with gall, which he did not take.) [24]They affix him to the cross. They divide his garments, casting dice, to see who will take them.

25 It was the third hour when they crucified him.

26 The inscription of the charge against him was written, "The King of the Jews." [27]They affix two thieves to crosses along with him, one on his right and one on his left. [[28]The scripture was fulfilled that says, "He was reckoned among lawbreakers."][1]

29 Passersby would blaspheme him by shaking their heads and saying, "Oh yeah! The man who was going to destroy the temple and build it in three days!" [30]"Save *yourself* by coming down from that cross!"

31 Likewise the chief priests too, making a mockery of it among themselves, with the scribes, were saying, "He saved others—he is

---

1   Verse 28 is omitted from some early manuscripts.

powerless to save himself! ³²The Christ! The king of Israel! Let him come down now from the cross, that we might see! That we might have faith!"

The men who were affixed to crosses with him also continued to mock him.

33 When the sixth hour came, darkness came over the whole land, until the ninth hour.

34 At the ninth hour, Jesus cried out in a loud voice, "Elöi, elöi, lema sabachthani?" which means, "My God, my God, why have you forsaken me?" ³⁵Certain men standing there, when they heard this, said, "Look, he's calling out 'Elijah'!" ³⁶Someone ran up, soaked a sponge in vinegar, placed it on a stick, and gave it to him to drink, saying, "Leave him alone. Let's see if Elijah comes to take him down."

37 Jesus let out a great cry and sent out his spirit.

38 The inner curtain of the temple was ripped in two, from top to bottom. ³⁹The centurion who was posted across from him, when he saw how he had sent out his spirit, said "Truly, this man was Son of God."

40 There were women looking on from a distance, among whom were Mary Magdalene, Mary the mother of the lesser James and of Joseph, and Salome ⁴¹—these are the women who followed him and served his needs when he was in Galilee—and many other women too, who accompanied him up to Jerusalem.

42 As it was already getting dark, since it was the day of Preparation, that is, the vigil of the Sabbath, ⁴³Joseph of Arimathea, an upright councilman who, moreover, was for his part looking with expectation for the kingdom of God, went boldly to Pilate and requested the body of Jesus. ⁴⁴But Pilate was surprised that he should already be dead. So he summoned the centurion and asked him if he had been dead for long. ⁴⁵Once he knew from the centurion, he relegated to Joseph care of the corpse. ⁴⁶So he bought a linen cloth,

took him down, and wrapped him in the linen cloth. He placed him in a tomb which was hewn out of a rock. He rolled a stone up to the door of the tomb. ⁴⁷Mary Magdalene and Mary the mother of Joseph were taking careful note of where he was placed.

Commentary

This chapter corresponds point by point to what Jesus, in Mark 10:33–34, says will happen. The account is matter-of-fact: no embellishments giving voice to emotions, no words of special emphasis, no lessons drawn, no accusations. The story is told with economy of expression, with detachment, and a general pity.

Mark for the most part avoids the historic present. As in the preceding chapter, much of the action takes place behind closed doors, where Peter did not witness it, and the events may have been too terrible to narrate in the present tense (see verses 20–24 for the contrast).

1–5

1 As soon as it was morning

That is, the scribes and the elders handed Jesus over to Pilate as soon as they could.

gave him over to Pilate

Avoiding a long digression, Mark does not explain the background to their plan. Jesus, whom they held to be a blasphemer, was worthy of death by Jewish law. By Roman law, he had committed no crime worthy of death. Lacking political sovereignty, the Jews had either to accuse Jesus successfully before Pilate of some crime under Roman law or to exploit Pilate's pragmatism.

They "gave him over" to Pilate—that is, they betrayed a fellow Jew to their enemy, the Romans, ceding control over his fate to Pilate when they understood that Pilate's designs were not beneficent.

2 "You are king of the Jews?"

Pilate's statement-question reveals that the Jewish leaders at first accuse Jesus of the crime of insurrection under Roman law. Pilate knows that Israel historically had both a priestly class and a hereditary monarchy. It is plain to him that Jesus is not an insurrectionist. Pilate is also superstitious, like other Romans. So he cannot rule out, and perhaps even suspects, that Jesus is the hereditary monarch.

"You say."

Pilate senses he is in the presence of someone like himself, with a sense of his own authority and dignity.

4 "You make no answer?"

Pilate believes that Jesus will deny the charges and can refute his accusers through cross-examination. It is clear that his accusers want Jesus put to death, but Pilate has the authority to put him to death. This is Jesus' chance to avoid that fate, and Pilate cannot understand why he is silent. It is as if he wants to be sentenced to death, and yet no man wants to be falsely accused and unjustly executed.

Pilate has little inherent interest in Jesus or sympathy with his plight. If the man will not stand up for his own interests, why should anyone else do so? Rather, Pilate represents Roman power. His concern is preserving and growing that power. It would be compromised if it were abused, especially if it were thought to be subordinated to the interests of the Jewish religious authorities. Pilate, then, must not simply ignore these authorities, as he would be doing if he merely released Jesus. He must silence or undermine them. So when the crowd gathers for the release of a prisoner on the festival, he gets the idea of appealing to the crowd against these authorities.

6–15

Jesus was first betrayed by one of his own, Judas, to the Jewish authorities, who, after condemning him, betrayed him to Pilate. Now

Pilate, through his stratagem, in effect betrays Jesus to the mob. When the mob, in turn, betrays Jesus to the executioner, the betrayal is complete on all sides.

8 A crowd formed

Not "a crowd gathered," Mark's usual expression. The wording here suggests an unruly crowd, already angry as they approach Pilate. Their anger pleases Pilate because he thinks they will then accept whatever prisoner he proposes to them.

9 "Is it your wish that I release for you the king of the Jews?"

The worldly Pilate recognizes the chief priests' envy of Jesus but misunderstands it. He thinks they envy his popularity with the crowd, while the real source of their envy is Jesus' favor with God. Moreover, when Jesus does not claim the title, king of the Jews, Pilate infers that the title, used widely of Jesus (as he was aware from informers), must have been given to him by the people. So Pilate thinks he can silence and defeat the religious authorities by playing the people against them.

11 But the chief priests had stirred the crowd up

The Jews were an occupied people. The angry crowd in Jerusalem would be attracted, therefore, to an insurrectionist. But they could easily be roused to contempt for one of their own who looked weak before the Roman authorities—and Jesus stood before them bound.

The contrast between Jesus' reputation as a wonderworker and his apparent powerlessness now before Pilate suggests that he is a fraud, reinforcing the mob's contempt.

12 "So then, what do you want me to do with the man you call the king of the Jews?"

The crowd's choice of Barabbas takes Pilate by surprise, but he still expects them not to care what he does with Jesus. Having got the man they wanted, he supposes, they will disperse now. And indeed they might have done so if Pilate hadn't taunted them with the phrase "king of the Jews," stirring up their contempt.

13 They cried out another time, "Put him on a cross!"

This cry is usually translated "Crucify him!" but our familiarity with that phrase hides what the crowd are saying. To put someone on a cross was to abandon him there, exposed and vulnerable, until he died of the hanging. It was a fate more like being thrown in a well than being shot.

But where did this particular, cruel demand come from? Did the chief priests maliciously incite the crowd to demand the worst possible punishment, or was this the crowd's own perverse improvisation? Or perhaps some had heard Jesus speak about "taking up one's cross" and now, out of anger and contempt, thought he should do what he was telling others to do.

14 Pilate said to them, "On what basis? What evil has he done?"

Did Pilate ask this rhetorically, unable to understand why a people who earlier that week had lauded Jesus as their king now demanded his crucifixion? Or did he think that, as governor, he needed to investigate whether Jesus had done something to merit such an extreme punishment?

15 He handed over Jesus to be scourged and affixed to a cross.

Pilate thought he could use the crowd to his purposes. He did not anticipate a riot. We might imagine he is angry with himself for it. But in any case, he is a busy man, and the matter has taken up too much of his time. He gives the crowd what they want so they will go away—as they do—and now, from his point of view, the problem is solved.

Scourging, which customarily preceded crucifixion, was inflicted by two "lictors," who alternated blows. The cords of their whips were knotted with bits of metal, designed to remove the skin quickly. Further blows tore into muscle and sometimes stuck in the victim's bones. The number of blows was limited only by the need to keep the prisoner alive for crucifixion. Scourged men were considered "half dead."

Given the enormity of this punishment and that Jesus had specifically foretold his scourging, one wonders that Mark mentions it only in passing, with a single word in the Greek. Possibly he and Peter found it too painful to report.

16–20

Jesus had foretold that "the Son of Man will be betrayed to the Gentiles, who will mock him and spit on him." Mark now describes the eerily precise fulfilment of those words. After the scourging, Jesus would be stumbling around with painful and open wounds, barely able to stand up, and, from a human point of view, in need of compassionate treatment. But the cruel soldiers turn his debasement into further reason for ridiculing him.

16 the praetorium

From the Latin *praetor*, which means "leader," it is the government palace.

17 a crown that they braided from thorns

What inspired one of the soldiers to take time to braid a crown? Had he done so before, in a game or out of malice, to torture a prisoner—for example, by placing circles of thorns around his thighs? The crowning with thorns was especially malicious if it was dreamed up just for this occasion.

19 They kept hitting.... They kept spitting....

The suggestion of Mark's writing: if they did any of these things even once, it would be horrible, and yet, unbelievably, they kept on doing so, again and again, and would not stop.

They kept hitting his head with a stick

The "stick" was probably something like a bamboo pole. They would have swung it as hard as possible, maybe aiming at the crown to press the thorns into his skull, no doubt hitting his face and mouth as well, possibly knocking out a tooth or two.

They kept spitting upon him.

Spitting emphasized Jesus' powerlessness and complete humiliation. Perhaps they had heard that besides "king" he was also called the "Anointed One," so they "anointed" his face with spittle. Whatever devilish expressions of cruelty and mockery we can think up were, without doubt, surpassed.

20 put him in his own clothing

They knew that each change of clothing ripped the scabs off his wounds.

20–24

21 Simon of Cyrene, the father of Alexander and Rufus

Sons were usually identified by reference to their fathers, but fathers were not usually identified by reference to their sons. We may conclude, then, that Alexander and Rufus were more familiar to some of Mark's readers than their father, Simon. In fact, it is reasonable to think they were Christians who at some point lived in Rome. (See Acts 13:1, Acts 19:33, Rom. 16:13.)

24 They divide his garments, casting dice, to see who will take them.

Mark does not point out what is clearly a fulfillment of Psalm 22:18. Why not? As we have seen, he wants his readers to focus on the Passion, and he avoids any kind of digression.

25–32

25 It was the third hour when they crucified him.

Literally, "It was the third hour, and they crucified him." The Romans divided the day into twelve equal hours, beginning at six o'clock A.M. The Jews divided daylight into twelve equal hours, beginning at dawn. As the Passover occurs near the spring equinox, these two methods of keeping time would coincide closely. By either method, the third hour would be roughly nine o'clock in the morning. John, however, says that it was "about the sixth hour" when Pilate handed Jesus over to be crucified (19:14), and tradition holds that Jesus hung on the Cross from noon until three o'clock.

Perhaps the best solution to this puzzle comes from St. Augustine, who suggests in his book on the harmony of the Gospels that Mark is referring to the beginning of the whole scene, when "they," the crowd, called out for his crucifixion. Others speculate that, since John composed his Gospel as an old man after having lived in Asia for many years, he used an Asiatic method of counting the hours, which began from midnight, not dawn.

26 "The King of the Jews."

The charge, written on a small plaque, was hung around the neck of the condemned man or carried in front of him in the procession to the place of execution. John says that it was written in Hebrew, Latin, and Greek (19:20), that is, in the local, official, and common languages.

The Gospel writers differ in what the inscription said:

"*This is Jesus, the King of the Jews*" (Mt. 27:37)

"*The King of the Jews*" (Mk. 15:26)

"*This is the King of the Jews*" (Lk. 23:38)

"*Jesus the Nazarene, the King of the Jews*" (Jn. 19:19)

If we take "This is" as indicating not what was written but the performative force of the inscription, then John gives the full inscription, and the others give only parts thereof—exactly the kind of variation one typically sees in truthful independent accounts of a single incident.

28 The scripture was fulfilled

Verse 28 is lacking in the oldest manuscripts and those judged most reliable.

29 Passersby would blaspheme him

Here again Mark expresses horror at the repetition of this ill treatment of the Lord.

"The man who was going to destroy the temple and build it in three days!"

An example of a false report that gets exaggerated and becomes the common way of thinking about something.

30 "Save *yourself* by coming down from that cross!"

An expression of contempt for someone perceived as powerless. Jesus' weakness was caused by others, indeed, but it soon becomes grounds for reproaching him.

31 "He saved others—he is powerless to save himself!"

But perhaps the mockers are not so sure. There seems to be an element of exultation in their words, for they are relieved that he (apparently) cannot save himself. For them, the crucifixion had the aspect of a test and proof.

32 "The Christ! The king of Israel!"

They say this sneeringly. But they do not say "the king of the Jews!" because they are upset by Pilate's inscription.

"Let him come down now from the cross, that we might see! That we might have faith!"

Here the chief priests and the scribes ridicule not only Jesus but also his followers. They have heard reports of how he dealt with lepers and blind men, praising them for their faith and restoring them to health. Thus, they mock him by pretending grotesquely that they are among his putatively gullible followers.

33–36

33 When the sixth hour came

If we follow St. Augustine's interpretation, we should take this verse as well to be a marker of time. The three hours of darkness, from noon to three o'clock, are the three hours that Jesus spent on the Cross.

darkness came over the whole land

Mark strikingly gives no explanation. He does not mention clouds, but the darkness could not have been caused by an eclipse. The Passover took place at a full moon, when the moon is opposite to the sun relative to the earth.

34 "Elöi, elöi, lema sabachthani?"

Mark gives the *sound* as well as the *meaning* of what Jesus cried. The line is the first verse of Psalm 22, which is as follows:

> 1 My God, my God, why hast thou forsaken me? why art thou so far from helping me, and from the words of my roaring?
>
> 2 O my God, I cry in the day time, but thou hearest not; and in the night season, and am not silent.
>
> 3 But thou art holy, O thou that inhabitest the praises of Israel.
>
> 4 Our fathers trusted in thee: they trusted, and thou didst deliver them.
>
> 5 They cried unto thee, and were delivered: they trusted in thee, and were not confounded.
>
> 6 But I am a worm, and no man; a reproach of men, and despised of the people.
>
> 7 All they that see me laugh me to scorn: they shoot out the lip, they shake the head, saying,

8 He trusted on the Lord that he would deliver him: let him deliver him, seeing he delighted in him.

9 But thou art he that took me out of the womb: thou didst make me hope when I was upon my mother's breasts.

10 I was cast upon thee from the womb: thou art my God from my mother's belly.

11 Be not far from me; for trouble is near; for there is none to help.

12 Many bulls have compassed me: strong bulls of Bashan have beset me round.

13 They gaped upon me with their mouths, as a ravening and a roaring lion.

14 I am poured out like water, and all my bones are out of joint: my heart is like wax; it is melted in the midst of my bowels.

15 My strength is dried up like a potsherd; and my tongue cleaveth to my jaws; and thou hast brought me into the dust of death.

16 For dogs have compassed me: the assembly of the wicked have inclosed me: they pierced my hands and my feet.

17 I may tell all my bones: they look and stare upon me.

18 They part my garments among them, and cast lots upon my vesture. (KJV)

Verses 9–10 may look out of place in relation to the description of his sufferings. However, they make sense if considered as directed at his mother, who was standing at the foot of the Cross (Jn. 19:25).

37-39

38 inner curtain

It would have been impossible for men to rip that curtain, and certainly not from top to bottom. But how could anyone have known that it was torn at the moment Christ died? Perhaps from some kind of lightning flash or loud noise.

39 when he saw how he had sent out his spirit

The verb rendered here as "sent out his spirit" can also mean simply to exhale; by extension, it can mean to exhale for the last time, that is, to breathe one's last. But the centurion's reaction gives it a stronger meaning here—that Jesus died by a free act of giving over or giving up his spirit. As Bede writes, "Now the cause of the centurion's wonder is clear.... For no one can send forth his own spirit, but He who is the Creator of souls."[2]

42-47

43 who, moreover, was for his part looking with expectation for the kingdom of God

Mark does not call Joseph of Arimathea a follower. A member of the council, he presumably admired Jesus in secret, believing that what he taught was true. In Mark's description of Joseph, a single phrase summarizes his belief—we might think of it as the original description of "mere Christianity": he "was looking with expectation for the kingdom of God."

went boldly to Pilate

Mark suggests that others were astonished that Joseph would attempt this. For all anyone knew, the unpredictable Pilate might have had such an inquirer arrested, perhaps even scourged and put to death.

---

2 Bede, quoted in Saint Thomas Aquinas, *Catena Aurea: Gospel of Mark*, trans. William Whiston (Grand Rapids, MI: Christian Classics Ethereal Library), p. 254.

44 Pilate was surprised that he should already be dead.

Fortunately for Joseph, Pilate focuses not on him but on the surprising swiftness of Jesus' death—exactly the sort of detail Joseph would have reported later to Peter.

So he summoned the centurion

Presumably the same centurion who stood guard at the Cross and confessed Jesus as Son of God. Only minutes after Jesus' death, then, there are two believers standing before Pilate.

45 he relegated to Joseph care of the corpse

The word for "relegated to" is quasi-legal language. Through this act the state relinquished rights over the body, and Joseph acquired them. Similarly, the word "corpse" seems quasi-legal in the context and presumably echoes Pilate's own language. For the rest of the chapter, Mark never refers to the "corpse" or the "body" but always to Jesus, referring to the body consistently as "him": "taking him down, he wrapped him in the linen cloth. He placed him in a tomb." This personalistic language presumably expresses Mark's conviction that Jesus, though dead, is still alive. His body, therefore, may be identified with him.[3]

46 He rolled a stone

Not "they" but "he." These stones for sealing tombs were usually set in a track and would be rolled downhill, where they would rest in a kind of slot. It was not difficult for one man to close the tomb, but it would be difficult to roll away the stone to open the tomb.

47 Mary Magdalene and Mary the mother of Joseph were taking careful note of where he was placed.

Which is to say, they know the tomb well enough to find it with assurance three days later.

---

3 Along these lines, note that in Catholic doctrine, the death of Jesus consisted of the separation of the soul of Christ from the body of Christ, but soul and body remained united with the Son, the Second Person of the Trinity, even while they were separated from each other.

CHAPTER 16

1 When the Sabbath had passed, Mary Magdalene, Mary the mother of James, and Salome purchased spices to go and anoint him. ²Very early on the first day of the week, they came to the tomb, after the sun had risen. ³So they were saying to themselves, "Who will roll away the stone for us from the entrance to the tomb?" ⁴They look up and see that the stone has been rolled away. (The stone was very big.)

5 After entering the tomb, they saw a young man sitting to the right, clothed in a white robe. They were filled with amazement. ⁶He tells them, "Do not be amazed. You are looking for Jesus, the Nazarene, the crucified. He is risen. He is not here. As you can see, here is where they laid him. ⁷But go, tell his disciples, and Peter, 'He is going before you into Galilee. You will see him there, just as he told you.'" ⁸They left and fled from the tomb, since trembling and agitation had seized them. In fact they said nothing to anyone because they were filled with fear.

9 After he had arisen, early on the first day of the week, he appeared first of all to Mary Magdalene, out of whom he had cast seven devils. ¹⁰She went and announced it to those who had been with him, who were in mourning and were weeping. ¹¹When they heard

this report, that he was alive and had been seen by her, they did not believe it.

12 After these things, to two men from among them who were traveling he showed himself in a different appearance when they were going to the country. [13]They went back and announced it to the rest. But they did not believe even them.

14 Afterwards, to the Eleven when they were at supper he showed himself. He rebuked their lack of belief and hardness of heart, because they did not believe those who had seen him risen.

15 He said to them: "Travel out into the whole world and proclaim the good news to the whole of creation. [16]The man who believes and is baptized will be saved. The man who fails to believe will stand condemned.

17 "These signs will accompany those who believe: they will cast out devils in my name, they will speak new languages, [18]they will grab snakes with their hands, and if they should drink a deadly poison, it will not harm them; they will place their hands on the sick, and they will become well."

19 And so the Lord Jesus, after speaking to them, was taken up into heaven. He took his seat at the right hand of God. [20]But they went out everywhere and preached, while the Lord worked alongside them and confirmed their preaching through the accompanying signs.

Commentary

1-4

1-2 When the Sabbath had passed.... Very early on the first day of the week

Christians do not celebrate the Sabbath on the last day of the week but the Lord's Day on the first day of the week.

to go and anoint him

Mark continues to refer to the body of Christ as "him" not "it."

they came to the tomb, after the sun had risen

Although Matthew says that they came to the tomb *when* the sun was rising (28:1), there is no contradiction if we suppose that Matthew tells us when they began their journey and Mark tells when they ended it. These different descriptions correspond to two different practices in the early Church for celebrating Easter: at first light and after sunrise.

3 "Who will roll away the stone for us...?"

Another concrete detail which has the ring of truth—because it is just like us to start on a journey to the tomb forgetting that a heavy stone blocks the entrance. They discuss the problem rather than just bemoaning the obstacle, realizing that there were Roman guards at the tomb but that they would not help them.

4 They look up and see

The historic present brings us into the scene, and the account sounds as someone who heard it from the women themselves might have told it. Note also the detail that they "look up." Perhaps the tomb was in an elevated place. Perhaps in the dim light of dawn they needed to pay attention to where they were placing their feet. Or perhaps they were looking at one another as they discussed the problem about moving the stone.

One can imagine that as they told their story—"we were wondering how we were going to move that stone when we looked up and saw it had been moved"—the women interpreted the unexpected moving of the stone as a favor granted in response to a prayer. This is how pious people think.

5–8

6 "You are looking for Jesus, the Nazarene"

The "young man" in white, interpreting their purpose, does not say that they are looking for the corpse, but for Jesus. To these women who loved the Lord, his body was precious, and they were going to anoint it piously at first light. But the angel knows they are seeking not the corpse but the person.

"Do not be amazed. You are looking for Jesus, the Nazarene, the crucified. He is risen."

The angel does not lack a sense of drama. Jesus was crucified, dead, destroyed, demolished, annihilated. But—(pause)—he is risen (just as he said).

"He is not here. As you can see, here is where they laid him."

The angel, knowing that these women took careful note of where the body of Jesus was laid, calls the scene to their minds: "Jesus, the Nazarene, the crucified, . . . here is where they laid him."

The angel shows the women that there is nothing where the body was left. The resurrection was a new creation, but creation is the bringing into existence of something out of nothing. He therefore invites them to imagine there, again, the nothingness of death from which the resurrection comes.

7 "tell his disciples, and Peter"

Peter would be especially fond of this detail. The first communication from the risen Lord, so dearly sought, mentions Peter by name, implying that he is restored to good graces and, despite his betrayal, remains the leader among the apostles.

"He is going before you into Galilee."

Jesus' immediate departure for his home country indicates that the center of the Church he is founding will not be Jerusalem. This remark, then, is the first announcement that the good news will go out to the whole world.

8 They left and fled from the tomb, since trembling and agitation had seized them.

The women say nothing in reply to the angel. They do not ask questions—about the resurrection, about the plans of the Lord, about where in Galilee they should first go, and so on. They do not express gratitude or praise. They do not wait to see if the angel has more to say. But they flee.

In fact they said nothing to anyone because they were filled with fear.

Mark's Gospel is characteristically frank about human weakness since Peter, its source, is very much aware of his own weakness. We learn that the women, instructed to proclaim the good news, ran away and said nothing to anyone—the first report of the resurrection muffled, as it were, by human fear. At the same time, their failing is presented as perfectly understandable.

Two of the oldest and most highly-regarded manuscripts for the New Testament end the Gospel of Mark with verse 8. But as explained in the preface, the following verses should be included as its ending. Admittedly, they have the appearance of an appended summary. Yet they share many characteristics with Mark's narrative, they provide an apt conclusion, and without them the Gospel would be unfinished.

Verses 9–14 report three resurrection appearances, verses 15–17 describe a commission, and verses 18–20 mention the resurrection and the beginnings of early Christian evangelization.

9–14

9 early on the first day of the week

This repetition from verse 2 suggests that this passage was written independently and later added to the Gospel, and yet it is characteristic of Mark to set the temporal context of an episode.

out of whom he had cast seven devils

Mary Magdalene having already been referred to in verse 1, this additional description of her seems to have been appended later. Nevertheless, the description is appropriate, for it implies that Jesus, who showed great mercy in saving her from evil, now honors her with being the first witness to his resurrection.

10 She went and announced it to those who had been with him

One would expect the narrator to note the contrast between Mary's prompt obedience now and her fear and silence earlier. That he does not is another sign that this is a later addition.

who were in mourning and were weeping

With this phrase, Mark gives color and detail to the scene, as is characteristic of his Gospel.

11 he was alive and had been seen by her

The report that "he was alive" precedes the report that he "had been seen by her." Here we do have a connection with what is recounted in verses 1–7, because the report that "he is alive" depended first on Mary Magdalene's seeing the empty tomb and hearing the angel. Only later did she see him.

they did not believe it

But why did they not believe it? Perhaps they regarded Mary's credibility as too slight, and what she reported as too unlikely. But if, out of love, and given what Jesus had taught, they had *wanted* the resurrection to be true, then shouldn't Mary Magdalene's say-so have been enough to settle it? Along a similar line, some have said that the reason that Mary the mother of Jesus did not go to the tomb is that she saw no need to confirm what she already believed.

12 he showed himself in a different appearance

This language suggests that Jesus had already shown himself in some guise to Mary Magdalene and that this appearance was different. That is, the language comports with the accounts in the other Gospels that he looked like a gardener to Mary (Jn. 20:15), and that he went unrecognized by the disciples on the road to Emmaus (Lk. 14:16).

who were traveling … were going to the country

Even in this short summary, Mark is careful to set the place and time.

14 when they were at supper

A concrete detail, characteristic of Mark, which summarizes the story Luke tells at greater length (24:36–43).

lack of belief

The "lack of belief" for which Jesus rebukes the disciples indicates an unwillingness to believe and accept, which in turn indicates a failure of love and friendship.

hardness of heart

A characteristic expression of Mark.

15–17

15 "to the whole of creation"

The word for the whole of the creation, *ktisis*, occurs two other times in Mark (10:6, 13:19) but never in another Gospel. This is more evidence, it seems, that Mark is responsible for the material added at the end of his Gospel.

It is fascinating that the good news should be proclaimed not only to men but also to creation more broadly. St. Gregory the Great minimizes the significance of the phrase by reading it as a reference to man as a microcosm: "Every man must be understood by *every creature*; for man partakes something of every creature; he has existence as have stones, life as trees, feeling as animals, understanding as have Angels. For the Gospel is preached to every creature, because he is taught by it, for whose sake all are created...."[1] And yet the idea seems

---

1 St. Gregory, quoted in Saint Thomas Aquinas, *Catena Aurea: Gospel of Mark*, trans. William Whiston (Grand Rapids, MI: Christian Classics Ethereal Library) p. 268.

to relate to other main themes of Mark's Gospel, such as the Lord's power over nature and his authority over devils.

The "proclamation of the Gospel to the whole of creation" implies that human skill and industry should be informed by the Gospel and that through sound government and culture, Christians should establish places where Satan is, as it were, expelled and the ravages of sickness are ameliorated.

16 "The man who believes and is baptized will be saved."

It is not enough to believe, because baptism provides the grace necessary for acting as our belief requires. St. Gregory astutely comments here, "But perhaps some one may say in himself, I have already believed, I shall be saved. He says what is true, if he keeps his faith by works; for that is a true faith, which does not contradict by its deeds what it says in words."[2]

"The man who fails to believe will stand condemned."

Jesus does not say "the man who fails to be baptized will stand condemned," since as we saw, the unbaptized Moses and Elijah were not condemned but were living and discoursing with Jesus on the mount.

17 "These signs will accompany those who believe"

Not these signs *only* but signs such as these. These seem to be miracles that were worked at the beginning of the Church, when they would aide in the rapid evangelization of pagan cultures. Throughout the history of the Church there has been no lack of miracles, mainly miraculous cures—although some great saints, Padre Pio, for instance, have worked unusual miracles such as bilocation or reading souls.

---

2 St. Gregory, ibid., p. 269.

19-20

19 And so

This phrase—*men oun* in Greek—unlike verse 8 above, marks a true conclusion of the Gospel. Compare Jn. 20:30, sometimes thought to be an earlier ending of that Gospel.

20 while the Lord worked alongside them

An allusion to the Holy Spirit. Although the Lord "took his seat at the right hand of God," he nonetheless remained with his Church.

they went out everywhere and preached

Our hypothesis is that Mark, having written his Gospel in Rome, added verses 9–19 in Alexandria. This verse, then, brings the story from the point where the women flee from the tomb and tell no one, all the way up to Mark in far-flung Egypt, as he has "gone out everywhere" with the other disciples.

Verses 9–19 are Mark's work without Peter. Missing are the broad and strong pastoral purposes that govern the selection and arrangement of materials. Gone are the vivid accounts of ongoing action. We are not shown "what it was like" to be there when the resurrected Lord appeared. There are no details pointing to an eye-witness, no memorable expressions. We are given a description and a perfunctory list, in no particular order, somewhat colorless and flat.

How remarkable that the energetic, passionate, and good-hearted personality of Peter lies behind Mark's Gospel! Through Mark's Gospel, that personality informs the other synoptic Gospels and indeed the entire tradition about Jesus. It is certain that Jesus chose Peter in part to insure that the written tradition would take the form that it does. Reading the Gospels today, one finds oneself under the pastoral care of that first among the apostles, Peter.

Finis.

Deo gratias.

ACKNOWLEDGEMENTS

My love for the book of Mark dates back to the summer between my sophomore and junior years at Harvard College. I had just converted to Christianity and was living at home in Hicksville, Long Island, with my parents. A high school friend, Jack Levison, who was attending Wheaton College, invited me to a weekly study of the Gospel at his house with his father. Those were humble and simple discussions, but Jack's love for the Gospel shone through and was contagious. Jack since went on to get advanced degrees from Cambridge and Duke Universities and is now a distinguished scripture scholar. Currently he holds the W. J. A. Power Professorship of Old Testament at SMU's Perkins School of Theology. So, to Jack: thank you, and may this book repay in part what you taught me about Mark's Gospel and the love of the Lord.

To my wife, Catherine Ruth Pakaluk, who has been the biggest fan of this book and a constant encouragement to continue with it and bring it to completion: thank you for your faithful and romantic Christian love and for your many prayers.

I wish to thank my literary agent, Giles Anderson, for his confidence in this project and my editor, Tom Spence, for his welcome and supportive enthusiasm.

Finally, I owe a deep debt of gratitude to Rebecca Ryskind Teti, who helped with the daunting task of editing this book in its final weeks: daunting, because although the book in manuscript had many fans, it wasn't until Regnery agreed to publish it that anyone did a word count and discovered it was almost twice as long as would be reasonable for such a book! It's hardly possible, and certainly not easy, for an author to edit down his own work so drastically. Really, only an editor can accomplish it. But how to find such a person? One needs someone who loves the work, possesses intelligence and subtlety, and is herself a skilled writer, but who at the same time can be practical and efficient in making cuts. Credit Catherine for seeing that Rebecca would be such an editor, and Rebecca for agreeing to take this project on and carrying it out so well!

Index

A

Abba, xvii, 241, 255–56

Abiathar (high priest), 29, 44–45

Abomination of Desolation, 226, 233, 235

Abraham, 129, 209, 215, 218–19

Acts (book of the Bible), 52, 55, 115, 117, 127, 219, 232, 273

Aenon, 10–11

Ahimelech (high priest), 44–45

Alexander the Great, 124

Alexandria, xiv, 289

Andrew, 2–3, 14, 16, 18, 36–37, 48, 160, 225

Anointed One, 1, 5, 129, 273

anthrōpos (Greek), 52

Antichrist, 233, 235, 237

Apollinarius, 257

Apostolic Succession, 102

Aquinas, Thomas (St.), 24, 45, 174, 255

Aramaic, xi, xvii–xviii, 56–57, 61, 92, 256

archē (Greek), 4

Arianism, 35

Aristotle, xii, 121, 158

Ark of the Covenant, 61

Asia, 274

Asiatic method, 274

Athanasius (St.), 257

Augustine (St.), xxiv, 12, 60, 122, 199, 229, 232–34, 256–57, 274, 276